SHIFTING SANDS

OTHER BOOKS AND AUDIOBOOKS
BY KATHI ORAM PETERSON

The Forgotten Warrior

An Angel on Main Street

The Stone Traveler

River Whispers

A Christmas to Remember

Cold Justice

Wanted

Deceived

Remembering the Joy of Christmas

Star Struck

Breach of Trust

A Familiar Fear

Bloodline

A Stranger Watches

Treacherous Legacy

SHIFTING SANDS

a romantic suspense novel

KATHI ORAM PETERSON

Covenant Communications, Inc.

Cover image *Man* © panic_attack, Istockphoto.com. *Woman* © CoffeeAndMilk, Istockphoto.com. *Wilderness Beach* © sharply_done, Istockphoto.com. *Dog* © Alexander Gabriel, Istockphoto.com

Cover design by Kevin Jorgensen
Cover design copyright © 2023 by Covenant Communications, Inc.

Published by Covenant Communications, Inc.
American Fork, Utah

Library of Congress Cataloging-in-Publication Data

Name Kathi Oram Peterson, author.
Title Shifting sands / Kathi Oram Peterson.
Description American Fork, Utah Covenant Communications Inc., [2023]
Identifiers Library of Congress Control Number 2022941909 | ISBN 978-1-52442-302-5
LC record available at https//lccn.loc.gov/2022941909

Printed in the United States of America
First Printing February 2023

28 27 26 25 24 23   10 9 8 7 6 5 4 3 2 1

PRAISE FOR KATHI ORAM PETERSON

"*Shifting Sands* by Kathi Oram Peterson is a love story involving a soon-to-be marine biologist and a sand pounder. Gloryanna Griffin is diving along with another student and her mentor to help save the ocean and earn a grant for a master's degree. When Gloryanna ventures alone a little too far, just below a vortex, she discovers that something is wrong with her tank and realizes that she won't stand a chance against the vortex that just caught her. Awake, Gloryanna finds herself on a beach with a dog and a man next to her. She learns that the man who rescued her had saved many other people from certain death, that he isn't an ordinary man, and that of all the people he saved she is the only one who can see him. Her rescuer, Jonathan Dawson, knows that the woman he just saved wasn't there by chance and that they met for a purpose.

I'm shamelessly addicted to the romantic suspense genre because of novels just like *Shifting Sands* by Kathi Oram Peterson. I was immediately sucked into this astonishing book, which is a gripping, richly atmospheric, and thoroughly enjoyable page-turner that left me breathless. It contains so many surprising, interesting facts combined with fiction, and irresistible protagonists that will convince you to make room for them in your heart. This is an absorbing read that I highly recommend. Romantic suspense fans and anyone who likes historical fiction will enjoy it and be rewarded."

—Readers' Favorite 5-star review

"Who doesn't love a mystery with a ghost? *Shifting Sands* by Kathi Oram Peterson is a fascinating tale guaranteed to intrigue readers of all ages."

—Paige Edwards, author of *Facing the Enemy*

for my father,
who served his country during World War II

PROLOGUE

Olympic Peninsula
Washington, USA
September 1943

"WHERE IS FRANK?" JONATHAN DAWSON scrubbed a hand over his face and beard. Worried about his teammate, he paced in the small confines of the crude shelter, followed by his faithful German shepherd, Max. During the time they'd been assigned here, Jonathan and Frank had made it as comfortable as they could for a place that had no running water or electricity and that was positioned only fifty feet from the jagged cliffs of Purgatory Point, the turbulent Pacific Ocean churning below.

Behind their shelter loomed a thick forest they'd hacked through to reach their post. That had been nearly six months ago. In only a week, their replacements would arrive. Jonathan could hardly wait. Oh, he was willing to serve his country, and he enjoyed living close to nature, but a guy needed a bit more in life. And truth be told, he'd grown weary of Frank Becker.

They had been together day and night as sand pounders, a division of the Coast Guard. Their assignment watch for the enemy should they come by sea, by air, or even on foot.

Frank had gone on patrol, but he should have been back a while ago. Since the war seemed to be winding down, they sometimes split up the work so they could get done faster. While Frank had checked the trail, Jonathan had gone back to prepare supper on the woodstove that not only cooked their food but also kept them warm. He'd heated up a can of stew instead of making fish chowder. He'd even added bits of jerky to give it more flavor. But that had been over an hour ago. The sun would set soon. Still, no Frank.

Jonathan stopped pacing and gazed down at Max. Brown doggy eyes peered at him. "Should we go anyway?"

Max's tail thumped the floor's wooden planks. Jonathan and the dog had trained together at Elkin Park Training Station in Pennsylvania. Because so many soldiers had been stationed overseas and the military was short on man power, they were only too happy to welcome his German shepherd. Jonathan assumed he and Max would be assigned beach patrol on the Atlantic because that was where a German U-boat had been spotted trying to smuggle spies into the country. However, they'd been sent to serve on the Pacific front, where Japanese submarines had shelled and bombed along the coastline.

"Frank's been gone too long." Jonathan patted the dog's furry head. "We've both eaten, and we're late leaving for our patrol." He checked his wristwatch. "In fact, we should have left a half hour ago." He scratched his bearded chin.

He should shave, but his beard kept his face warm. The dress code for sand pounders wasn't nearly as strict as other units in the military, especially since Coasties, another nickname for their division, lived in continual harsh weather. In fact, instead of wearing uniforms, both he and Frank wore logger clothing heavy boots, wool shirts, blanket coats, and oilskin ponchos.

"We gotta head out." Jonathan moved the pot away from the heat, closed the mouth of the cast-iron stove, and made sure no sparks escaped. He grabbed his poncho from the wall hook and pulled it over his head. He looped his Mark 28 binoculars around his neck and picked up his rifle. "Frank can heat up what's left when he gets here."

Max waited patiently for Jonathan at the door.

Bracing himself for the cold wind blowing off the Pacific, Jonathan pulled on the latch and slipped out of the shelter, Max at his heels. Salty sea air scrubbed his face. He jerked the hood of his poncho over his head, and after securing the door, he headed down the trail Frank would have taken. Then he stopped. So did Max.

"You don't suppose he went to the point, do you?"

Max tilted his head.

"Why would he, you say? Well, it makes no sense, but when has Frank ever made sense?" Jonathan's partner was a blond surfer from California, a freeloader, and a big talker filled with get-rich-quick schemes. "Maybe he saw something at the point that looked like a treasure. He's forever telling us that when the war is over, he plans to pan for gold in Nevada. That's where the next big strike will be. Nevada, of all places."

Reluctantly, Jonathan started for the point. Max kept pace with him.

Jonathan had different plans when the war was over, and it didn't involve panning for gold. Though shortly after he'd enlisted, his sweetheart, Mary Ann, had sent him a Dear John letter, he still believed in true love and wanted to find his soulmate, have a flock of children, and settle down. That was why he'd bought Max. A family needed a dog they could count on.

And Jonathan counted on Max. From the moment his eyes had locked onto the German shepherd's in the animal shelter's window, he'd known the dog was meant to be his. They had an unspoken understanding, a trust.

Jonathan pulled his poncho more closely around him and continued toward the point. During the months stationed here, he'd learned how to work through his fear of heights by only getting close enough to the edge to accomplish his job. Following the path, he stepped as close to the precipice as he could stand.

What if Frank had fallen? If he had, the tide would have pulled him under by now, and the current would have sucked him out to sea. Chances of him being there were slim to none, but still, Jonathan had to check.

Peering from the grassy vantage, he gazed below at the angry ocean crashing against jagged rocks. No sign of Frank.

About to turn away, Jonathan caught a glimpse of strange movement by the beach. "What the . . . ?" He strained to see if it was a sea otter or a beached whale. He couldn't tell, and he wasn't stepping closer to the lip of the cliff to find out. No, he and Max would hike down there to make sure all was well.

Max growled and took off behind him.

Jonathan spun around.

There on the path to the point stood Frank, but he wasn't alone. A group of wet and bedraggled men waited behind him.

Max attacked a big burly guy, latching onto his forearm. The dog's teeth sank through his coat. The man screamed, twisted, and turned as he tried to fight off the animal.

"Max!" Jonathan yelled. "Release!"

The dog ignored him, which concerned Jonathan. Max always obeyed.

One of the other men took hold of Max and pulled him off his buddy. Max snarled and snapped at the intruder, and then the animal leaped at the man he'd first gone after. The huge guy kicked the dog, sending him flying through the air and over the cliff.

Jonathan gasped, shocked by the rapid turn of events.

Time stopped.

Even the wind ceased.

Jonathan stepped past his one-foot perimeter and peered down the cliff. There on the jagged rocks below lay Max. No yelp. No whine.

A huge wave crashed over the craggy shore. As water receded, Max disappeared. Vanished!

Anger torpedoed through Jonathan, the white-hot rage surging in his veins. He whipped around and aimed his rifle at the cocky guy who had killed Max. The man swiped the back of his hand over his mouth and gave Jonathan a look that said, *Bring it on.*

Jonathan's finger slid to the trigger, but Frank knocked the gun out of Jonathan's hands and blocked his path.

"Are you crazy? Get out of the way!" Jonathan would take Frank out too if he tried to stop him.

"You weren't supposed to be here." Frank stepped closer to Jonathan, backing him up to the ledge Max had gone over only moments ago.

"What's wrong with you?" Jonathan couldn't grasp what his friend was talking about. "That idiot killed my dog." He pointed at the lug dressed in what looked like a German uniform. In fact, all the men wore the same uniforms and carried packs on their backs, all except one. He was dressed like a Japanese military attaché.

The man who had killed Max stepped up to Jonathan, and in a strong German accent, he said, "No mongrel bites me and gets away with it."

Jonathan tried to elbow past Frank, but his friend grabbed hold. Incensed, Jonathan yelled, "Let go of me!" He yanked on Frank's arms.

Their eyes met. The partner Jonathan had lived with, had served with for over six months, had disappeared. Gone was Frank's California smile, replaced with . . . an enemy's void expression. Frank took a deep breath, but then he shoved hard against Jonathan's chest.

Jonathan's feet slipped at the edge of the cliff. Flailing his arms, he caught himself momentarily, but the weight of his body shifted and dragged him over the cliff. He frantically clawed at the long grass, the blades cutting his skin.

Frank bent over, reaching his hand out, but then shook his head, straightened, and stomped on Jonathan's fingers, grinding the heel of his heavy logger boot into Jonathan's knuckles.

Despite mind-numbing pain, Jonathan held on, but the grass uprooted, and before he could grab more, he plummeted in a free fall. As he went down, the wind sucked away his breath and fear shot through his gut.

All at once, he slammed against the rocks.

Oddly, he felt no pain.

As he fought to remain conscious, he saw a woman . . . his true love—he just knew in that moment that she was. Long curly brown hair with highlights of blonde caught in the sun. A smile warmed her flawless face. Big, luminous eyes with flecks of copper zeroed in on him as she drew near. Behind her came Max's playful yip.

Jonathan blinked, and her face blurred. The air became cold and misty.

A wave crashed over him. Water filled his nose and choked his throat as the sea dragged away his life.

CHAPTER ONE

Present Day

GLORYANNA GRIFFIN GAZED THROUGH HER scuba mask at scaly green sea kelp hypnotically swaying in the surge. The constant noise of the regulator to her oxygen tank and the bubbles that emerged seemed to accompany the dancing kelp. Urgency pulsed through her veins. This critical dive could establish two things it could help her on her quest to save the ocean, and it could help her earn a grant for a master's degree.

If she didn't get the grant, she'd have to put her plans to become a marine biologist on hold until she earned enough money. And who knew when that would be? Her parents couldn't help her, and with Grandpa being ill, she might not have another opportunity for years. All she had to do was publish an article in a noteworthy scientific magazine, and that would keep her in the running.

She wasn't alone on this dive. She looked over at her fellow divers studying a sickly bed of coral on her right. Thomas Clifford, another student at Western Washington University competing for the grant and also her ex-boyfriend, and next to him was Professor Nakano Takahashi. The Japanese-American woman was one of the smartest people Gloryanna knew. The professor had quickly become Gloryanna's mentor and the only reason Gloryanna had come on this dive only a few days before earning her bachelor's.

Though many believed coral was found only in shallow tropical waters, divers were surprised to find erect, soft gorgonians in some of the underwater canyons of the Olympic Coast. But they, too, like coral around the world, were dying. Could the cause be mercury poisoning? She hoped not. She loved the ocean and wanted to do all she could to preserve it. All three divers wanted to make this expanse a "hope spot" to preserve sea life, but the coral in its current condition could endanger such efforts.

The professor and Thomas seemed fascinated with what they'd found, but Gloryanna wanted to scope out the rest of the area. Deciding to go a little farther, she kicked her full-footed, free-diving fins. The vortex current would be dangerously strong, but she'd avoid that. After all, she wasn't a rookie.

The new scuba dry suit with special seals and zippers her father had insisted on buying allowed her to wear black fleece undergarments to stay warm in cold water. As she dove deeper, she shone her compact torchlight through green water to a glove sponge nestled among vibrant orange sea cucumbers. On the edge of the chaotic and frantic whirlpool of the current, she also found a collage of dark-purple and vermilion red-painted sea anemones. She wanted to get some close-up shots of those. Their coloring wasn't quite right.

A shadow swam by. Her heartbeat quickened as she shone her light on a curious sea lion checking her out. Relieved it wasn't one of the transient orcas Professor Takahashi had warned them about, she adjusted her regulator attached to her aluminum tank. She wished she had a steel HP 100 scuba tank like Thomas had, but it cost a lot more.

And then she saw something else, something that looked like . . . a conning tower from the top of a submarine? It rested deeper on the ocean floor and just below the vortex. She couldn't tell if a submersible warship lay beneath it. Could her grandfather's delusional ramblings of a sunken sub be true? She swam closer. The pull of the deadly current drew on her. If she was going to get a picture of the anemones and the conning tower, she'd better do it quickly.

She grabbed her camera from its holster on her wet suit. Well, it wasn't her camera. Ralph Wagner, her boss and the owner of Fish Tail Café and Scuba Supplies, had loaned it to her. He'd insisted his beloved camera would take better pictures, which she needed if she wanted a chance at winning the grant. She adjusted her hold on the camera, but just as she moved it to get a better grip, the clasp broke on her wrist, and the camera floated out of her reach and toward the vortex current.

She had to retrieve it. Swimming for all she was worth, she felt the tug of the current, but it was nothing she couldn't handle. She kicked harder and then, to her horror, realized her regulator didn't sound as loud as it had before. Fewer bubbles emerged. Something was wrong with her tank.

She let the camera go as she turned her light on the gauge. The regulator was losing compression, and it was low.

Too low.

So low she might not make it to the surface.

If she ascended too fast, it could damage her lungs and cause decompression sickness. Or if the professor and Thomas were close, they could help her. She frantically scanned the area but couldn't see them. Her only option was to go topside as fast as she could; it was a risk she was going to have to take to stay alive.

As she feverishly kicked up, the vortex's swirling waters pulled at her. She fought against it. But her arms and legs had grown numb. Her vision blurred. All at once, the current swallowed her.

This was not happening!

Not to her!

She'd been diving since she was a kid. She knew what she was doing. She needed to relax and not fight it. Panic was her enemy.

But then her regulator completely quit.

No bubbles. An odd tingling sizzled her skin as she convulsed.

Her mind raced for solutions until, suddenly, flashes of a mysterious man's bearded face overpowered all other thoughts. Dark brows shaded his kind and caring eyes. A warm smile drifted to his lips, as if he recognized her.

And then he vanished along with her last sliver of air as she lost consciousness.

***

Darkness thinned to light. Gloryanna blinked several times. She no longer felt the mouthpiece, and she could breathe, though she lay facedown. Her blurry vision soon cleared. Through her scuba mask, she saw sand mixed with pebbles. A heap of sea kelp loomed to her right.

A beach?

Where?

She pressed her gloved hand against the ground to help her roll to her side, then tugged her mask over her head, sucking deep drafts of air through both her nose and mouth.

Weak, she managed to pull her arms from the straps of her BCD and push herself to a sitting position, where she jerked off her gloves. She pulled the dry suit diving hood off and removed the cloth beanie she wore beneath to keep her head warm and her hair dry. She scanned the horizon over the ocean, looking for Professor Takahashi's boat as she nervously undid her braid, allowing the ocean breeze to blow through her messy hair, making her feel alive, which was miraculous in and of itself.

No sign of the boat or the dive markers they'd placed in the water.

Tugging off her fins and willing energy into her core, Gloryanna stood and turned around. A high cliff rimmed by a thick forest backdrop stood before her. This unfamiliar coast looked hardly touched by man. The vortex current must have pulled her miles away from the others, down the coast of the peninsula to the primitive area only reachable by foot. But where exactly?

Trying her best to gain her bearings, she studied the ocean again, hoping to see something familiar. Movement by her side jerked her gaze down. A German shepherd stood next to her, sniffing at the booties covering her feet.

She reached to pet the animal, but he shied away and dashed behind her. She turned to see where he was going and stopped short.

A bearded man dressed in what looked like a plaid logger shirt and canvas pants leaned heavily on a walking staff and stood in a pathway that led to the top of the cliffs. There was something vaguely familiar about him, but she really couldn't tell this far away. Obviously, he had not been the one who had rescued her, but maybe he'd seen what had happened.

To be heard over the crashing waves, she yelled, "Hello there!"

His dark brows pinched together, and his mouth dropped open. He stared at her as if she were some sort of sea monster. His dog hid behind him.

Maybe she should move closer so he could hear her better. She started toward the man, but then a dizziness threatened to topple her. She stumbled a little but righted herself. As she drew nearer to him, his expression changed from astonishment to relief and even a smile—a smile she recognized. And then it came to her. She had seen flashes of this man's image just before she'd passed out. Why?

CHAPTER TWO

THE WOMAN STUMBLING TOWARD JONATHAN in some sort of scuba-diving suit could actually see him.

Amazing!

As time had slowly ticked by day after day after his human life had ended so long ago, he'd saved many people from certain death, but none of them—not a single one—had ever seen him.

But now this woman looked straight at him. Spoke to him.

Phenomenal!

He wanted to answer her, but after using his gift to pull her from the current, he could barely stand. He'd never discovered where the power came, but he could remain on dry land and, using his mind, zero in on a flailing diver or swimmer trapped in the undertow and bring them ashore. Mind over matter, he supposed, though he could use it for only a short amount of time.

And he wasn't alone in gaining a gift. Max, Jonathan's German shepherd, could be inside their shack above the cliffs and know someone was struggling in the water below. The dog had been blessed with a hypersense of knowing.

The woman he'd just saved strode toward him, her luscious, brown, curly hair with golden highlights bobbed every which way. A feeling of déjà vu befell him, as if he'd been with her before. But that didn't make sense. He had no idea who she was.

Unable to place her, he concentrated on the swirling dark mass that hovered behind her like a storm, though transparent. Maybe the aura of her near-death lingered, but he didn't think so. The menace stalking her may have had something to do with her almost drowning. However, that would have dissipated once she'd reached the beach and taken a breath.

Whatever it was, this woman meant something to Jonathan, or why else could she see him? Either he needed to help her, or she needed to help him—or both. He very well might be standing on the threshold of changing his state of being because of this woman. All he needed was to learn the true events of how he and Max had died. He had no memory of how they had perished. And without that knowledge, they could never move on to wherever the dead were supposed to go.

Still weak from his overexertion in willing her to safety, he couldn't work his tongue. Couldn't speak.

She brushed sand from her diving suit as she walked. As she drew closer, his energy grew stronger, which was extraordinary. He usually had to return to his shelter above the cliffs to feel a resurgence of vigor.

She stopped only a few feet away. "You've got a friendly dog there."

Max stood beside Jonathan, ever watchful.

She stared at him. "Have we met before?"

Though he'd had the same thought when he'd first laid eyes on her, he knew it was impossible. With more of his energy restored from her nearness, he cleared his throat and said, "I highly doubt it."

She shivered, but her eyes never left him. "Well, since you're completely dry, I know it wasn't you who saved me." She took a deep breath, then continued, "But did you notice someone else in the water?"

"No."

"Well, there had to be someone who pulled me to shore." She took several deep breaths.

He studied her, not knowing what to say. He'd always believed telling the truth was best, but he didn't know if she could handle this incomprehensible reality.

Maybe the one who couldn't handle it was himself.

"Where exactly am I?" Again, her eyes scanned their surroundings.

"Purgatory Point." He nodded toward the cliffs.

"I know it sounds absurd"—she placed her hands on her hips—"but I shouldn't be here. I should be out there." She pointed to the ocean. Her bottom lip quivered. "I should be . . . well . . . dead."

Maybe that was why she could see him. Maybe she, too, was dead.

But if she were, he and Max wouldn't have needed to rescue her.

"I didn't enter the water from shore." She put her hand to her chin as she stared at the turbulent waves crashing to the beach. "I went diving from a boat several nautical miles from Neah Bay with two other people, and we were separated." She stole more breaths. "Oh, I hope they're okay." She turned once again to face him. Her brown eyes, flecked with copper, focused on his face, and she asked again, "Did you see anyone else come out of the water?"

He shook his head, mesmerized by her.

"They didn't dive as close to the vortex as I did. They should be all right . . . I hope." Her forehead pinched with worry. "Do you have a cell phone I could use? I need to make sure my diving partners are okay."

"No. I'm sorry." He had no idea what a cell phone was, but he knew he didn't have one.

She bit at her fingernail as concern for those she'd been with took priority over her own well-being. Such a noble trait. She definitely wasn't dead. She was beautifully alive but was stalked by an intimidating shadow. Jonathan had to calm her down to see why this threatening entity was connected to her.

To do that, he needed all his energy. Though he felt renewed from being near the woman, he had to return to his shelter. It quickened his rejuvenation.

"I can't explain it." Her shoulders slumped. "You must think I'm crazy. I swear on my life I don't know how I came to be here." She bit her lips together for a second, then said, "I really should have drowned in the vortex current and—" She stopped midsentence. Her hand hit her chest. "Ralph's camera! What am I going to tell him?"

The stalking darkness turned black as ink. Was it a warning? But for whom? Her? She seemed oblivious to the entity. Maybe it was a sign for Jonathan, that he needed to continue to take care of her. He stared at the beautiful woman before him. She was waiting for him to answer her question. He cleared his throat. "I assure you, miss, I don't know what you're going to tell him. I didn't see a camera."

Fearful bewilderment flushed her face. He could understand her confusion. One minute, she'd been with her friends, and the next, she was alone here on the beach.

She swayed.

On reflex, he reached to catch her, then stopped as she righted herself. Their paths had merged for a purpose. If he was going to learn that purpose, he needed answers to his questions. But first, he had to make her feel comfortable and safe. "My name is Jonathan Dawson. Would it make you feel better to know that I've been assigned to this stretch of beach to protect people such as yourself?"

"So, it was you." Relief flushed her face. "You saved my life. But what about the others?" She eyed him again. "And how come you're dry?"

"I'll tell you all that I know, but you've been through quite an ordeal. Let's talk where we can be more comfortable. I have a shelter on the cliffs." He fully intended to tell her the truth as far as he knew it, but not here. They were both ready to collapse.

She held out her hand. "My name's Gloryanna Griffin. If you don't have a cell phone, do you have a CB radio of some kind?"

Unable to accept her handshake, he said, "I used to have a radio, but it disappeared." A lot of things had vanished on that horrible, mixed-up night so many years ago. After waking up on the beach, Jonathan and Max had returned to their shelter. Frank, the other sand pounder assigned here, and all his things had been missing along with the radio.

Jonathan had tried to hike out to find his friend, but every time he and Max had reached the mountain meadow just past the first stand of thick forest, they'd suddenly found themselves back in the shelter, as if they'd never left. After several more tries, they'd quit.

How in the world was he going to explain teleportation to this woman who was worried about her friends? He didn't understand it himself. He'd tell her when the time was right. No sense in overwhelming the poor thing right now with the mysteries that surrounded his and Max's beings.

The woman tilted her head as she studied him and his dog. Curiosity filled her gaze, as if she found them to be an intriguing puzzle.

In an attempt to sidetrack her from trying to get ahold of her friends, he said, "Gloryanna. Wasn't that the name of the faerie queene in Spenser's poem?"

"I don't know about that, but I'll take your word for it. I'm named after my late grandmother." Again, she trembled. She still fought the threat of shock. And who wouldn't? A near-death experience would jolt anyone's nervous system.

"Forgive me. I was an English major, and we had to read that complex book. Anyway, Gloryanna, I'm exhausted. I've got to go up. I'm sure the fire in the camp stove will help fight off your chills. We can have tea and talk over what happened to you and your friends."

She cast her gaze toward the sea. Big, black, billowing clouds with streaks of lightning flashing through them hovered over the ocean. The storm would be here soon. She shivered. "Ordinarily, I wouldn't, but with what looks like heavy rain heading toward us, I must admit tea sounds very good right now." She quivered, peering up at the cliffs. "That's some climb. And what about my gear? I can't just leave it there." She pointed to her scuba equipment on the beach. "The incoming tide could take it, or someone might steal it."

Jonathan wished he could do the gallant thing and move her tank for her, but for his energy to fully return and render him more of a mortal-like body, he'd need to be closer to the shelter. The force that anchored him to the structure allowed him to touch, feel, and eat, as if he still had flesh and blood. Though he felt surprisingly revived already, he didn't dare push his luck. "Not a lot of people come here, but if it makes you feel better, you can hide your things among the black twinberry bushes near the spruce trees where the tide can't reach them. And don't worry, Max will alert us if someone comes near."

"From up there?" She glanced at the cliffs above.

"Max has a sixth sense about this beach. He's the one who alerted me that you were in trouble." The German shepherd wagged his tail on cue.

Though weakened from her ordeal, she retrieved her things, stopping every once in a while, which made him feel like a heel. To try to remedy her thinking him a jerk, he guided her to the bushes, where she plopped down her gear. As she inspected the tank, the darkness shadowing her increased. "I thought I'd find a hole or crack, but nope. No sign of damage, although the gauge shows no air, which is crazy. It had plenty when I started the dive."

Again, worry lines creased her face. Jonathan needed to get her away from her scuba things so she could relax. "Let's go topside and discuss it."

He led the way up the trail carpeted with spongy mosses, banked by thick ferns, and canopied by Sitka spruces, western hemlock, and red cedar trees. He glanced back every once in a while to check on her. She seemed to grow more and more perplexed as she studied her surroundings, but she said nothing.

As they neared his hut, he felt new energy pour through him. He grabbed a few logs to feed the fire he'd left in the stove. Even in early summer, the wind had a chill, and with the storm fast approaching, and after all his guest had been through, she would need to get warm fast.

He showed her inside his one-room shack. The foreboding backed off and stayed outside as she entered. He nodded to a chair she could sit on by the table and then loaded the woodbin. He opened the mouth of the stove, placed a log on the red, inviting coals, then moved the kettle still containing water from this morning's breakfast over the heat. "That shouldn't take long. In the meantime, you might want to change from your diving suit."

"I don't have anything else to wear." She held her hands out to the flame. "I mean, I have undergarments on beneath this suit, but my clothes are in Professor Takahashi's van parked at Neah Bay harbor. It's so strange that the current took me so far away from our diving site." She shook her head like she still couldn't believe what had happened. "Do you have a map?"

Jonathan thought of the map he'd been given when he and Frank had been posted here. But it, like the radio, had disappeared with Frank. "I used to. You'd best change. I have some things you can wear."

He pulled a bin from beneath his cot and found a flannel shirt and a pair of pants. For good measure, he grabbed some woolly socks and set it all on his bed. "Why don't you change while I pick some spearmint leaves?"

"Pick?"

"Yes. To make your tea. Fresh is always better. With that storm brewing, I won't be long. When the water starts to boil, just set the kettle on the back of the stove." He and Max ducked out.

Once she relaxed, he'd question her more. He needed to figure out if the darkness shadowing Gloryanna came from within or if it was a warning of something about to happen to her. Either way, he felt compelled to protect her.

***

With a tremendous struggle, Gloryanna peeled off the dry suit and the wet, muddy booties from her feet. Her underwear, though a bit damp from perspiration, was amazingly dry. She quickly dressed as she worried. The professor and Thomas must be looking for her, if they were still alive. But she could do nothing to help them right now. She had to remain calm and think. Her mind turned to Ralph.

What was she going to tell him about his camera? He believed in her. Put his faith in her to take care of it. And now she'd have to face the music and tell him what had happened, that she'd made a rookie mistake reading her tank and then everything had spiraled downhill from there. She'd buy him a new one. Her main concern was making certain Professor Takahashi and Thomas were okay and then getting back before someone told her family she'd gone missing.

She stopped a moment. Ralph had filled her tank. He'd be very upset with himself for not doing it right.

And Thomas had helped her put it on. Could he have done something to it without her noticing?

What was she thinking? Why would Thomas want to kill her? Four years ago, they'd been dating. And even though they hadn't been in a relationship for three years, they were still friends.

Albeit, competing friends. Friends vying for the same grant. Which didn't make sense at all. Thomas's father was none other than Seymour Clifford, one of the richest men in the state. In fact, he'd donated so much money to the university that they'd named a building after him Clifford Hall.

Maybe Grandpa's dementia and paranoia is contagious. Her ninety-nine-year-old grandfather suffered from congestive heart failure and the rigors of old age. Unable to care for himself, he'd moved in with her parents. She could hardly wait to tell him that she thought she'd seen a conning tower that could prove a sunken submarine was down there. When he was having one of his "senior" moments, he'd talk about a submarine he'd been on during World War II.

No one believed him because he'd actually served on an aircraft carrier. Besides, after all this time, some scuba diver would have come across such wreckage. Mom chalked up his rambling to his watching too many war movies and merging those stories with his real life.

Steam billowed out of the teapot, and it whistled. The canvas pants Jonathan had loaned her were way too big, so she held them to her waist and trekked in his woolly socks closer to the stove. Both Jonathan's black-and-red-flannel shirt and the heat from the fire calmed her shivers. After moving the teapot, she turned so her backside would get warm too. She scanned the interior of the shack.

In the kitchen area next to the stove stood a table and two chairs held together with some type of rope. The craftsmanship that went into building the furniture, though hindered by crude materials, made them appear well built. A cupboard with no doors hung on the wall and had bottles of various sizes on its shelves. It all made her appreciate the comforts of her mother's stylish kitchen and even her own small apartment. At least she had a bathroom. Poor Jonathan. He must really be down on his luck.

Her eyes drew to his bed. It looked like an army cot, as did the ugly dark-green blanket on top. Near the pillow rested a tattered book, the cover unreadable. Maybe she could talk her father, a contractor of his own construction company, into building Jonathan a decent bed for saving her life.

On the other side of the shack, a crate held an old-fashioned crank phonograph record player, but it appeared brand new. Gloryanna's grandfather had a similar one. It was among his most treasured possessions.

Holding the pants up, she tramped over to take a closer look. Several albums leaned against the crate. They were in extremely good condition. The first one had the face of a pretty woman with a 1940s hairdo. Her image had been placed above the Cliffs of Dover. A train, with steam billowing from its smokebox traveled beneath World War II planes flying overhead. In the lower right-hand corner, a couple embraced. The album's title was *The Very Best of Vera Lynn*. Grandpa had one of her albums. Since Grandma had died, he'd play *We'll Meet Again* over and over. Gloryanna browsed the room some more. This was like a time capsule.

Black binoculars hung by the windowpane. Scuffed and scratched, they appeared pretty beat-up. She took them off the peg and tried peering through them out the window. She caught the image of Jonathan returning to the shack.

He was amazingly handsome. And he reminded her of someone. With striking clarity, she suddenly knew. He reminded her of Jim Caviezel in the old movie *The Count of Monte Cristo*. Jonathan had the same wind-tossed hair, expressive dark eyes, and beard.

Those frantic moments when she'd fought for her life while on the dive returned. Why had she seen her movie heartthrob? Talk about weird. Why hadn't she seen her parents or someone close to her? How odd was it that she'd seen a man who looked so much like Jonathan?

Fighting blustery winds, he headed for the shack with a handful of fresh spearmint. His dog, Max, dutifully trotted by his side. Their images grew blurry. She tried to focus the binoculars but couldn't. She turned them over. On the base, it read Mark 28.

Jonathan stomped his feet as he opened the door. She quickly hung the field glasses on their peg, not wanting him to know she'd been spying on him.

Max entered first, followed by his master. Jonathan went to the kettle, broke the leaves from the stems, and dropped them inside. "We'll let that steep for a bit. Feeling better?"

Rain pelted against the window. "I'm worried about my friends. I hate to think of them caught in this storm, though there's not much I can do about it." She pulled out a chair for Jonathan, then sat on the other one. "But I have a ton of questions for you."

"Like I said before, I didn't see your friends. Only you. What would you like to know?" He settled onto the chair.

Since he couldn't set her mind at ease about Professor Takahashi or Thomas, she decided to focus on something he might be able to answer. "I know that the mind can play tricks on a person when they've been underwater and oxygen deprived, but I have to know how you saved me. You weren't even wet."

"I've thought about how to tell you." He sat tall. "And determined I should just be honest. It's very simple how I rescued you. I'm a ghost."

CHAPTER THREE

THE WALLS OF THE SHELTER closed in on Gloryanna as she stared at Jonathan. He looked perfectly sane. Maybe she'd heard him wrong. Had the vortex current done something to her hearing? She cleared her throat and leaned toward him. "Excuse me?"

"I'm a ghost. And so is Max." He pointed to the dog, which had come over to rest at her feet.

That was what she'd thought he'd said. He was obviously a bit of a nutjob. She'd need to be careful if she were going to get away from him. Wanting to pretend to give him the benefit of the doubt, she slowly bent over and stroked Max's head. "If he's a ghost, why can I touch him?"

"I don't know exactly. I believe it has something to do with the shelter." He glanced around his one-room shack, then at her. "And if I'm being honest, you."

"Me?" She stood. The pants almost dropped from her waist, but she snagged them in time. "Why would it have anything to do with me?"

"I'm not sure." He stroked his bearded chin. "But in all the years since Max and I died, no mortal has seen us until you came along. That's why I believe it has something to do with you."

"Look, I don't want to play this weird game of yours." She scanned her surroundings. "I have a very hard time believing I have anything to do with you or your dog. And your shack doesn't look magical or extraordinary or even haunted, for that matter."

He lifted his shoulders as if he were out of ideas. The man's mind must have lost its rudder, and after everything she'd been through today, she jumped from being upset to being blasted infuriated. "If you could please tell me the best way to reach civilization, I'd appreciate it. I need to let my friends and family know I'm all right."

Jonathan leaned back in his chair. "You can't leave yet."

Fear rippled over her. Was he going to keep her here against her will? She had to play this cool and calm. Going along with the conversation, she asked, "Why?"

"For one thing, it's raining. For another, a darkness followed you from the beach. I think you're still in danger." He leaned forward. Staring into her eyes, he said, "You nearly died, but you survived, so the shadow of death should have left. It disappeared once you stepped into my home, but I fear it may return once you go outside again."

Bewildered, she didn't know what to say. He was right in that she should have died. But his claim that he'd saved her and that some death shadow followed her to his shack was a bit much. She was in deep trouble here, especially if she let him know she was unnerved. Playing along, she said, "Do you mean the Grim Reaper?"

"No. I've battled him before for others—and won, I might add." He placed his elbows on the chair's well-crafted armrests. "The enmity stalking you is something different, a danger ready to pounce, but it hasn't."

Was he talking about himself? Was he some kind of sick pervert who toyed with his victims?

"I see doubt in your eyes." He steepled his hands together. "Look, Max and I died many, many years ago. We've been stuck here since. I'm sure you've checked around my place?"

Creeped out by everything he'd said, she wondered where he was going with this question and uttered a leery, "*Yes.*"

"What did you see?" He pulled a pipe from his coat pocket, then got up and retrieved one of the jars off the shelf. He returned to the table.

"Crude furnishings, a book, records, and stuff." She hesitated. "I know the phonograph and records are old, but they look new."

"That's because they are." He sat down, opened the jar, and loaded his pipe with dried aromatic leaves. "For some reason, the shelter has been suspended in time, like Max and I have been. We're stuck somewhere in the middle between life and death. As for the furnishings, Frank and I made most of it when we first got here, and the Coast Guard furnished the rest." He swiped a hand over the wooden table.

He set his pipe down, rose, and pulled the blanket off the cot. "It's stamped with a date. They made tons of these during the war. With our troops stationed all over the world, there was a high demand for blankets." He pointed for her to take a look.

Gloryanna warily walked to him, and sure enough, there was a military stamp dated 1943. "This should be thread-worn or faded. It's 2023 now."

"Are you telling me eighty years have passed?" His complexion paled, if that was possible for a ghost. However, right now, he seemed very mortal to Gloryanna.

"I guess so."

He let out a deep breath. "I knew it had been a while but not that long." He seemed to quickly shake off his astonishment, and instead of asking what had happened in the world over the years, as Gloryanna had expected him to, he went to the phonograph and picked up the conversation from before the discovery of how long he'd been here. "I packed this in myself. Didn't want to be stuck without some form of entertainment."

That he didn't ask about what had gone on in the last eighty years or who had won the war amazed her. Maybe it was because he knew and he was blowing proverbial smoke in her face with this tale of being a ghost and her having a dark shadow following her.

He'd conveniently sidestepped the time blip. Maybe if she got him to acknowledge he was spinning a tale, he'd tell her the truth. She whipped around and looked at the stove. "Did you pack this in as well?"

"No. The Coast Guard brought it to us on a mule. We were mighty happy to get it too. Frank and I about froze our tails off those first few months until it arrived."

Frank? He had a buddy? This was not good. Maybe he was keeping her here until his friend returned. She couldn't let panic dictate her actions. She had to gain the upper hand before she was outnumbered. "Look, I'm not buying your story. How does this prove that you're a ghost? And who is Frank? Do you have a friend here with you?"

"Frank was my teammate. Our job was to patrol the coastline during the war."

Testing to see if he'd slip up, she asked, "What war? The Korean? Vietnam? Afghanistan?"

"I've never heard of those." His mouth formed a grim line. "Were they after World War II? Who won World War II anyway?"

"You know very well that we did, just like you know when those other wars were." She'd had enough and started gathering her scuba-diving suit and booties.

"I'm glad we won, but I can't believe, after all we went through, that more wars would follow." He shook his head and returned to his chair. "Did humanity learn nothing?" His voice cracked.

Concern and deep sorrow furrowed his forehead. His shoulders slumped. He seemed truly crestfallen. Either this guy was a darn good actor, or he truly believed his story. But that was all it was. *A story.*

He desperately needed help. Did she dare stick around to learn a little more about him? She tentatively sat on the cot, still holding her scuba gear. "So, you and this Frank fellow were stationed here during World War II?"

"Yes. We were sand pounders."

"Sand pounders?" She'd heard of them in the nautical history class she'd taken. "They came into being in the late 1800s and were on the East Coast."

"You're right. There was another division called that before ours. When the US was pulled into war with Japan and then Germany, even though those battles happened far away from our homeland, America soon realized her own coastlines were vulnerable, especially after a German U-boat tried to smuggle spies into our country from the Atlantic. The army and marines had their hands full, so the Coast Guard formed a special division, which they called sand pounders, to patrol our beaches."

She made a mental note to look this up when she returned home. And right now, she had to get the heck out of Dodge so she *could* get home. "I need to leave. Thanks for the clothes. I'll bring them back. I promise." She walked to the door.

"Gloryanna." His voice was low and gentle, almost a whisper. And he didn't sound like a predator. He sounded genuine.

She glanced at him. He sat on the chair he'd claimed he'd made, with his elbows on the armrests. The sad pleading in his gaze, heightened by his bearded and chiseled face that looked even more ruggedly handsome, made her insides tumble with an unexpected warmth. Her heart skipped a beat, and her breath caught.

She was totally losing it.

Perhaps her near-death experience coupled with meeting this gallant, though slightly delusional man had played with her jumbled emotions. Shaking her head, she said, "I can't stay here."

"Even though I told you about the shadow that follows you?"

"Well, I don't see it." She checked behind her. "Besides, I'm not afraid of shadows."

He gave a long sigh. "All right. The storm has let up a bit. But there's no way you can walk out of here following the beach." His calm voice pulled her to a stop. "High tide makes that impossible. And if you take the wrong trail through the forest, you could get lost for days. Even the trail we made using shortcuts takes a good day to hike through to the next shelter, where they may have automobiles and access to a road to take you back to a town. If you leave now, in late afternoon, you'll be caught in the forest overnight."

Total frustration pulsed through her. She dropped her scuba suit to the floor. "What am I going to do?" She smoothed irritating hairs away from her face. "By now, Professor Takahashi will have notified my family—that is, if she and Thomas are still alive. I can't stay here. I have to leave now."

"Even despite the warning I gave you about a darkness chasing you?"

"Look, if you mean to scare me into staying, it's not going to work. Even if darkness is 'chasing me'"—she did air quotes—"I can't sit around and wait for it, can I?" She surprised even herself with her logic.

He took a deep breath. "As you wish, but Max and I will travel with you as far as we can and make sure you're on the right trail." He rose to his feet.

"No, that's all right. I can find my own way." She'd be better off alone in the forest than with this crazy man.

He shook his head and grabbed an odd-looking flashlight with an angled top. "You're going to need this." He handed it to her.

"Do the batteries still have a charge? I mean, if you've been stranded here for eighty years, surely they're dead." She checked the base of the housing on the brass-bodied device and saw the word *Eveready*. Then she flipped the switch. To her astonishment, it beamed a light.

"As you can very well see, it's fine."

That the old flashlight worked shored up her suspicion that he was crazy and not a ghost. He'd had to have bought batteries for the light recently. She tried to bundle her diving suit under her arm but dropped half of it.

"Why don't you leave that here? You can pick it up when you come back to get your tank and return my clothes." He took her suit from her and set it on his cot.

She fought the urge to argue. The day was fast ending, and she needed to get going. Opening the door, she glanced down at her feet and realized she had no shoes. "This will ruin your socks."

"I happen to have an extra pair of boots." He went to the cot and pulled out his box again. As he dug deep into the contents, he said, "The dress code for sand pounders wasn't nearly as strict as other military units. Instead of wearing uniforms, both Frank and I opted to wear logger clothing." He pulled out some well-worn standard-issue military boots. "I quit using these when I got my Danner Loggers. They might be too big for you, but they'll keep your feet dry." He handed the boots to her.

"Thanks." She sat on the floor and tugged them on, quickly tying the laces as tightly as she could while he banked the stove and pulled the kettle to a cold spot. He came over and took his poncho from the wall peg. "Here. You're going to need this."

"No. I can't take it." She already felt indebted to him enough.

"Yes, you can. It's still raining some, and you'll be glad you have it." He placed it over her head and pulled it to her shoulders, letting the rest drape to her ankles. "You can bring it back when you return for the rest of your things."

She stepped outside. The cold wind slapped her face, stealing her breath. Jonathan followed. "Are you certain you want to leave now?"

"I have to." She prayed in her heart she'd find civilization sooner than he'd said she would.

"Then Max and I are going with you, and I'll hear no more arguments." He started down the trail.

***

Jonathan watched the shadow following her again. If it was a sign that he needed to protect her, what would happen when they reached the mountain meadow and he and Max were transported back to the shack? She'd be on her own to fight it.

He pondered this dilemma as they hiked the trail. With his energy renewed during their stay at the shelter, he was able to walk at a good pace, and surprisingly, Gloryanna kept up even though she struggled a little with his boots that were clearly too big for her.

Maybe Jonathan could get Gloryanna talking while they hiked, which might help him figure out what to do. He'd unnerved her with the truth and needed to calm her down. Besides, he'd missed conversing with another human being. "Your family must mean a lot to you for you to risk traveling through this primitive forest by yourself at night."

"They do." She walked at his side. The hood of the poncho covered her head, but locks of her hair peeked out and had become wet and dangled loosely. "They're my world. My parents have always been there for me, which probably sounds pretty childish."

"No. Not at all. In fact, I'm quite envious." He glanced at her. He couldn't help but think of Allred Orphanage, where he'd been taken as a toddler during World War I and had spent most of his youth. He had no idea what his parents or grandparents had been like. The orphanage had been a horrible place filled with haunting memories.

She tripped and stopped, adjusting something beneath the poncho. "What's wrong?"

"I'm surprised you can't see with your ghost vision." She shot him a mischievous look, then seemed to regret it. "I'm having a horrible time keeping your pants up."

"Ghost vision?" He chuckled. "I should have given you some rope to use. Wait, I know." He stopped and unbuckled his own belt. "It's easier for me to go without one than you."

"I can't take your belt. Besides, it will never fit."

"It'll adjust to you." He pulled it from his pants.

"Okay, but I can put it on myself." She kept her distance but reached out for it. She acted as if being close to him made her uncomfortable.

"These basic rigger belts can be tricky. The tip needs to pass through the buckle and feed back to the locking bar."

"I've put on a belt before." She impatiently gestured for him to hand it to her.

Since she seemed to know what she was doing, this might be a good chance to test the shadow. If Jonathan were to come too close to her and the cloud darkened, that would mean it came from within Gloryanna. He took a step, invading her personal space.

She grimaced and stepped back. The shadow stayed the same. So it had to be a warning of danger to come. Careful not to touch her, he dropped the belt into her hand. "Sorry. Are you angry?" The last thing he wanted to do was make her upset with him. Now that he knew the danger was more likely a warning, he worried about her leaving him.

"No. I'm just not used to a ghost giving me his belt." She slipped it on and seemed to have no trouble at all. "And I have to say you seem very tangible to me. You even smell like my grandfather's Old Spice cologne."

Old Spice. Something familiar from his forgotten life. As was the orange-blossom fragrance he smelled on her. "The pants shouldn't cause you any more trouble, but I can't say the same about the boots."

"The boots are keeping my feet dry, so I can manage." She stood close, and her breaths became short, shallow. Her gaze trailed to his face. He peered into her luminous brown eyes that he could get lost in. She gulped and muttered, "Thank you," then abruptly broke the spell by turning away.

They started walking again.

The rain had turned to a mere drizzle, and the sun was beginning to set. In another mile or so, they'd reach the edge of the forest that he couldn't leave. Beyond that point was the meadow he and Max were unable to cross. Maybe it would be different this time with Gloryanna.

Things had already started to shift she could see both him and Max. Plus, he was fairly certain he was supposed to protect her from the foreboding at her heels. He wanted to keep her talking as much as he could in case she said something that would help him understand what he was to do, but he also wanted to lock the sound of her voice to memory. "Tell me again why you would put your life at risk by hiking through the forest at night?"

"*And again*, I say, I'm worried about my friends and my family." And then she sighed. "But mostly, I'm afraid news that I'm missing might very well kill my grandfather.

Her words sank deep within him. The pain of not having his own family had been a perpetual wound.

"Are you okay?" She stared at him.

"I was just thinking how very lucky you are." He didn't elaborate.

"You mean, despite nearly drowning and having some threatening shadow following me?" She stopped. "Sorry. I don't know what to think of you, Jonathan. You tell me you're a ghost, which is absurd. You live out here in the middle of nowhere, like some Unabomber."

"Unabomber?" He didn't understand what she meant, and she seemed even more upset than before. To calm her, he said, "I'm trying my best to be honest with you."

She huffed. "Okay, then, tell me about your family. If you've been stuck at the beach in your shelter all these years, is there someone you would like me to get in touch with to see how they're doing?"

"I never knew my parents." He hated admitting it.

"Of course not."

"I grew up in an orphanage."

Her shoulders drooped a little as his words seemed to register. Still walking, and with more sincerity than before, she said, "That had to be tough."

"It's okay." He didn't want to tell her what he'd lived through as a kid.

"So, did you have a girlfriend?" A light trace of hope threaded her words.

"Mary Ann wrote me a Dear John shortly after I was stationed here. I thought she was the one, but it probably worked out for the best since I died. She would be a hundred now."

Gloryanna had paused when he'd said he died. She stared at him now. "Let's drop this charade. If she's that old, you must be a hundred and ten, but you don't look a day over thirty."

He had to try again to help her understand. "Remember I told you the shelter is frozen in time. I myself don't understand why. I think it has something to do with when or how I died. I seem to have stayed the age I was then."

She said nothing, just continued to stare at him. In the forest's shadows, her eyes became dark sparkling orbs. Her wet hair framed her worried, porcelain face. He'd never been acquainted with a woman like this. Not only was she stunning, but her character was also impressive.

Down the trail in a few hundred feet, things would change, and he and Max would be whisked away to the shelter. He had to make her believe him. But he could think of no other way to do it.

She started walking again. The flopping sound of his boots that she wore only endeared her to him more.

Before they reached the meadow, he had to tell her what he could and hope that she would somehow help him. Keeping up with her, he said, "I can't remember what caused my death. All I know is on that horrible night, Max and I left the shelter to find Frank. He was late returning from patrol. It was growing dark, much like it is now. But that's where my memory fades. I don't know what or who killed me, but I think if I learned that, Max and I could move on to where we're supposed to be."

She stepped in front of him, arms folded. "Okay, it's not like I believe your ghost story, but if it will make you feel better, once I'm home, I'll do a little research to see what I can find."

"I knew you were sent to help us, just like I'm supposed to help you." It was all he could do not to reach out and hug her, but he'd already pressed his luck. He didn't want to freak her out any more than he already had.

"Don't say that." She rubbed her temple.

"What?"

"That I was sent to help you. You're putting a lot of pressure on me."

"Sorry." Though he wasn't. For the first time in decades, he felt hopeful.

"And I can't promise I'll find anything." She bit her bottom lip. "I mean, it's been such a long time. And I have my hands full trying to help my parents with Grandpa and trying to win a grant so I can continue my education; plus, there's my job."

This beautiful, complicated woman he'd saved from the depths of the ocean had agreed to help him. He couldn't stop the grin that pulled at the corners of his mouth.

She threw her hands up. "And wipe that smile off your face. Whoever heard of a happy ghost stranded in a shelter next to the beach who saves peoples' lives? I must be hallucinating."

"You're not. You, Gloryanna Griffin, are a noble soul. God has put us together for a reason. You'll see. When the time comes, we'll be there for each other." He hoped he was right, that he and Max could continue to follow her and keep her safe.

She stared at him, and a warmth settled in her eyes. Was she starting to believe him, starting to care about his predicament? But then she abruptly walked away. "And there you go, saying I'm noble."

They were dangerously close to the part of the trail where he and Max could be sent back to the shelter. Just in case, he had to let her know he believed in her and that what he'd said was true. She was in danger. The only thing he could think to do to convince her was to touch her. Before, when he'd rescued her from the ocean, it had been with his mind. This would be different. This would be physical.

But what if his hand went through her?

She'd be terrified.

He had to take the risk.

He reached out and took hold of her arm. The simple touch awakened his mortal senses. It had been so long since he'd made contact with another human being. It reminded him how very alone he'd been. When she left, he would not be able to experience such sensations again. Intense loneliness waited for him. He yearned to hold her, to smell her hair, to keep her with him. He could hardly stand the thought of returning to the empty shack.

She seemed mesmerized at first, and then she flinched away. "Stop it."

Coldness rushed in. "Just . . . give me a second." He touched her again, drawing her closer and closer. Her glare melted away. Her breathing slowed.

As he'd lain dying on the craggy rocks below Purgatory Point, he'd seen *her*. Touching her, he studied her creamy face and her brilliant eyes. She was the woman who had come to him in his last moments of life. It wasn't déjà vu. He had this one chance to show her how much he cared.

All at once, she stepped away. "What do you think you're doing?"

"Proving a point." He didn't blame her for recoiling. After sharing that powerful knowing gaze, she had to be confused and in denial.

"The point that you're crazy?" She turned around and started walking.

Jonathan and Max followed. Her image began to fade, becoming blurry. The tingling sensation of teleportation's greedy fingers wrapped around him, pulling him back to his prison.

Before he could say a word, Gloryanna disappeared.

CHAPTER FOUR

STILL REELING FROM THE ODD sensation that had filled her senses from his touch, Gloryanna didn't know what to say, what to do. A strange, enchanted warmth had emanated from him to her. Did she really just experience some odd metaphysical awareness?

No.

She'd crossed over to crazy-ville.

She had to stop this line of thinking and see it for what it was. Feeling surer of herself and the proprieties of being with a new acquaintance, she said, "I mean, you just don't haul off and touch someone you hardly know."

She had to make Jonathan understand that he'd crossed the line. She walked farther out into the mountain meadow, expecting him to defend his actions. But he didn't answer. She swung around.

He and the dog were gone.

She tripped on his massive boots, righted herself, and rushed back to the forest line, peering into the growing shadows. He'd been right there on her heels the entire time, and now he was gone.

No, he had to be hiding. "This isn't funny, Jonathan. It's been a very long and trying day. Come out."

No answer.

No movement.

She stared at the giant trees and the underbrush. An eerie quietness settled over the forest. Why didn't he answer?

Fear prickled her spine.

So, was he a ghost?

She had no idea. She only knew that ever since she'd regained consciousness on the beach where she'd first laid eyes on Jonathan, she'd been living in a surreal existence, and it seemed as though that hadn't been the first time she'd seen him. Maybe as she'd been deprived of oxygen deep in the ocean, it had been Jonathan—not Jim Caviezel—who had come to her.

A shudder took hold.

This was mind-blowing stuff beyond her reasoning.

Not to mention Jonathan had warned her about a shadow following her. Filled with the urgent need to run, she turned around and took off, sprinting as fast as she could.

Midway through the mountain meadow, she stopped. There were no more trees for him to hide behind. But now she stood in the open where he could see her. How stupid was she?

Racing as fast as she could, she made a mad dash through the wild meadow, keeping her focus on the next stand of trees waiting for her. At least she'd have shelter there.

The path led to giant, foreboding, druid-like pines that swayed from a sudden wind. Scurrying noises came from the brush. Probably squirrels or rodents. Not bears or cougars, even though it very well could have been one of those animals.

An owl hooted above. Gloryanna hesitated. In the meadow, she'd had moonlight guiding her. But in the forest, it was dark.

Eerily dark.

Hauntingly dark.

She clicked on the flashlight Jonathan had given her.

This was a bit too *Twilight Zone*-ish.

Walking timidly down the trail, she shone the light in the direction of any sounds. But gratefully, every time, she saw only foliage and kept walking.

With each step, a whirlpool of unanswerable questions mingled with undeniable truths and swirled in her head. She couldn't put the puzzle of Jonathan Dawson together. And she was terribly alone.

She swiped a hand over her face, hoping to vanquish the man's memory, and continued to follow the trail. She wished she'd grabbed her scuba-diving watch from the shack. She hadn't bothered because it was outdated anyway, but it could have at least given her the time. She had to have been walking for hours. Every muscle in her body ached. Still, she kept going.

She tried thinking happier thoughts time with Mom shopping, time with Dad playing a game of hoops, and time with Grandpa listening to him spin his good-ole-days tales of riding the seas. But despite her best efforts, her mind drifted to Jonathan and the shadow of darkness he said followed her.

What if the darkness meant something had happened to her family? Maybe Grandpa? Or Mom and Dad? Or what if the shadow was Thomas's and Professor Takahashi's ghosts?

If that were the case, wouldn't Jonathan have seen them too?

Tripping on a rut in the trail, she shone the light on a large rock. She needed to be more careful. She focused on the path. *Just keep walking, walking, walking.* She repeated the mantra over and over.

She thought of Jonathan's shack and his records. The Vera Lynn song "We'll Meet Again" played in her mind.

Jonathan's face came to her. His smell. His touch.

The sound of a twig snapping sounded from her left. She shone the light in that direction. The shadow of a man blended behind a huge pine draped with moss.

"Jonathan!" she shouted.

Had he been following her through the forest all this time? Too late, she realized whoever it had been was much shorter than Jonathan.

Terror seized her. Prickling needles of fear raced over her skin. Was this the darkness Jonathan had warned her about? Too scared to scream, she spun around and immediately fell down, dropping the flashlight.

She scrambled to her feet, grabbed the flashlight, and raced down the craggy, rut-filled trail the best she could in oversized boots.

The terrifying sound of someone or something crashing through the brush came right at her. He'd be on her any second. Her heart sledgehammered against her ribs. Fighting for breath, she bolted ahead.

Thumping footsteps grew closer and closer, gaining on her with every second.

She ran for all she was worth, ignoring the knifing pain in her side. Her feet pounded the ground. Her lungs felt ready to burst.

All at once, strong arms grabbed her, and she screamed.

CHAPTER FIVE

"Ma'am!" A man fought to hold her. "Ma'am, I'm not going to hurt you." He flinched and deflected each blow she gave him until she finally stopped fighting and quit screaming.

She shone the flashlight into the face of the stranger with a long shaggy beard and hair. He wore animal skins and smelled of the wilds. She pushed him away, and he finally moved back.

He nodded as though he understood her need for space and held out his hand. "Name's Branson White."

Leery, she didn't take his offer but instead asked, "Why did you chase me? Why are you out here?" She had a hundred more questions to ask but thought she'd start with those as she caught her breath and stared at the man who had scared the living daylights out of her.

"I didn't want you running into a tree or something, as scared as you were." He chuckled, but Gloryanna could find nothing funny.

He continued. "We've had trouble with a bear getting into our garbage. He does it close to dawn, so I thought I'd sneak out to try to lure him into a trap."

"Did you say bear?" She quickly glanced around, shining her flashlight at the bushes around them. No bear, only looming trees and underbrush.

"Yes, ma'am." He stroked his beard. "If I trap him, the park service will take the animal to higher ground."

Gloryanna drew a deep breath and focused on the man and getting out of here. "Do you live close by?"

"Yes."

"Do you have a cell phone?" Was it too much to hope he did?

"I don't, but my wife does. She's back at the cabin. She'll be very happy to see another woman." He started down the trail, leading the way. The dark of night slowly evaporated into silvery grays. "Ma'am, can I ask what in the world you're doing out here by yourself?"

She cautiously followed him and figured she might as well tell him. "I got caught in a vortex current in the sea and found myself on the beach below the cliffs. A man claimed he saved me, but he wasn't even wet."

He stopped and stared at her. "Are you Gloryanna Griffin?"

Surprised that he knew her name, she replied, "Yes."

"Oh my holey socks! You're the woman everyone has been searching for." He shook his head. "How in the world—" He stopped and stared at her. "You said a vortex current got you?"

"Yes." She hated admitting to a rookie diving mistake. "Were they also searching for two other divers?" She hoped for the good news that Thomas and Professor Takahashi were safe.

"No. Just you. You said a man saved you but he wasn't wet?" He stared at her, making her feel like a child about to be scolded.

"You think I'm crazy, don't you?" She hesitated, gaining fresh courage, then added, "He showed me this trail and then disappeared."

"Well, I'll be." Branson shook his head. "Our ghost is at it again, though I've never heard of anyone actually seeing him."

"Ghost?" She needed this man to confirm what she knew in her heart. Not that Jonathan Dawson was a ghost but that he was a sad, lonely man.

"Ma'am, I'm no authority when it comes to phantoms and what they can and can't do. But in the last ten years since my wife and I moved here, I can't tell you how many people come out of this forest claiming that someone saved them from drowning in the ocean. They say it had to be a ghost. But none of them ever saw who their rescuer was."

Gloryanna didn't know what to think.

Still fighting to find the truth, she felt pretty certain that Jonathan was no ghost. And neither was his dog. When she reached home and everything calmed down, she needed to see what she could find out about Jonathan. She might even do some research about the sand pounders assigned to this beach during World War II. Even if he was delusional, Jonathan had saved her life. She would find what she could and bring it to him when she returned for her tank and dropped off his clothes.

***

Alone with Max in the shelter, Jonathan paced back and forth in the small room. "Why was I stupid enough to touch Gloryanna?" He stopped and looked at the dog that stared at him.

"Okay, it was ill-advised, I'll grant you that. Especially when our very existence hinges on her help." He drove his fingers through his hair. "And I confess, touching her was an impulse. A desperate impulse." But deep in his heart, as he'd stood there staring at Gloryanna, he'd been overcome with the need for human contact. The thought that he may never see her again had overtaken his emotions and blocked his logical thinking. "But I'm not sorry, and I'm not apologizing."

Max whined and leaned against Jonathan's legs.

"So you do understand." Stroking the dog's head and rubbing his soft ears, Jonathan relived the moment. He'd been unprepared for the flood of feelings that had sprung to life. "I'm so glad I could touch her. I wasn't certain I could."

He marveled. "She was the one, Max. The woman I saw before I died. We were destined to meet. And I was so certain I was supposed to protect her. I even thought we might be able to follow her through the meadow. I know she'll help us. But how long will it take? And did she believe me?"

With no answers to his questions, he rubbed the back of his aching neck.

"She had to have believed, don't you think?" He gazed at Max. The dog stared at him, his eyes full of sympathy.

Jonathan answered for his four-legged friend, "Maybe?"

Doubt rushed in. "Why would she believe me? To her, I'm some crazy person claiming to be a ghost living in a shack in the forest." He looked at the dog. "And ghosts only happen in stories, right? They're fiction. We're fiction. Yet, here we are." He paced again.

Max blocked his path.

"What's wrong?" If someone needed to be rescued, Max would bark, not stop him.

The dog cocked his head. Even he questioned whether she'd help them.

"You're right. There's no way she'd believe I'm a ghost. I screwed up bigtime. I was dumb, imprudent, and wrong."

Max merely stared at him.

Jonathan dropped onto his knees. "I know you can't understand, but it has been so long since I've touched another human. I had to do it. I was desperate. Touching her seemed the answer, flawed logic now that I think back on it. But we need her help. Unless you like living in limbo."

Max licked Jonathan's chin.

"Thanks for understanding, old boy. We're in this together, aren't we?" He gave the dog a hug. Pulling back, he gazed into Max's eyes. "You liked her, didn't you?"

The animal dipped his head the other way.

"I know you did. You went right up to her on the beach. You've never done that with the other people we've rescued."

Again, Max licked Jonathan's chin.

"So, we agree. She's pretty special." He stood. "She should be home sometime today, back with the family she loves. Imagine that, Max. Having a family that you love and who loves you in return. Wouldn't that be something?" Again, memories of the orphanage he'd grown up in threatened to surface. But he wouldn't let them. He'd overcome those haunting times from his long-ago childhood.

Max went to the door and scratched.

Jonathan checked out the window. The sun had risen. Time to go on patrol. He reached for his poncho. It was gone. He'd given it to Gloryanna. Glad that he'd done so, he instead grabbed the binoculars from the wall peg. "Let's see if someone needs our help."

Max's tail swished back and forth as he danced from one front paw to the other.

Jonathan opened the door a crack. Max nosed it wider, allowing himself to leave first. They really didn't need to patrol since Max had a sixth sense, but through the years, they'd kept to their routine of hiking the trails and checking the beaches. It gave them purpose and made Jonathan feel normal and not dead.

Dead.

To the world, that was what he was, but here in this bubble that had captured him and his dog, he was alive and well.

Max started following the path to Purgatory Point.

"You know we can't go over there." Ever since their passing, Jonathan hadn't been able to bring himself to walk the trail to the ledge. Images flew at him like pesky seagulls. Flashes of faces he didn't know nearly drove him insane from the pain they brought. "Max, come."

The German shepherd stopped and doubled back.

Jonathan had chalked up his inability to walk the path to his old mortal fear of heights. It had stuck to him even in death. The anxiety became as powerful as a sucker punch to the jaw. He didn't understand his qualms.

The thought reminded him of the shadow he'd seen following Gloryanna. Danger stalked her, hunted her. He had told her about it, hoping she would be mindful and wary, but had he done enough? Had he been too absorbed in his need to entice her to help him and Max? What if he'd played right into the hands of the threat? What if by helping him, she'd opened herself up to a menace that would risk her life?

It made sense. The shadow had followed Gloryanna from the water Jonathan had saved her from. And she had come right to him, which could have been what the ominous darkness had wanted.

Worried that he might have been derelict in protecting her and that he could have put her in even more peril, he sat on a moss-covered tree stump and hoped he was wrong.

***

Gloryanna awakened to a throbbing headache, and at first, she didn't know where she was. She glanced around the room happy daisy wallpaper, framed pictures of her in the pink prom dress Mom had made years ago. That was right. She'd spent the night at her parents' place. After all the hubbub of yesterday morning and being found, how could she have forgotten? She pulled herself to a sitting position.

Her gaze went to Jonathan's clothes draped on the chair beside her bed. She supposed everyone thought she'd gotten them from Mr. White and his wife. No one had questioned her about them. Sitting on her dresser was Jonathan's flashlight that had guided her footsteps throughout that terrifying night.

And then there was Jonathan's touch.

His theory that some higher being had brought them together resonated. But why? There had to be a reason. It wasn't like she needed a man in her life. She had a plan earn her degree and help other professionals save the ocean. Where did Jonathan fit in? He didn't. So why did she yearn for his touch and the scent of his Old Spice?

She wished she wouldn't have pushed him away. She should have asked him more questions. But seconds later, he and his dog had vanished. She almost wanted the memory of him to vanish as well; then she wouldn't be in this turmoil. He had been desperate for her help. She should have told the authorities about him. But something, some odd feeling, wouldn't let her.

She smelled bacon and toast cooking, and her stomach growled. She hadn't been able to eat much after returning, but now she was ravenous. Plus, she needed to tell Grandpa about the conning tower she thought she'd seen. By the time she'd gotten home last night, he'd been asleep, and Mom didn't want her waking him.

She leaped from the bed and dashed to the closet. She kept some clothes here for the times when she stayed to help with Grandpa. She grabbed a pair of jeans, a T-shirt, and tennis shoes and quickly dressed, then she swirled her out-of-control hair into a bun on top of her head and fled downstairs.

Seated at the kitchen nook, Mom stared at her phone, probably reading the headlines of the day. Her blue-rimmed reading glasses rested low on her nose, and instead of wearing her nurse's uniform, she had on her flowing blue caftan that heightened the color of her eyes. Blue was her mother's favorite color. Her usually happy face had become more drawn and lined with wrinkles since Grandpa had come to live with them, and she'd had to go back to nursing part-time at Mercy Hospital.

Gloryanna had been surprised when she'd been rescued that her mother hadn't lectured her about the dangers of scuba diving. She'd never liked that Gloryanna had become consumed with taking care of the ocean. She didn't understand why her only child would rather go on a dive than do anything else. Gloryanna braced herself for the inevitable argument about to take place, but the time had come to face the music.

Dad manned the stove, cooking breakfast. He raised his graying brows that matched his beard and hair upon seeing Gloryanna. "There's my Little Sand Dollar."

Dad had dubbed her his little sand dollar when was a child because she had been fascinated with sea creatures. She slid her arms around her father's middle and gave him a squeeze. "It's good to be home."

He leaned over and gave her a kiss on top of her head. No one would think this no-nonsense guy whose scowl could make a shark turn tail and swim away had the most tender heart, especially toward his family.

Her father grabbed plates for the three of them. "I need to get back to the job and my crew in Spokane, but I'm bidding to do the construction on that new shopping mall in Enumclaw."

"You're working on Sunday." Dad never worked on the Lord's day.

"No, sweetheart." Mom set her paper down. "It's Monday. You've missed a day. Of course, that's to be expected after all you've been through."

I've missed an entire day. "I'm so sorry. Since getting off the helicopter, things and people have kind of blurred together. I remember you two were there to meet me along with Professor Takahashi and Thomas."

Her mother nodded. "Your professor blamed herself that you went missing. She and Thomas looked and looked for you. Didn't she say Thomas used up most of the oxygen in his tank?"

Her father bobbed his head. "She did. Thomas seemed devastated, acting almost like you two were still dating. You're not, are you?"

"No. Of course not." Gloryanna didn't want her father worried about her getting back together with the guy. He never really liked Thomas and had seemed relieved when they'd broken up.

Her mother took a sip of coffee. "The media descended on us like locusts."

When Gloryanna had stepped off the helicopter, reporters had immediately shouted questions at her. Questions she couldn't answer, like, How had she gotten over sixty miles away from the dive site, and did someone save her? She'd told them about the vortex current and let it go at that, not wanting to mention Jonathan and Max. "I'm just glad the medical team at Mercy Hospital swooped in and saved me." Then her father's words sank in. "Enumclaw? If you got the job there, that would mean you could come home at night."

Gloryanna knew her father was a go-getter when it came to his work. By all rights, he should retire, but he wanted to keep working until he could no longer physically do the job. Whereas, Mom had other desires.

Before Grandpa had become ill and had come to live with them, Gloryanna's mom had talked of traveling and seeing Europe. Paris, to be exact. She wanted to visit the Louvre and hoped to paint landscapes while they were there. Oil painting had been her passion before Gloryanna was born, before she had interrupted her mom's dreams.

"You look a little flushed." Mom got up and felt Gloryanna's forehead. "But you feel normal."

Dad brought a plate filled with crispy bacon and scrambled eggs to them. He'd placed a cover on another plate of eggs and bacon to keep it warm for Grandpa until they were ready to bring it up.

"Your mother and I wanted to talk with you." Her dad motioned for Gloryanna to have a seat across from her mother. He sat next to Mom.

They were about to rehash the same old lecture they always touted.

Dad took a breath, looked at Mom, then said, "We want you to promise us that you won't dive again."

"That's impossible. My degree is in marine biology. Diving goes along with the territory. This isn't coming from you, Dad. It's Mom." She stared at the woman who seemed to want to snuff out her hopes and dreams.

Her mother reached across the table, taking her hand. "Sweetie, you've proven your point. You've earned your bachelor's degree. Surely there's some desk job in that field."

Gloryanna pulled her hand away. "None that I want."

"At least promise us you'll never dive in that area again." Dad's serious listen-to-me face stared at her.

The dive had scared her, and she really had no desire to return to the site. Plus, she always had a hard time saying no to her father. "Okay, I promise."

He stood. "Good. Now, let's eat." He went to the fridge and brought the orange juice over.

"Toast and coffee was enough for me, honey. I'll take Dad's meal up to him. He's been so upset the last few days, worried about you." Her mother looked at Gloryanna. "His dementia comes and goes, but he's getting worse, and his spells last longer."

"I wish I could have seen him when I came home." She loved her grand-father. He was the one who understood her passion for the ocean.

"I know." Her mother grabbed the tray. "Why don't you come say hi to him when you're finished with breakfast. I need to make him do his exercises, get showered, and sit up for a spell." She stopped. "I have the evening shift at the hospital tonight. Do you feel well enough to stay with him?"

"Of course. I should probably run by my condo, check the mail, and feed the fish, but I won't be long."

"That would be very helpful. Thanks. Now, eat your breakfast. You look like you've lost ten pounds because of your adventure. You need to build up your energy." Her mother left, breakfast tray in hand.

Sitting across from her in the booth, Dad dished up his plate. "You'd better do what she says and eat something." Without waiting for her permission, he scooped scrambled eggs onto her dish and topped them with two bacon slices.

She reluctantly picked up her fork. On a whim, she asked, "Dad, have you heard about the sand pounders who guarded the Pacific coastline during World War II?"

With a forkful of eggs poised to go in his mouth, he stopped. "What brought that up?"

"Just wondering." She took a couple of bites, trying to act normal, as if it weren't important enough to interrupt her meal.

"Can't say that I have." He continued eating too. In between bites, he said, "I wasn't even born when the war was going on. I'm a baby boomer. So is your mother." He took a sip of orange juice. "You know, if your grandfather is having a more lucid moment, he'd be the one to talk to about that." He glanced at the wall clock over the catch-all desk in the kitchen. "Look at the time. I need to get going." He shoveled several forkfuls of scrambled eggs into his mouth, chewed, and swallowed, then he stood and gulped down the rest of his juice. "Mind cleaning up here?"

"Of course not." She was only too happy to help out.

He kissed the top of her head again. "I'm so glad you're all right. Wish me luck." He grabbed his briefcase and left through the back door. A few minutes later, Gloryanna heard him start his three-quarter-ton Ford truck, its diesel engine making its familiar rumble.

As she finished eating and clearing the dishes, she realized Dad was right— she should ask Grandpa about the sand pounders. He'd been in the war, had lost several friends. Besides, she needed to tell him about the conning tower. She only hoped his usual fogginess wouldn't cloud his memories this time.

***

Gloryanna had looked into Grandpa's room before leaving home, but her mother had taken him to the shower. Gloryanna decided to run errands while she waited. First, she needed to stop by her place to make sure everything was all right.

On her way up the steps to her condo, she stopped to get her mail. She inserted the small mailbox key into the slot and opened it only to find it crammed with junk mail. No envelope with an explanation from Northeastern apologizing for losing her application. But she didn't need them now that she had a shot at a grant that would allow her to stay right here to complete her master's. Bundling the papers under her arm, she turned to rush up the stairs to her condo and bumped into Thomas.

"Geez! Why didn't you say something?" She walked around him. He was the last person she wanted to see. She'd already apologized for going off on her own during the dive, and she'd already thanked him for searching for her. Done and done.

"I just had to drop by to make sure you were okay." He followed behind her.

Could he be the shadow that Jonathan claimed followed her? She had wondered if he could have done something to her tank. Maybe he'd come to finish the job.

She quickly glanced at him. He gave her his boyish smile that had fooled her into thinking he was a nice guy years ago. She supposed he was; he just couldn't be faithful to one woman. But a murderer? No.

Still, she didn't want to deal with him right now.

Reaching her door, she fumbled with her keys, trying to find the one to turn the lock while also keeping the mail under her arm against her body.

"Let me do that." Thomas took the keys from her.

She reached to take them back, but he turned away, blocking her from the door. Trying to make a point, she said, "As you can see, I'm fine."

He easily slid the correct key into the lock and opened the door almost in one fluid motion. He'd done it many times before when they'd been dating.

He stepped aside, allowing her to enter first. She took her keys from him. This was her chance to get rid of him. She swung around, ready to close the door. "Thanks."

He stuck his foot on the doorjamb, preventing her from shutting it. "Don't be this way, Glory. I was worried about you. I didn't get much of a chance to talk with you the other day after you were rescued."

Gritting her teeth at the nickname she couldn't stand, she said, "Thanks, but I'm fine. Please move your foot." She waited.

He waited too. "Nope. I'm not leaving until you talk with me."

Was she really going to keep him out because she believed what a man who claimed to be a ghost had said about a shadow following her? No.

Thomas was just being Thomas. Not wanting to argue anymore, she slipped off her shoes and left them on the doormat. She went to the kitchen to toss the advertisements in the recycling bin.

When she came back, Thomas had taken off his shoes as well and was sitting on her couch just like he used to when they'd been dating. But that had been years ago. He may be worried about her, but that didn't mean he could make himself at home.

She might as well use his presence to her advantage and ask him some hard questions. That might make him leave. "You know, during the dive, something happened to my tank. It lost compression. Later, when I checked it over, there was no air. You didn't accidentally do something to it when you helped me put it on, did you?" She knew even if he had, he'd never confess to it.

"What!" He appeared stunned. "Are you accusing me of sabotaging your tank?" He could act offended with the best of them. His minor at the university had been theater.

"It's a question I have to ask."

"I didn't." He reared back. "Do you think Ralph did something to it?"

Yep, Thomas was good at deflecting blame. Always had been. When she'd broken up with him, he had blamed her because she'd never asked him not to see other girls. Even so, she had wondered the same thing about Ralph, but she had dismissed the thought because she'd checked the gauge herself after picking up her tank.

She suddenly wished she'd never brought up the subject. Trying to hurry him along the best she could, she said, "I'm only here for a minute. I have a ton of stuff to do today."

"So, you're all right accusing me, but when it comes to your friend Ralph, who can do no wrong, you change the subject?" He glared at her like he used to when they'd argue.

She counterglared that she wouldn't dignify his question with an answer.

"Look, you scared me, going off on your own like you did." He gazed accusingly at her. He had the higher ground with this argument.

"I shouldn't have. I'm sorry." She went to her goldfish bowl and sprinkled in a little fish food. Herman, the sole occupant, swam up and began eating. She usually fed him once a day. He'd been without anything for too long, and though a goldfish could live a couple of weeks without food, she felt bad that she hadn't been there to feed him. Turning to Thomas, she said, "The vortex current got me." Remembering the camera, she slapped her forehead. "That reminds me, I need to run by the Fish Tail."

"Are you going to ask Ralph if he did something to your tank?"

"Don't be absurd." She'd never tell Thomas that the thought had crossed her mind.

"Then why talk with him? You're not diving again, are you?" His brows rose high over his brown eyes that stared at her as though she'd be crazy if she did.

"I don't account for my time with you." She went to the door, hoping Thomas would take the hint and leave.

"Mind if I get some water before you show me out?" He headed for the kitchen before she could stop him.

He was stalling. She heard him open her cupboard and get a glass.

He came back into the room, drinking water, and handed the glass to her. "Professor Takahashi was worried. Blamed herself. I've never seen her so upset. Promise me, whatever you do today, you won't go diving alone." He slipped his shoes on, then came to stand close to her. Too close, like he had when they'd dated.

"I'll speak with her. Now, if you don't mind, I need to get going." She added meeting with the professor to her long to-do list. She would have to give Professor Takahashi a good explanation about what had happened.

"Where are you off to?"

She stepped back. "What is with you all of a sudden?"

He huffed out a breath. "I guess when you went missing and as every second ticked by and there was no sign of you anywhere, I realized something." He clenched his jaw, then rolled his shoulder. "You mean more to me than just a casual friend I once dated. I care about you."

Gloryanna stared into his eyes and saw what looked like genuine concern. Surprised and confused, she didn't like the seriousness covering his face. She didn't know how to handle it. This was foreign territory for their relationship. Years ago, she'd yearned to have him look at her like this, yearned for him to be honest with her. But she'd learned the hard way that he didn't know how to be truthful. Wanting to stop this from going further, she said, "You're only saying that because you want to know what I'm planning to do for my article so you can top it and have a better chance at publication."

"No." He took her hand. "Though the grant *is* important to me. I said it because I realized I have deep feelings for you. I've known it for some time now, but the dive showed me that I needed to tell you how I feel."

She didn't know what to think. Was he sincere? Had she severely misjudged Thomas? She thought of the day she'd found him making out with another woman in a restaurant while he had been dating her. No. He hadn't a clue what sincerity was. But she didn't want to drag up ancient history. "Sure you do. That's why you brag about getting an occasional better grade than I do. Which doesn't happen that often, I might add. Or how you put down my ideas in class and tease me relentlessly."

His face froze. "I had no idea that's how you saw things. Bragging, putting you down, and teasing? I'm sorry. Sure, I've been confused about my feelings for you, but I wouldn't ever have wanted you to feel those things."

She didn't trust him. And she didn't want to, because if he was sincere, she'd have to stop to rethink her feelings for him as well. And she didn't want to do that either.

Just in case he was being straightforward, she needed to be gracious. "Thank you. I'm having a hard time accepting what you say, but I appreciate your trying to be truthful." If that was what he truly was doing.

Or did he feel guilty because he had messed with her tank?

She shouldn't think such thoughts, but she couldn't get Jonathan's warning about a shadow following her out of her mind. And Thomas had had many opportunities to sabotage her gear. She had to get him out of here so she could think. "I'm sincerely grateful you looked for me. But as you can see, I'm fine."

"Not exactly what I wanted to hear. But it's okay. I'm patient. And always know this if ever you need me, I'll be here for you." He gave a slight nod and left.

Gloryanna closed the door. Talk about a surprise. She had never *ever* thought Thomas would say something like that to her. After they'd first broken up, she used to daydream that he would confess what he'd done and tell her that he loved her. Even though he hadn't said the *L* word just now, he had implied it.

She pushed that thought aside. She couldn't stand here going over the past and trying to figure out Thomas and his true motives. She had things to do talk to the professor, check in with Ralph and confess to losing his expensive camera, and then research Jonathan's story. Plus, she needed to go back to her parents to be with Grandpa.

She quickly packed her makeup and her comfortable PJs into a travel bag, then headed out the door, locking the perplexing moment she'd shared with Thomas inside.

***

Gloryanna sat staring at Professor Takahashi across her massive desk.

The professor inhaled deeply. "This man, who you said saved you, told you he was a ghost?"

The tone in her voice made Gloryanna wonder if she'd made a mistake sharing with her mentor what had happened. She hadn't planned to, but then they'd started talking, and it had slipped out. This might make the professor rethink recommending her for the grant. Maybe she needed to give more details. "Yes, and he said he was a sand pounder during World War II. He wants me to help him find out how he died."

The professor stood and walked around her desk. Dressed in black, from her blouse to her leather boots, she smoothed her ebony hair over her shoulder. "You know, you were deprived of oxygen for a while. That might have played tricks with your mind, like making you think you saw a conning tower."

"You might be right about that." She'd told the professor about her grandfather's delusional claim of a sunken submarine a week ago. Professor Takahashi had scoffed at the idea then, like she was now. And she had a good point. Gloryanna had been oxygen deprived. Still, she couldn't let the issue of Jonathan drop. "But I have the clothes he lent me. If he were a hallucination, I wouldn't have those, would I?" She waited, keeping her focus on the professor.

The immaculate woman shrugged and leaned against her desk. "What else did he tell you?"

"Just that he and his dog, Max, are the ones who saved me from drowning."

The professor reared back. "So, if he was a ghost, how could he do that?"

"I don't know. His clothes weren't even wet." Gloryanna wrung her hands together. "And the strange thing is, while he stayed around his shack and that area, he seemed like a normal person, with a body."

Professor Takahashi put her head to one side in a questioning manner.

"I know it's weird, but his shack seems suspended in some type of time warp. And the amazing thing is . . ." Gloryanna hesitated. She didn't know if she should tell her about the magical sensation she'd felt when he'd touched her or his Old Spice scent. She'd keep those to herself. "*The thing is* when he tried to step out of the forest into the mountain meadow, he and his dog disappeared."

The professor folded her arms, gazing at Gloryanna. "You actually saw them vanish?"

"Well, no. I had my back to them when they left. When I realized they were gone, I couldn't find them anywhere. One second they were there, the next they weren't."

Professor Takahashi stared at her. After what felt like an eternity, she said, "What did he say his name was?"

"Jonathan Dawson."

The professor grabbed her phone and took notes on an app. "And he said he was a sand pounder?" She glanced at Gloryanna.

She nodded.

"Okay, I don't want you spending any more time worrying about this. Let me do some research, and you start working on your article. Were you able to get some idea of what you want to base your paper on?"

"Before the vortex got me, I saw sickly looking anemones." She didn't want to bring up the conning tower again, so she skipped that part. "I was going to take a picture, and that's when I noticed a problem with my air. I'd like to dive there again." Wait. She'd promised her parents she wouldn't dive in that spot again. "Or maybe even check out other areas to see if the same thing is happening."

Professor Takahashi tapped her index finger to her lips. "It would be best to return to the ones you saw in case you missed something. Give your parents a few days so their emotions aren't so high " She thought a moment. "Wait until after graduation. It's the day after tomorrow. When that's over, I want you to check with some of the local divers to see if they've noticed a change to the ecosystem. But get your strength back first. Are you staying with your parents?" She returned to her seat behind the desk.

"Yes. At least tonight. Thanks for your help, professor."

"No problem. I should be able to find something about this"—she glanced at her phone and what she'd written—"Jonathan Dawson. Let me know when you plan to return his clothes and pick up your tank. I want to go with you."

"Are you sure?"

"Yes, I'd like to meet this man who claims to be a ghost." Surprisingly, a smile tugged at Professor Takahashi's lips.

Gloryanna didn't know if the professor was making fun of her or not, but at the moment, she didn't care. Her mentor was going to help her.

CHAPTER SIX

Pulling up to the Fish Tail Café and Scuba Supplies shop, Gloryanna saw Ralph taking garbage out to the dumpster. He was dressed in Polynesian board shorts and a loud Hawaiian shirt in colors of pink, yellow, and green on a turquoise background. His straggly hair hung to his shoulders. He looked like an old beach bum from the sixties.

He glanced up, and when he saw her, his long Scooby-Doo face split into a huge grin. He waved at her as she shut her car door. How was she going to tell him about his camera?

"You've been all over the news for the last two days." He walked toward her. "I called your folks, and they let me know you'd been found. Super glad you're all right."

"It was quite an amazing experience."

He put his arm around her shoulders as they made their way toward the building. "I want to hear all about it. Come into my office. Skip can watch the store, and Minnie does better if I let her take charge of the grill." Skip, a drifter until he'd met Ralph, had been a good friend of his for years. Minnie, a magician when it came to making juicy burgers, had been the real reason for the café's success.

He opened the back door. Boxes of scuba gear were stacked along the wall. He guided her to his crammed office, where more boxes were stacked not only on the floor but also on the chairs. He moved boxes from one. "Haven't had time to put these on the shelves yet. Have a seat."

She eased down as she tried to think how she was going to give him the bad news.

He sat on his rickety swivel chair with a loud creak and clasped his hands together. "So, tell me what happened."

"Well, I hate to admit it, but the vortex current got me."

"The vortex?" His face pinched. "You're lucky to be alive, my dear. I've known some men who have been caught in one and ended up in Japan or Alaska."

"Japan or Alaska?" She wasn't buying it.

"Well, I may have exaggerated a touch, but they died and weren't found for many a day. I'm just glad you survived." His frown morphed into a smile. "Did you at least get some good pictures?"

Now was as good a time as any to tell him, while he was still grateful that she'd survived. She took a deep breath. "Here's the thing . . ."

He sat there patiently waiting.

"I lost it."

He froze for a moment, then said, "You mean you panicked. Who could blame you? I know I would have."

"No. I lost your camera when the vortex got me. But I'll buy you a new one." She'd charge it on her credit card since she was strapped for cash.

The smile left his face, and he didn't move.

"A better one."

He didn't blink.

Giving it all she had, she said, "One that will give you amazing pics. And will last forever and ever. And I'll work for free for a week. No, a month. Please, Ralph. Say something."

He shook his head. "Yes, the camera meant a lot to me, but you mean more." He took a hesitant breath. "I've been watching you go on dives since you were a pup. You're like a kid sister to me." He gave her a forced smile, as if everything would be all right. She knew it wouldn't be.

He'd said the words she needed to hear, but she'd lost his trust. It would be a long time before he'd offer to lend her his equipment, which was only fair. His faith in her had been shaken.

But her faith in him wasn't exactly solid right now either. Her tank had been compromised, and Thomas had accused Ralph of doing something to it. She knew Ralph would never purposely hurt her, but she had to ask if he'd noticed a problem with her gear. "The weirdest thing happened on my dive."

He'd started shuffling papers on his desk, not making eye contact. "What was that?"

She had to go about this in a different direction. "I found some anemones that looked pretty sad, and beyond them, I thought I saw a conning tower. I was about to take a picture of it and the anemones, and that's when my regulator stopped working. In fact, it acted like there wasn't enough air in the tank."

His eyebrows rammed together. "Skip filled it. He'd better not have screwed up." A red flush came to his cheeks as if he were going to rake Skip over the coals.

Gloryanna didn't want to get the man in trouble. "I checked it before going out, like always. And it seemed fine. Do you think I could have had a leaky line or something?"

"Let's take a look. You brought your gear with you, right?" He stood and started for the door.

"Sadly, no. I had to leave it with the guy who saved me." She said it before thinking.

"Guy. What guy?" He stopped, staring at her.

She'd only told the professor about Jonathan. Oh, and Branson White, the Grizzly Adams man who had let her use his wife's cell phone. So, she'd told a few people, but she didn't want the press to get wind of a person living a private life on the coastline.

The damage was done with Ralph, though, so she might as well tell him the rest, or, at least, some of the rest. "Yes, this guy on the beach helped me walk out of there, but I had to leave my tank behind. He was gracious enough to say he'd keep an eye on it for me."

"As soon as you get your tank back, bring it in. I want to check it myself." He took a deep breath. "If Skip did something that caused you this trouble, I'm sincerely sorry."

About to ask if that meant he forgave her for losing his camera, she stopped when a tap came on his office door, followed by a gravelly smoker's voice. "Boss, there's a customer out here says you promised that you'd service his gear for free."

"Tell him to cool his clams. I'll be out in a minute." Ralph rolled his eyes. Looking at Gloryanna, he said, "You're not coming in to work, are you?"

"No, I have Grandpa duty tonight. But I had to stop by and tell you what happened." She wished she could work. The more she was around Ralph, the sooner this oddness between them would fade. The next time she came, she'd bring him a new camera to replace the old one. Replacing the camera as soon as she could should go a long way to getting things back to normal.

"Good. You need to rest and take care of yourself. Don't give the Fish Tail a second thought. But do drop off your tank as soon as you get it." He left and went to the front where the anxious customer was waiting.

Gloryanna dodged out the back. Telling him about the camera had been tough, but at least it was over. And she'd known he'd be concerned about her tank. She was hesitant to bring it in and have him look at it. If he found that Skip had done something wrong, Ralph might fire him.

Not wanting to think about it, she hurried to her car. She'd accomplished almost everything on her list. Now she could go home, relax, and listen to Grandpa tell his stories.

***

When Gloryanna walked into Grandpa's room, she found her parents there. Mom, dressed in her nursing scrubs, sat on the edge of Grandpa's bed; Dad stood at the foot, a huge smile on his face.

Grandpa was sitting up. His wrinkly, lidded, sunken blue eyes focused on her, and he reminded her of Gandalf from *The Lord of the Rings*.

Dad put his arm around her. "Hey, Little Sand Dollar, I got the job in Enumclaw. As soon as the crew finishes construction in Spokane, we can start."

"That's fantastic." She hugged her father. "It will be great to have you home more."

"You're telling me." He gave her a squeeze. "I should get going. I need to drive to Spokane tonight. I want to be there bright and early so my crew can wrap things up in time for me to make it back for your graduation." He went to her mother, leaned over, and kissed her. "I'll call you later tonight. And, Captain"—he looked at Grandpa—"take care of our girls, will you?"

"Always do." Grandpa gave him a nod. Dad called him "Captain" because Grandpa had owned a whale-watching boat that he'd named *Pequod*. His favorite book had been *Moby Dick*. Sometimes Gloryanna wondered if he fancied himself as Captain Ahab.

Dad saluted him and left.

It had been a long time since Gloryanna had seen her father so happy, other than when he'd hugged her after she'd returned home from her ordeal. But that was more a relieved happy, not a happy-with-good-news happy.

Mom glanced at her watch. "I need to shove off too, or I'm going to be late for my shift." She gave Grandpa a hug. "Behave yourself."

She motioned for Gloryanna to follow her into the hall. "He's had his evening meds, all but his sleeping pill. He needs to take that at around nine thirty." She stopped and looked at Gloryanna. "How are you doing, sweetie? Did you get everything done that you wanted to do today?"

"Yes. Don't worry about Grandpa and me. We'll be fine. It's great about Dad getting that job." She wanted her mother to dwell on someone else.

"It sure is." Mom gave her a brief hug. "Call if something comes up." She turned and hurried through the hallway, disappearing down the stairs.

Returning to Grandpa's room, Gloryanna expected him to be asleep since everyone had left, but he surprised her and was wide awake. He patted his bedside. "Come, tell an old sea captain of your adventures. You had us very worried."

She did as she was told and sat beside him. "Grandpa, I think I saw a conning tower."

"A conning tower?" He squinted at her.

"Yes. Remember a couple of weeks ago, how you told me you were on a submarine that sank during the war?" She hoped he'd remember.

A guilt-ridden expression flashed over his face, which morphed into concern. "My dear one, I served on an aircraft carrier. Not a sub."

So, he'd forgotten the conversation. She didn't want to make matters worse by dwelling on it. Instead, she said, "Well, my adventure was quite amazing." She told him about her tank losing oxygen, getting caught in the vortex and passing out, and then coming to on the beach below Purgatory Point. "And that's when I saw Jonathan." Her list of people she was telling about that man kept growing despite her intentions.

Grandpa's scraggy gray brows rose on his age-spotted forehead. "Jonathan?"

"Yes." She hesitated only a second before telling him about Jonathan's rescuing her.

"Ah, my little Starbuck, I may mix up my stories every once in a while, but even I know he couldn't have saved you without getting wet unless he was Houdini." He gave her that look he'd used when she was a little girl and had fibbed about eating his candy.

"Just hang on. I'm getting to that." She told him about going to Jonathan's shelter and how quaint the furnishings had been. "It was like a time capsule of World War II."

Grandpa's forehead wrinkled as he stared at her. "And where did you say this was?"

"Purgatory Point, in the wilderness area of the Olympic Peninsula." She hated to say it, because even as the words left her mouth, she knew how crazy they sounded.

Grandpa rubbed his forehead with his trembling hand. "I've had the *Pequod* caught in a strong swell, so I understand how off course you can get in a situation like that, but how could that vortex current have taken you so far off course? Why not out to the ocean instead of near the beach?"

"I know! I didn't understand why either." And even though she'd lived through it, she still didn't get it. And yet, she did.

Jonathan.

Grandpa cleared his throat. "I think you're keeping something from me."

She should have known he'd catch the missing link she didn't want to tell him but needed to. "Well, here's the deal. He told me he was a ghost."

Grandpa choked and coughed as if he'd swallowed down the wrong pipe.

"Are you okay?" She quickly poured him a glass of water. Mom always made sure a carafe of fresh water and a clean glass waited on his nightstand.

Gloryanna held the glass to his lips and helped him drink.

After a swallow or two, he pushed her hand away. "I'm fine, child." He took several deep breaths, then focused on her once again. "A ghost. And you believed him?"

"I don't know what to think. He seemed so real, and he loaned me some clothes. Do ghosts even have clothes. I mean, why? And yet, at his shack and even as he walked with me through the forest, he seemed real. I even touched him." That moment that they'd shared resurfaced, and her cheeks grew warm. She pressed on. "He even insisted I use his flashlight." She stood. "Do you want to see it?"

Grandpa gave a nod.

Gloryanna hurried to her bedroom to grab it from her dresser, then rushed back to Grandpa. Settling in the chair beside his bed, she handed the Eveready to him.

He studied it, then gave it back. "Sure looks like the ones we had during the war. Does it still work?"

"Yes. I don't know what I would have done without it." To prove her point, she flipped on the beam, but her finger pressed a second time, taking the switch to another setting. The light blinked three short times, then three long, then back to three short on the wall. It repeated the cycle over and over.

"Hmm." Grandpa watched with great care. "That's SOS in Morse code."

"Are you sure?" She studied the constant blinking. "You're right. Jonathan didn't tell me it did that."

She flipped off the beam, and there, standing where the light had been, was a startled Jonathan and his dog, Max.

CHAPTER SEVEN

JONATHAN STARED AT HIS NEW surroundings, trying to figure out what had just happened. One moment he and Max had been settled in front of the camp stove for the night, and then the familiar tingling sensation and pulling of the teleportation had started. They hadn't been at the edge of the forest where it usually happened. He didn't understand, nor could he do anything to stop it. When the feeling finally subsided, he found himself and his dog in a strange room, standing before a sickly old man and . . . Gloryanna.

Did his eyes deceive him? He closed them and looked again. No. There she stood, staring at him like she'd seen a ghost—which he supposed she had. Just behind her lurked the dark shadow that had stalked her on the beach, except it had grown more intense.

"Harbinger!" The elderly guy screamed in obvious fear as he pointed at Jonathan.

He saw him!

Jonathan didn't know what to do. The only person who had seen him in all the years since his passing had been Gloryanna.

"He's evil incarnate!" The wizened fellow tried to crawl from his bed as he stared at Jonathan as if Jonathan were Satan.

"Starbuck, get below deck! Sound the alarm!" he yelled at Gloryanna, who was trying to calm him. "Heaven have mercy on us. It's an ill wind that's brought him and his canine minion. Take cover!" With his blue-veined hands, the elderly fellow pulled his blankets over his head.

"Grandpa, it's all right." Gloryanna glared at Jonathan like this was all his fault, then turned her attention to her cowering grandfather. She pulled his coverings from his head and stroked his arm. "It's okay, Grandpa. He won't hurt us."

Her grandfather glared at Jonathan as though he were a mighty whale circling his ship. "Ignorance is the parent of fear. You said he was a ghost. He's not. He's the forerunner of doom."

Gloryanna turned to Jonathan, a look of exasperation on her face. "Would you and Max please wait for me in the hall? You're upsetting Grandpa."

That was an understatement. Without receiving a reply from Jonathan, she focused on the trembling man, stroking his thinning gray hair and blocking his view of the source that caused him such trauma.

Jonathan wondered if the old guy could also see the ominous aura stalking his granddaughter. No. Surely he would have mentioned its presence as he railed against Jonathan and Max showing up.

Going to the door, Jonathan reached to open it, but he couldn't grip the knob. Odd. Another strange phenomenon he hadn't noticed was that both he and Max had no matter, and they were floating.

Max passed through the door, so Jonathan followed. One moment, he was in the room, the next in the hallway. He leaned close to the door and listened to Gloryanna's lyrical voice as she spoke kindly to her grandfather to soothe him.

Jonathan struggled to understand why her grandfather would think him a harbinger. He wasn't a forerunner of anything. He wasn't an omen. His thoughts returned to the darkness following Gloryanna. It was a sign of danger, and he wondered if he had been summoned here to protect her.

In order to prove his theory, Jonathan needed to know what catalyst had brought Max and him to this place. And why? In the many years they had been suspended in time at the shelter, they'd never been allowed to venture elsewhere. And now they were here.

Wherever *here* was. Whatever had brought them, it had to do with Gloryanna.

Marveling at his new situation, Jonathan studied his surroundings. On the corridor walls hung family pictures. One large family grouping had Gloryanna standing behind a nice-looking couple the woman had Gloryanna's eyes and slender nose; the man had the same hair color and noble brow. Another picture was only the couple, in younger years. Close by were individual pictures of Gloryanna.

Finally, she exited the room he and Max had crossed through and quietly closed the door. "So, you really are a ghost." She stared at him, which made him look down at himself.

His matter was gauzy and transparent at the same time, like it should have been since his passing. But at the shack he'd had a mortal image. He didn't know what to say, but at least she now believed him.

"And you're here," she added. "I wasn't sure, especially after you disappeared through the door."

"I'm sorry about that, and I'm so sorry to have upset him—I assume he's your grandfather." Jonathan couldn't abide it if she was mad at him. He needed her more than ever now. And by the looks of the shadow that still followed her, she needed him too. Maybe even more so.

In one hand, she held the flashlight he'd given her. She motioned for him to follow her downstairs and into a room that had to be the kitchen. But he'd never seen one this size before. The vast room had marble countertops, redwood cabinets, and hardwood flooring.

She set the flashlight on the counter. "Why are you two here?"

Max wagged his tail when she looked at him. He went to her. She reached to pet him, but her hand went through the dog. "I don't understand. At the shack, I could pet him, but now I can't, and you're both floating, and you appear to be . . ."

"Ghosts." Jonathan nodded. "Only at the shack and its surroundings do we take on a mortal form, though unseen by other people until you came along. We're stuck in some type of middle between death and life, and the shack serves as our base. But we've never been able to venture away. I'm as baffled as you are why we're here."

"Grandpa saw you. I've never seen him so upset." Gloryanna went to the cupboard. "I'm going to give him his sleeping pill early. That will help him rest." She pulled down a small amber bottle, opened it, and took out a pill. "I'll be right back." She fled up the stairs.

Jonathan paced. "We have to figure this out, Max, old boy. Why do you suppose her grandfather can see us? Maybe because he's related to Gloryanna? Something else bothers me though. Why don't we have the mortal abilities we have at the shack? And gravity holds no power over us. I wonder if we still have our gifts." Could Jonathan use his mind-over-matter ability? And could Max's hypersense of danger still work? Testing to see, Jonathan stared at his old flashlight Gloryanna had set on the counter. He willed it to come to him.

At first, the device wobbled but an inch. He concentrated harder, and the flashlight flew through the air toward him. He willed it to stop and return to the counter.

Immediately, he felt a drain to his ghostly energy much like he experienced at the beach whenever he rescued someone. His shack had replenished him. What would help him now? What would restore him? He stayed suspended in place, hoping that would shore up some energy.

Max stared at him like he should have known better.

"I had to see what my limitations are. Why have we been brought here?" Max looked toward the stairs.

"Yes, I, too, think she brought us. We have to protect her from that danger that nips at her heels. You saw the shadow, didn't you?"

Max tipped his head.

"Though I sense something more is going on." Jonathan thought a moment. Try as he might, nothing fit. He heard footsteps on the stairs.

Gloryanna entered the kitchen; worry lined her face, and the ominous, cloudlike shadow still followed her. "I think he's settled, at least for a little while, if not the whole night. He calls me Starbuck all the time, but when he started quoting Melville, it was a clear sign his brain was overtaxed."

The flashlight caught her attention. "I wonder if this had something to do with you being here. I was showing it to Grandpa, but this time, when I pressed the switch, it started flashing. Grandpa said it was Morse code for SOS."

"Yes." Jonathan was aware the light had such a function. "We could use the setting in emergencies. But I never did."

As she studied the flashlight, she said, "Do you suppose the SOS summoned you?"

"It appears so." He should have thought of that. It had been part of the shack, part of his unending probation there.

"Why?" Her gaze met his.

He stared into her caring eyes and felt a different tingling spread through his being. It was the same sensation he'd had when they'd touched in the forest. Attraction? What good would attraction be when he had no physical matter? Only frustration would follow. He had to think of the emotion on a different level. Something higher . . . But an explanation failed him.

He realized he hadn't answered her question. Reverting to the subject at hand, he said, "The flashlight's SOS signal is the catalyst that transported me and Max to you. I believe that you, and perhaps even your grandfather, are vital to Max and me—to figuring out why we're still in this state of limbo between the living and the dead."

She stared at him, confusion playing over her face. How could he put this in a way that would make more sense? "We need you to help us move on to the next stage in our afterlife progression. But something more is going on. Remember I told you at the shack that a darkness stalks you? It's here, even now, like it was on the beach when you nearly died."

And then some of the puzzle pieces fell into place. "Someone wants you dead. Someone tried to kill you by tampering with your diving tank. Max and I saved you, and that's why we've been brought together again, so we can protect you."

As soon as he spoke the words, the darkness evaporated. He must have been right. The shadow had served its purpose. Now it was up to Jonathan to fulfill his mission to keep her alive.

"But why would someone want to kill me?" She set the flashlight on the counter "I have no enemies."

"Whether you choose to believe me is up to you. But you were fighting for your life in the ocean." Jonathan hoped that hit home and jogged her memory. "And did you not tell me that your diving tank was out of oxygen?"

"Well, yes. I must confess that the thought that someone tried to kill me has crossed my mind. Since I can't think of a rational reason why someone would want me dead, I've decided what happened was faulty equipment. I told Ralph about it, and he wants to check my tank after I collect it from your beach. You didn't happen to bring it with you, did you?" She gave him a hopeful yet teasing smile.

"I left in a bit of a hurry." Jonathan could play along. It eased the tension. "Seriously, though, do you trust this Ralph person?"

"Yes. He would never do anything to hurt me. And when I told him what happened, he was very upset and genuinely worried." She wrung her hands together.

"Was he? Or was he upset because he'd failed?" Jonathan hated pointing out that the person she'd placed so much trust in could have ulterior motives. "How well do you know him?"

"I've known him for years. Besides, Ralph didn't actually fill my tank. His employee Skip did." She walked to the stove and set the kettle on the back burner, then she took down two mugs. "Want some?"

He patiently waited for her to realize he couldn't drink.

She expectantly looked at him, then all at once, she said, "Oh, I'm sorry. You can't now that you're away from the shack. Do you mind if I do?"

Max barked, which startled both Jonathan and Gloryanna.

"What's wrong?" She reached her hand out to calm him, but Max darted away, running to the stairs and barking.

"Something's not right up there," Jonathan said. He wasn't sure, but he couldn't dismiss his dog. "Perhaps you should check on your grandfather. Max must still have his ability to sense someone in jeopardy."

Gloryanna fled up the stairs, but this time, Jonathan followed her. She burst open the bedroom door and flipped on the overhead light. The elderly man lay sprawled on the floor.

She dropped down beside him. "Grandpa!"

He winced and muttered, "Yes, child."

"Why are you on the floor?"

Instead of answering her, he drifted off.

"Why would he get out of bed?" she asked.

"He must have still been upset at seeing me." Guilt riddled Jonathan.

She checked the elderly man's arms and legs. His limbs moved freely, so it appeared there were no broken bones. "Grandpa, I need you to get back in bed."

He moaned and nodded but didn't open his eyes or move.

She tried to pull him into a sitting position, but his bulk proved too heavy. "The sleeping pill makes him groggy sometimes, especially when he's been upset."

"Let me try." Jonathan drew on his power. Levitating the frail man off the floor took extreme concentration, draining what little energy he possessed. Yet, he had enough to float him toward the bed.

Gloryanna gawked at Jonathan, then scrambled to pull back the blankets as he set her grandfather softly on the sheet, not disturbing a single hair on his head.

She tucked him in and exhaled deeply. "That's how you saved me, isn't it?"

"Pretty much."

"If I hadn't seen it with my own eyes, I never would have believed it. Thank you for rescuing me and helping Grandpa. I think he'll stay put now." She turned out the light. Leaving the door open, she left the room.

"I don't know what I would have done if you hadn't been here. But if he hadn't seen you, he wouldn't have been upset." She looked at Jonathan. "You're fading. Are you all right?"

"Using my gift is very draining." He didn't want her to worry. "Remember at the beach, after I saved you?"

"Yes."

"I didn't help you move your tank because I didn't have the strength after bringing you out of the water." He followed her through the hall and down the stairs.

Max stood by the stove and growled. Jonathan went to him. "What's wrong?"

Gloryanna went to turn on the stove. Fire exploded from the burner. Flames leaped at her face. She dropped to the floor.

"Turn it off!" Jonathan would have, but it was all he could do to remain visible.

She eased up carefully to a stand. The control knobs were on the back panel. The blaze reflected in her fearful eyes as she leaned away from the inferno. Somehow, she reached her arm around the fire. Her fingertips brushed the knob. She recoiled. "It's melting."

"You almost had it. You can do it!" Jonathan pressed. If she didn't turn it off soon, the entire house would become engulfed.

With more determination, she once again reached around the flames, her fingers inching toward the controls until she finally flipped the knob.

Flames dissipated in a poof. Smoke hung in the air along with the scent of gas.

She opened the back door, then went to the kitchen sink and held her hand in cold running water. She looked at him. "What happened? I don't understand."

"There must have been a gas leak. Are you all right?"

She held up her hand. The back and the tip of her index finger was red.

"You have a flash burn. Keeping it in cold water should help." He studied her face. Her brows, eyelashes, and bangs were singed, but her face was miraculously unharmed. "It could have been so much worse. Max tried to warn us." He patted the dog's head.

She grabbed a small plastic bag and filled it with ice from the freezer. Placing it on her hand, she sat down. "I'm going to have to call the gas company in the morning and have them check things out."

"Do you still think no one wants to kill you?" Jonathan hated stating the obvious, but she had to realize that she and maybe her entire family were in grave danger.

"This was a fluke. I'm sure there's a reasonable explanation." She took a deep breath.

"What is it going to take to make you realize your life is in danger?" He wanted to shake her but didn't have the umph. "When I told you someone is trying to kill you, that shadow that stalked you faded away. The message it was trying to send was finally delivered. You need to believe me."

"I guess a person should believe a ghost." She stared at him.

"I should think." Finally, he was getting somewhere. "Is there any reason someone would want to hurt you?" Relieved that she was finally on board with what he suspected, he waited for her answer.

"The thought that someone is trying to kill me has crossed my mind, but stating it out loud and talking about it makes it real." She shook her head.

Jonathan empathized with her. "No one wants to believe that someone means them harm. But you need to try to think of who it could be."

"I'm in competition with another student, Thomas, for a grant. He went on the dive with me. And before you bring it up, I asked him if he did something to my tank, and he said no." She shrugged. "It seems ridiculous that he'd want to kill me over something like that."

"A grant is money in the bank. And you know what they say about money."

"It's the root of all evil." She nodded. "But his dad is rich, so I don't think that would be the reason." Her forehead wrinkled.

The way she talked about this Thomas person bothered Jonathan. "How well do you know Thomas?"

"Very well. Years ago, we used to be in a relationship. At least, that's what I thought. But he believed we were just friends who 'made out,' which he seems to do with every girl he takes to dinner. I broke up with him. And like I said, it was years ago. It's not him." She shuddered. "I went on that dive with him and the professor."

"So, a man you used to date but broke up with and this professor had access to your equipment?" Jonathan added both to his list of suspects.

"Yes, but the professor would never hurt me. And Thomas caught me at my condo this morning and told me that when he couldn't find me, he realized he had feelings for me." She moved to the couch in the small sitting area adjacent to the kitchen, a cozy alcove with a fireplace and a wooden rocker.

"Love is the oldest reason in the book to justify murder." Though he'd never seen Thomas, anger pulled at Jonathan for the way the man could be manipulating her. "Don't you see what he's doing?"

"Yes. He's trying to unnerve me, and it's not because of 'love,' which was what *you* said, not him. He was very careful not to use that word. He only wants to rattle me because we're in competition for the grant that would be a full-ride to earning a master's degree." She leaned back and rested her head on a couch cushion.

"But you said his father was loaded. Why would Thomas need a grant that badly?" Jonathan was thinking out loud.

"I have no idea."

"What stories do you read?"

"What do you mean?"

"In every murder mystery, the two major reasons a person kills are for love or money, and your Thomas is tied to both. He's definitely one to watch." Jonathan hoped he'd convinced her.

"I suppose. Hey, seeing as you're a ghost, could you spy on him for me?" She sat straight up.

"Honestly, I don't know." He looked at her, grateful that he and Max had been here when the explosion had happened. Though he hadn't stopped the near disaster, Max had tried to warn them. "But I hesitate to leave your side in case your nemesis shows up."

"I guess that's a pretty good excuse to stay." Holding the bag of ice to her hand, she stood. "I should check on Grandpa again." As she passed the back exit, she took a deep breath, then closed the door.

Even after her very life had been threatened, she still worried about her grandfather. Jonathan couldn't help but admire such love and devotion. As he watched her hurry up the stairs, a swelling of gratitude and a sense that he was where he belonged fell on him. He'd do everything he possibly could to keep her safe. He prayed it would be enough.

CHAPTER EIGHT

Gloryanna stood at the threshold of Grandpa's room. He breathed deeply as he slept and seemed undisturbed. Why had he become so agitated when he'd seen Jonathan? She'd already told Grandpa about him and that he was a ghost. But maybe seeing the real deal was more than he could take. She'd had a hard time believing it too, and she had all of her faculties.

But now more than ever, she wondered if she and Jonathan were destined to be together. The thought seemed ludicrous, but she couldn't shake it. Why else would she have seen him before passing out in the vortex? Why else would he have saved her? And why else would he have shown up at her parents' house when he had? So many things seemed to add up but not lead to clear, defining answers.

And what was the matter with the kitchen stove? It had been working fine this morning when Dad had made breakfast. And Mom had been home all day with Grandpa. But her family rarely locked the back door, so it was possible a stranger could have entered the house. Or someone posing as an employee with the gas company could have stopped by. Her mother would think nothing of letting such a person in to have a look. If that person did do something to the gas line, they would have had to do it with Mom and Grandpa upstairs at the time.

That thought chilled her to her core. Wait. If someone was trying to kill her, why wouldn't they do something to the gas in her condo? Why here? Unless that person knew she was staying with her grandfather and didn't care how many people died to get to her.

Thomas knew. And he had pretty much forced his way into her condo. Had he gone there to do something to her gas line but then changed his mind when he learned that she was going to be at her parents' house? That was a very long line of "ifs," but it kind of made sense.

Who else knew where she was tonight? She'd told Ralph, and she'd told Professor Takahashi, but neither of them would do such a thing.

Her mind shifted to Jonathan. He believed she was meant to help him and Max move on from this world, and he also thought that he'd been sent here to protect her. Maybe he was right.

She hurried downstairs. Entering the kitchen, she looked for Jonathan and Max but couldn't see them. What if they'd left, gone back? Worried, she called, "Jonathan?"

"I'm here." His voice came from over by the fireplace in the alcove off the kitchen, but she couldn't see him.

As she stared, his being barely appeared. "You've faded even more. What do you need to recharge your energy?" Even though his arrival had been stressful, the thought of him leaving scared her more.

"I'm not sure." He moved toward her, and his image grew a little brighter.

"That's strange."

"What?" He stopped.

"As you moved toward me, you became more vibrant. Did you feel more energy?"

"As a matter of fact, I did."

She placed the bag of ice in the sink and rubbed her throbbing head. "Why would that be?"

"I noticed on the beach, where we first met, that as you walked toward me, I felt my energy restore." He came closer. "We're supposed to be together . . . for some reason."

She could see more clearly his groomed beard and mustache and even the short hairs that brushed the tops of his ears. His deep, dark eyes drank her in, making her want to fall into his arms and never leave.

What was wrong with her? He. Was. A. Ghost. How could she think of him in such a way? She'd breathed in too much gas fumes, that was how. And it had made her loopy.

The throbbing in her head grew to a pounding. Not knowing what to say, she went to the cupboard and grabbed the bottle of Tylenol from the second shelf. She got a glass and filled it with water. Tossing two pills into her mouth, she drank the water, gulping down the medicine. That accomplished, she turned around to face him once again, but to her surprise, he'd moved to stand right beside her.

She jumped. "You startled me."

Little lines between his eyes deepened as he squinted. "Sorry, but if I'm going to help you, I need my energy replenished."

"What about Max?" She glanced at the dog.

"I think he gains his strength from me." Jonathan shrugged his shoulders.

"I'm glad we've got that figured out." She motioned for him to follow her as she moved to the alcove where she'd be more comfortable. She sat on the couch. "Now, let's see if we can figure out who might be trying to kill me."

He rubbed his palms together. "Okay. Let's get down to business. I checked the doors and windows while you were upstairs. No broken glass, and the door locks don't appear to have been tampered with."

"You know, it's one thing for them to try to kill me while I'm on a dive but quite another while I'm home." Her eyes widened. "I've put my entire family in danger." She pressed a hand to her forehead. "Maybe when Mom gets home, I should return to my condo."

"Maybe so." Jonathan dipped his head. "Or you could stay here. There's strength in numbers. Max alerted us to your grandfather falling down and to the gas leak. He's very good at what he does. Together we won't let anything happen."

Maybe Jonathan was right. She'd much rather stay here with those who loved her. "If you really believe you two can keep us all safe, I'll stay."

"Yes, I do."

She bit her bottom lip when another thought came. "Do you think other members of my family will be able to see you? I mean, Grandpa did. It would make life so much simpler if someone else could too."

"That could be true, but it could also be because he is close to crossing over to another life. He's sensitive to the spirit world."

Gloryanna couldn't stand the thought of losing her grandpa. Yes, she knew he was old. And yes, he was sick. But he was her grandpa, and he had always been there to encourage her, be her champion. Grief rippled through her. She couldn't speak. She didn't even know what to say.

Jonathan seemed perplexed by her silence, as if he couldn't figure out why her grandfather's being on the verge of dying was so unthinkable. But he wouldn't since he was dead. Blunt reality regarding her grandfather stung.

An I'm-sorry-to-be-the-bearer-of-bad-news expression overcame his face. "We'll find out if the other members of your family can see us soon enough." He reached to touch her but stopped.

Gloryanna wanted the reassurance of his touch like she'd felt when they'd stood in the forest. She placed her hand on him, and though she couldn't touch his being like before, a warmth breathed over her skin as if she'd stuck her hand in a pool of comforting water. She glanced up at Jonathan.

His eyes were closed. A soft moan issued from his lips, and when his eyes opened, a wise, knowing expression erased the worry lines over his brow. "I feel your anxious soul. But fear no more. Max and I have been sent to watch over you." He leaned nearer. "You need to sleep. Don't worry." He rose, making room on the couch so she could put her feet up.

"How can I sleep? Someone wants to kill me." Despite her words, she yawned and covered her mouth. Had Jonathan cast a spell on her? No, he was only a ghost. A deep tiredness pulled her head onto the armrest as she curled onto her side. She felt a blanket cover her as she drifted off to blissful slumber.

***

Jonathan stood amazed by what had transpired between them. Words were inadequate to describe the mingling of their emotions when she'd touched him. They were meant to be together.

He, more than anyone else, knew how very precious life was, and he'd do everything in his power to make sure she lived and fulfilled her destiny on earth, whatever that might be.

He settled in the rocker, which seemed to mold to his spiritual form. As his energy replenished, he pondered and cherished his new circumstance. Max circled and lay beside him. The dog needed rest as well. They'd all had a very unsettling yet revealing evening.

Jonathan should take this slight reprieve to form a plan. He wished he could leave to find the suspects he believed could have motives to harm such a noble soul as Gloryanna. He gazed on her sleeping. Her beautifully sculpted face relaxed. The tips of her long lashes were bent from the fire, yet they lightly feathered her high cheek bones. Her curly hair made him want to touch it, but he wouldn't even try. He had to stay on task, which seemed impossible with her nearby. But he had to.

To solve why some lowlife scum would want to kill Gloryanna, he needed to understand why the two of them were important to each other. The first question that came to mind was, Why would he, a ghost from the forties, need someone's help eight decades later?

He thought of their first meeting. Max had warned him that someone was caught in the vortex current, so they'd gone to the beach, where he could save the person in trouble. They had done this many times. What had been different was Gloryanna. She was the main component in solving the puzzle. But why did she make the difference? What was different about her?

The sea had a way of protecting its own. What could Gloryanna have stumbled upon during her dive? He had to find out what she'd taken a picture of. Sea life? Or some foreign matter that wasn't supposed to be there? That had merit.

And what about this Ralph, whose camera she'd been so desperate to save that she'd risked her very life? Why had he loaned her his expensive camera? Did he want to see what pictures she'd take? What could have been on the ocean floor that he'd need to see? Was Ralph a genuinely good guy trying to help out a fair maiden? Possibly. Or was there something else driving his motives?

So many questions with no answers.

Jonathan's theorizing had hit a wall. He wished he didn't need Gloryanna to do research, but with his having to stay close to her to regain his energy, leaving her side became impossible. It was vital that he stay near her.

It made sense because she was his purpose for being here. Why else would the flashlight have beckoned him and Max to come? His mind drifted to their problem they couldn't leave the limbo they'd been stuck in for decades.

Why were they in this indeterminate state? That had been the question he'd wrestled with for so long. He'd always thought it was because he couldn't remember how they had died, but what if it was something else, something more? His gaze went to Gloryanna sleeping, oblivious to his mental torture.

He now had a beautiful woman in his life who gave him purpose. If only they'd met while he'd been alive.

He couldn't dwell on "if only." He had to stick to the facts. What a strange and frustrating predicament they were in.

The back door opened, and in walked a woman dressed in some type of operating scrubs, like he'd seen physicians wear during the war, except these didn't go on the outside of her clothing. They were her clothing. She set her purse on the counter near the flashlight. Upon noticing the Eveready, she glanced around the room.

Would she see him and Max?

She walked toward him, and as she neared, he realized this was the woman from the portraits in the upstairs hallway. Gloryanna's mother.

Max uncurled himself, prepared to greet her. She looked straight at them.

Jonathan braced himself, expecting an army of questions. But she said nothing and walked by.

She couldn't see them.

He reached and petted his dog. "Relax, old boy."

Max sat on his haunches and gave a big doggie yawn.

The woman stood beside Gloryanna, looking at her with the love of a parent. Her being was calm, which was a trait of a caregiver. This was a good woman filled with love. A woman who would do anything for her family. Jonathan couldn't help but envy Gloryanna for having such a person in her life.

Gloryanna's mom reached toward Gloryanna and moved a lock of curly hair away from her daughter's face. She leaned over and kissed her brow, lingering but a second before straightening her stance and going to the kitchen.

She dug in her purse, pulling out a strange handheld device that she set on a round disk plugged into the wall. It pinged, and a green light showed from the disk. Satisfied, she turned off the kitchen light and disappeared up the stairs.

She obviously had no idea Jonathan and Max were there. Oh, what mortals missed by not being able to see the spirit world.

He had about six hours before Gloryanna would awaken. He wanted to have some answers to give her. He just needed to find them.

CHAPTER NINE

GLORYANNA AWAKENED WITH A STIFF neck. She lifted her head off the arm-rest of the couch, rubbing sore muscles at the base of her skull.

"Did you sleep well?" A deep, masculine voice startled her for a second.

Jonathan is here. How could I forget? He must have been watching me sleep all night.

"Strangely, I did sleep pretty well. But next time, I'll make sure to grab a pillow." She slowly sat up. The thought of him guarding her actually gave her great comfort, especially when she remembered the moment she'd touched him. They'd shared something, a heightened awareness of each other, an assurance that they could face whatever challenge lay ahead of them together. Should she say something about it?

What if he didn't feel the same way? She thought he had last night, but this morning, she couldn't tell. Maybe it would be better not to talk about it. They had enough on their plates without examining feelings she didn't really understand. It might be better to keep things light between them.

As she continued to massage her neck, she noticed a throw had been placed over her. Jonathan must have tucked her in. Either that or her mother had. "Is Mom home?"

"She wandered in about an hour after you dozed off." He steepled his hands together but didn't move from the rocker. Max lifted his head, then relaxed again.

"Did she see you?" If her mother had seen him, Gloryanna was fairly certain their conversation would have awakened her.

"Rest assured, she did not." He leaned back.

Feeling self-conscious and wanting to get the attention off herself, she said, "Dad won't be home until the day after tomorrow, so we won't know about him seeing you for a while. Maybe before he gets home, we'll find the answer to our predicament, and you can go back to your shack or move on to wherever you're supposed to go."

"True." He rested his elbows on the rocker's arms. "I did a lot of thinking last night." He paused.

"Did you have a good time?" She couldn't help herself and tried to hide the grin pulling at her lips.

"Funny." No smile. His face stayed serious. "We have our work cut out for us today."

She turned, and the pain in her neck caught her. "Before we try to solve what's going on, I need to take a shower to see if that will help relax my stiff neck." She carefully rose to her feet, tossed the throw across the back of the couch, and glanced at the clock on the wall. "It's six thirty. Mom usually sleeps until eight, so you and Max will be undisturbed for a little bit. I'll hurry. I also need to make Grandpa's breakfast. After having such a bad night, he's going to be very hungry. Then you can tell me what you thought of, okay?"

Not waiting for his reply, she went to the kitchen desk and grabbed a piece of paper and marker. The back of her hand was still red, but it didn't sting anymore. Nor did her finger. She wrote "Don't use" and laid it on the stove, then started for the stairs. "You two stay down here." She'd said it more as an afterthought, but she seriously didn't want to worry about Jonathan walking in while she showered. She didn't think he would, but she wanted to cover her bases.

The thought of spending the day with Jonathan and Max exhilarated her, but the deep reason that they were here, plus worry over her family, overshadowed any pleasure at being with him.

As she passed Grandpa's room, she peeked inside. He hadn't moved, and she could hear his snores. Good. He needed his rest.

Hurrying to her room, she quickly showered, changed clothes, swirled her wild hair into a bun, slapped on a little makeup, and headed downstairs. Entering the kitchen, her eyes immediately went to the alcove where she'd last seen Jonathan and Max. Her heart stopped. They weren't there.

"Jonathan?"

"Who's Jonathan?" Her mother sat in the breakfast nook in her bathrobe, drinking her morning cup of herbal tea and reading headlines on her cell phone. Gloryanna hadn't seen her there. Had her mother seen the note on the stove?

The note was still where she'd left it, and the teapot rested on the front burner. Good. Her mother must have heated her tea in the microwave. Trying to ignore the question, she went to the fridge and pulled out some OJ. "I'd fix you some eggs, but there's something wrong with the stove. It was leaking gas last night. Did someone come by yesterday to look at it?"

"Good way to start the day, answering a question with one of your own." Jonathan's voice sounded right next to her.

Startled, Gloryanna nearly dropped the juice. He stood beside her, smiling with his arms folded.

"No, I noticed your note," her mom said. "I'll call and get it looked at. I'm not very hungry anyway." Her mom was completely unaware of the ghost and his dog in the room.

Gloryanna glared at Jonathan. How dare he? Wasn't it bad enough that she was the only one, besides Grandpa, who could see him? Now he'd decided to tease her in front of her mother? Well, she wouldn't let him rile her here. But when they were finally alone, she'd let him know such behavior was not acceptable.

Whenever her mother had an especially trying time in the ER, she didn't have much appetite the next day. Still, Grandpa had to eat. Retrieving oatmeal from the cupboard and milk from the fridge, Gloryanna turned her full attention to her mother. "Bad night?"

"You know me too well. There was a pileup on the freeway. We lost two, and three more are in the ICU." She set down her cell. "I don't want to talk shop. And by the way, you haven't answered my question. Who is Jonathan, and why would you think he would be here?"

What could Gloryanna say? How was she going to get out of this?

"Tell her the truth." Jonathan waited beside the counter.

"No!" Gloryanna spat out.

"No? That's hardly an answer." Mom left the nook, bringing her cup of tea. She nearly passed through Max, who quickly dodged out of her way.

She placed her cup in the microwave and turned it on before studying Gloryanna's face. "Your cheeks are flushed. And your lashes are singed."

"When I turned on the stove last night, it shot up a huge flame. But I put it out. No harm done." She tried to downplay what had happened.

"I'm glad you're okay. Still, sitting with Grandpa was too much for you so soon after your ordeal. Are you feeling well, darling?"

"Tell her," Jonathan insisted.

"No." She wished he'd quit badgering her.

"Oh, honey, I'm sorry." Mom retrieved her cup. "You sit down, and I'll make your grandfather's mush. Jumping right back into life after what you've been through then having the stove go bonkers on you, is it any wonder you're not yourself yet?"

"Mom, I meant to say yes, I'm fine. I don't know why I said no." She glared at Jonathan over her mother's shoulder.

"Are you sure?" Her mother felt her forehead.

Gloryanna pulled away. "I'm sure. But speaking of Grandpa, he had a tough time last night. After I gave him his sleeping pill, he got out of bed and fell. I was able to get him back in without too much trouble."

"You're welcome," Jonathan interjected.

Gloryanna did her best to ignore him. Besides, she'd thanked him for his help at the time. She hated deflecting her mother's attention from herself by telling her about Grandpa's upsetting evening, but she was worried about him and knew that if he told her mother he'd seen a ghost, her mother would chalk it up to his dementia, which wasn't fair at all. She hated the position they were all in.

"Was he all right?" Her mother glanced toward the stairs.

"Yes." She had to set her mother's mind at ease. "No broken bones. Not even a red mark."

Her mother started for the stairs. "I looked in on him this morning, but he was sleeping. Maybe I should check on him again."

"Tell her about me." Jonathan spoke from Gloryanna's other side.

"Wait, Mom."

With her hand on the rail, she stopped.

Gloryanna debated if she should tell her. Her mother, though a wonderful person, didn't believe in the afterlife. What would she say if Gloryanna told her about Jonathan and that he was now standing in the kitchen with them? Baffled, she searched for the right words.

Mom came back and stood directly in front of her, waiting.

Taking a deep breath, intending to fess up, Gloryanna couldn't do it, so she said, "Do you really think Dad will make it to my graduation?"

"You know he'll do his best to be here. In fact, your father was in such a good mood yesterday, I wouldn't doubt if he got here sooner."

Gloryanna opened the oatmeal and put a single serving in a bowl, then added milk. "Why don't you wait to check on Grandpa until his breakfast is ready?" She put a couple of pieces of bread in the toaster. He loved to dip toast in his oatmeal.

"You're probably right. No sense in disturbing him, especially if he had a rough go last evening." Her mother picked up her cup of tea and settled back into the nook.

"Chicken," Jonathan taunted.

"You don't understand," she hissed at him, wishing he'd leave her alone and let her tell her mom about him when and if she felt like she should.

"What don't I understand, sweetie?" Her mother picked up her cell.

"What?" Gloryanna struggled for words.

"You said that I don't understand, and I asked about what?" Mom leaned back. "Are you really okay? Maybe I should make breakfast. It's nice that you and your father think I need a break from cooking in the mornings, but I'm perfectly capable of using the microwave." She held up her cup of tea, showing the evidence.

"I'm sorry, Mom. I can do it." She started the oatmeal cooking, keeping an eye on it so it wouldn't boil over. "I have a lot on my mind is all."

"That's an understatement." Jonathan again.

Ignoring him, Gloryanna continued. "I need to work on that article for the grant, and that's going to take a ton of research. With everything that's been going on . . ."

"Honey, don't worry." Her mother took a sip of tea. "Remember what Grandpa always says 'It will all work out in the end.'"

Gloryanna stopped the microwave and stirred the oatmeal while glaring at Jonathan. He shook his head. She'd obviously been a great disappointment.

She didn't care. He'd have to learn that if they were going to work together, he was going to have to let her handle things her way and quit pestering her when another mortal was in the room.

***

Jonathan had hoped that if Gloryanna had told her mother about him, her mother would be her companion when he couldn't. Though he firmly believed that he and Max were brought here to help her, he wasn't sure how long he could stay. Maybe they'd already fulfilled their purpose by coaching her during the crisis with the blaze last night, and at any moment, the unstable teleportation could shift and send them back to the shack.

He hoped it wouldn't, but he had to plan for every contingency. At least he'd told her someone was trying to kill her. That seemed to have been the purpose of the shadow that had stalked her, that she be warned. But the shadow had also laid the burden of her protection at his feet. If he weren't here, who could Gloryanna count on as a strong ally?

He went back to the alcove next to the fireplace, where Max had retreated, to watch the mother-daughter variety show playing before him. The dog might have been right. It was best to keep his distance and let Gloryanna handle things.

It had been fun teasing Gloryanna while she'd tried to have a conversation with her mother. He'd done it only to help . . . at first. But then it had become a game. He'd delighted in watching Gloryanna's eyes sparkle with the challenge.

Jonathan settled into the rocker while Gloryanna fixed a tray for her grandfather. When her mother got up, she glanced toward the alcove and stopped. Jonathan realized he was making the chair rock back and forth. He immediately quit.

Her mother shook her head, then ignored what she had seen, gave Gloryanna a loving hug, and took the tray upstairs.

Once she'd left the room, Gloryanna made a beeline to him. "What is wrong with you? I can't tell her that you're here. She'll think I'm still suffering from my near drowning."

He said nothing.

"As you heard, Mom's going to call a repairman to check the stove. Do you think she'll be all right if we leave?"

"The killer is after you, not her. And now you want my opinion?" Jonathan couldn't help but ask. He had a reason for his persistent teasing and injecting himself into her conversation with her mother even though he stood on shaky ground.

"I know you're upset. But my mother doesn't believe in life after death." Her shoulders rose. "If I'd told her about you, we would've been in for a very lengthy discussion that I don't think we have time or patience for right now. Plus, she'd probably make me go to bed to rest. And besides, if by chance she does believe, knowing about you would be an enormous burden on her." Gloryanna rubbed the back of her neck.

"I see. Please forgive me." He had never asked a woman to forgive him before. It caused a strange sensation.

She blinked and did a double take, standing there for a moment. "Did you just apologize?"

"Yes. If I'm wrong, I gladly say so. And in this case, I was in error." He felt better each time he said it, especially after seeing a flicker of a smile cross her face.

"Well, all right, then." She returned to the kitchen and grabbed her purse and Jonathan's flashlight. "I have to say, it's nice to have a guy readily ask to be forgiven."

"Surely your father has made mistakes." Jonathan and Max followed her.

"But it usually takes a couple of days for him to work up the courage to say it. He and Mom bicker until he finally realizes life will never return to normal unless he admits he is wrong and apologizes." She slung her purse strap over her head, put the flashlight in it, and opened the door. "Shall we?"

Jonathan and Max went out into the beautiful morning that awaited them.

She nodded toward a bright red truck in the gravel parking lot. "Let's get going."

"This is your vehicle?" Jonathan marveled at the sleek work truck, so different from the six-wheel-drive military utility trucks they'd nicknamed *beeps* during the war. Certainly, vehicles had evolved since 1943.

"This was Grandpa's, but he gave it to me when he quit driving. It's a classic. Not many of these babies are left." Gloryanna sounded proud. "When he wasn't at sea, he restored old cars. Come on. Let's get going." She walked to the driver's side and turned the grip down. Amazingly, the door opened.

He inspected the truck before getting in. "This is remarkable." He admired the sleek interior, padded bench seat, and shiny chrome details. "There's so much leg room. And look"—he peered at the interior without getting in—"the windows give an increased range of sight."

"This truck was built in 1953. Wait until you see what everyone else is driving." She motioned for him to move inside.

Max barked at the rear tire and dug frantically at the ground.

"Maybe there's a cat under there," Gloryanna said.

"No." Jonathan knew something more was going on. He went to Max. "What's wrong, old boy?" He stroked his German shepherd, then checked under the carriage but couldn't see a problem. He inspected the tire. It appeared fine. "I don't see anything."

"Something's bothering him, and after last night, I'm going to check." Gloryanna got down on her knees and peered beneath the vehicle. She saw movement on the ground headed straight toward her. "It's a garden snake!" She leaped to her feet and climbed onto the running board. "Let's leave it alone and get going."

Jonathan guided his reluctant dog into the cab. "He doesn't usually react to serpents like that."

***

"No, no, no!" Gloryanna's foot hit the floor again. She gripped the wheel hard until her knuckles turned white. "We don't have brakes."

"Don't panic." Jonathan had been in an older truck than this when the brakes had failed. He needed to remember what he'd done.

They were coming dangerously close to the car ahead of them. Another couple of feet and the vehicle would be in their laps.

Gloryanna pressed her foot on the clutch and shoved the gearshift into second gear. She brought the clutch to the bar point, and the truck slowed a little.

But the car ahead braked.

"Look out!" Without thinking, Jonathan used his mind to turn the wheel.

They careened down the barrow pit. Weeds slapped the side of the truck.

Gloryanna once again pressed down the clutch, but she also pulled up on the emergency brake. The vehicle slowed and then hit an abrupt dip that jolted them. The truck still slid forward but had slowed a great deal. A railing suddenly appeared, and they slammed into it, propelling Jonathan out of the vehicle and onto the hood. He quickly checked Gloryanna.

The hair clasp she'd put in her tresses had failed, and her wild mane sprang in all directions. Her dark eyes peered at him from a pale face.

He drifted to her side. "You handled that great."

"Is that why you took over the wheel?" Her hand trembled as she smoothed a hair behind her ear.

"It was a reflex. I didn't mean to, but it happened so fast, and you were busy with the pedals." He felt bad, not because he'd taken over but because Max had tried to warn him again and he'd missed the clues.

A man with long wool-like hair and a camouflage T-shirt rushed up to the window and tapped on it. He shouted, "You okay, lady?"

Gloryanna rolled down the window. "Yes, I'm fine. Thank you."

"You're lucky to be alive." He stared at her a moment. "Hey, aren't you that woman who went missing on a dive a day or so ago?"

Gloryanna gave a hesitant nod.

"Oh man. And then you nearly bit it in a car accident. What made you swerve like that?" He stared at her; a twitch squinted his left eye.

"The car in front of me braked. I was too close, so I had to bail off the freeway."

The guy nodded while still staring at her. "Soon as we saw you leave the road, my girlfriend called the police." He pointed to his sedan parked up on the roadside. His girlfriend waved and then beckoned him to return. "They should be here in a few minutes. I'll wait up there so I can show them where you are. They'll never see you down here." The guy gave a nod and returned to his car.

"I can't believe this." Gloryanna shook her head. "My life has become a nightmare. Not only did someone enter the house and fiddle with the stove, but they also must have cut my brake line." She looked at Jonathan. Fear welled up in her eyes.

Without thinking, he reached to hug her. As his arms slipped through her, a warmth filled his being, reminding him what it was like to be human. The yearning he'd experienced last night stirred within him so intensely it caught him off guard.

She gasped and blinked her amazing bright eyes at him. "Did you feel that?"

He moved away from her. "Yes. I'm sorry." He'd stepped over the ghost/human line again. But he didn't regret it. Not. One. Bit.

"No, don't be." She stared at him. "I could have been killed, and it's nice to have you here to comfort me. I felt this, whatever it is between us, last night too. I didn't want to talk about it this morning 'cause I didn't understand it, and I didn't know if you felt the same thing."

"A tingling yet comforting sensation?"

"Yes. What does it mean?"

"I believe it's some kind of assurance that we're on the right track. I only wanted to hold you just now so you wouldn't worry." He didn't know what else to say.

"Thank you." She turned her gaze out the window.

Their little interlude had distracted them both from the very real danger they faced. He wouldn't allow himself to cross the line again. He needed to stay focused and learn to console her in a different way. Perhaps just provide a listening ear.

She wiped at her tears and sniffed.

"I'm glad you finally believe someone is trying to kill you. I just wish I'd found what had Max upset before we left your parents' house. I promise to be more diligent." He had to do a better job if she was going to stay alive.

"I believed you last night." She bit at her bottom lip. "I'm generally pretty rational and can remain cool, calm, and collected. I have to be to scuba dive. But at this moment, I'm not."

Jonathan saw lights flashing up by the road. "I think the police have arrived."

"I guess that's good. I'd better get out." She grabbed her purse and slid off the seat, but instead of climbing up to the police, she went to the front of her truck where the fender and hood were crunched against the railing.

Jonathan and Max watched and waited while the officer dressed in blue spoke with her. "Ma'am, can you tell me what happened?"

She recounted the tale.

The officer asked a few more questions. Jonathan stayed right beside Gloryanna, marveling at how well she presented herself.

"You're the woman who went missing out at sea, right?" the police asked.

She nodded.

"How did that happen?" He studied her, no expression on his face.

"My scuba tank malfunctioned, and I got caught in a current. I really can't say how I survived, but I woke up on the beach."

"And today you claim your brakes went out?" His face gave no hint of empathy.

Gloryanna squinted as she focused on the man. "They didn't work, so instead of slamming into the back of the car ahead of me, I drove off the freeway."

She glanced at Jonathan, worry flickered in her gaze.

"Ma'am, I don't want to scare you, but it doesn't sound like an accident to me." He watched her every twitch.

"Do you really think it wasn't?" Gloryanna's voice sounded so surprised and afraid. Perhaps having a live person say what Jonathan had been telling her brought it home. "But I don't have any enemies. I don't even have a lot of money. Why would someone want to kill me?"

"Don't know, ma'am," the officer replied. "But if you notice anything strange, call the police." He dug in his pocket and pulled out his card. "Call me. The two incidents could be a coincidence. But I think you should take it easy for a while and stay home." He wrote something on his clipboard. Jonathan moved closer so he could read it. Scribbled on the pad was "may need a psychiatric evaluation."

Jonathan was shocked and offended for Gloryanna that the man believed she needed a psychiatrist. Though, being under evaluation might be the safest place for her. He felt deep inside that things would only get worse, especially if she told a doctor about him and Max. He had to think how to get her out of this.

When the officer called someone on his portable phone, Jonathan whispered in Gloryanna's ear. "You need to get away from this man."

"I'm trying."

A huge tow truck rolled slowly off the highway, pulling up close to her truck. At the same time, another patrol car parked at the side of the road.

The trooper who had questioned her had her sign a paper. When she was finished, he pointed at the patrol car. "He can take you where you need to go. And please, be careful."

Maybe his note about a psychiatric evaluation would go in a file about her.

Gloryanna climbed up the embankment. Jonathan and Max hustled to catch up and slipped into the back seat with her.

The guy in the front seat turned. "I can drop you at home. Bleggi"—he nodded to the willowy guy hooking her truck to huge chains—"he'll do a good job repairing the damage."

"I'd rather go to my parents' place." She gave him the address, and they were off. They sat in silence all the while a boiling of questions bubbled within Jonathan. Tempted to talk with her, he decided against it. After what the other policeman had written, he didn't want her acting peculiar in any way.

They got out at the driveway to her parents' home. Walking toward the house, Jonathan said, "That could have been worse."

"Yeah. I could have died. I want to scream and yell and cry all at the same time. What am I going to do?" She kicked up bits of gravel.

The kitchen door opened, and her mother came outside. She must have seen Gloryanna from the window. "Why did the police drop you off? What happened?"

"I had a little problem with my truck. And the nice officer offered me a ride home." She walked toward her.

"Take my SUV. I'm not going anywhere." Her mother turned toward the house.

"Mom, you need to have a car available in case something happens to Grandpa."

"You're probably right." She glanced up toward his bedroom window. "I couldn't get him to eat much. He was worried about you, said something about a harbinger and that we were all in great danger."

Jonathan felt bad that the elderly man was so afraid of him. But in a way, he was right.

Her mother went on. "He became hysterical. I had to give him a sedative, and he fell back to sleep." Her gaze returned to Gloryanna. "It's so sad what's happening to him. But bouts of dementia are expected with someone his age. Guess we should be grateful he's been as healthy as he has been." She folded her arms. "Who were you talking to as you walked up the drive? I could hear your voice from the kitchen." Her mother looked around.

Jonathan couldn't wait to see what she'd say, so he moved behind her mother.

Gloryanna avoided his eyes and looked at the ground. "I was scolding myself. I had a feeling a week ago that I should take the truck in for a tune-up, but I ignored it."

"Uh-huh. But you were acting like someone was with you." Her mother waved her hand. "Oh, never mind. I'd offer to drive you home, but I don't dare leave. Wish your father were here."

Light came to Gloryanna's eyes. "I'll take Dad's motorcycle."

Did she say motorcycle? Jonathan hadn't seen one since the war. It had been an Indian model 841 issued from the army, powered by a 45-ci, side-valve, V-twin, air-cooled engine. That baby could go.

"I don't think that's a good idea." Her mother shook her head. "You know how protective your father is of his bike. The last time you took it, he was upset for a month."

"I'll be more careful. Promise. I'll see you tonight." She didn't wait but turned around.

Her mother shrugged, gave a half smile at her determined daughter, and went back into the house.

Gloryanna dashed off to the garage, leaving Jonathan and Max to follow. Entering the building, she pushed a button, and the garage door lumbered open.

Jonathan stood there, staring. How did it move by itself? Some type of box contraption hung from the ceiling, and a track connected to it with what looked like sturdy wire, which seemed to pull the door. Amazing!

The motorcycle was parked next to what looked like a supply truck. Jonathan noted how different the vehicle looked from those in his time period, but he stopped short at the bike. This was a much different machine than he'd ever imagined. The color wasn't green like the ones he was familiar with; it was burgundy with a winged logo on the gas tank that read Harley-Davidson.

She grabbed a key from a peg over the workbench. "Have you ever ridden on a Harley?"

"Never."

She picked up the helmet that had rested on the seat and put it on her head, fastening the chinstrap. Inserting the key, she leaned the bike up, and kicked the stand into driving position. Throwing a leg over the machine, she started the engine. "Hop on," she shouted.

Jonathan didn't know how this would work a ghost and his dog riding on the back of a motorcycle. But he was about to find out.

CHAPTER TEN

DRIVING HER FATHER'S HARLEY EXHILARATED Gloryanna much like scuba diving did. Jonathan and Max managed to stay near. She couldn't see if they floated or how they stayed close, but she sensed that they were behind her. She lived only four or five miles from her parents', so before she knew it, they'd arrived at her condo. Gloryanna pulled into her underground parking space and stopped. She felt Jonathan and Max move away, so she lowered the kickstand and shut down the rumbling engine before she got off.

She removed the helmet. She could just imagine what her unruly mop was doing. She glanced at Jonathan and his dog. They patiently waited for her as she swooped her locks away from her face. "Did you enjoy the ride?"

"Between holding on to Max and staying on the seat, I guess so." He appeared a little windblown.

"Good." Gloryanna paused a moment. "Do you think whoever cut the brakes on my truck will know this is my father's Harley and do something to it?"

"Don't worry. If Max gets upset if we try to ride it again, we'll do a thorough check before leaving." Jonathan bent over and patted the dog's head.

Relieved, she said, "Good. Let's go up to my condo." As she led the way, she dug her keys from her cross-body purse and was ready when they reached the door. She unlocked it and stepped aside. "Welcome to my home."

Jonathan and Max went in and looked around her living/dining area. Jonathan gazed at the scuba-diving pictures with vivid colors of marine life she'd hung on her walls.

She loved having scenes of the ocean deep around her. "As you can see, I love the sea."

Max jumped up on her couch and lay down, making himself comfortable. She watched as Jonathan noticed the fireplace in the corner and, across from that, a small farmhouse dinette with white legs and bare wooden seats. She'd left her laptop on the table.

Kicking off her shoes and looping her purse over the back of a dining chair, she opened her computer and turned it on. Without thinking, she said, "Would you like something to drink?"

"Um, that would be a no, but thank you." Jonathan stared at her laptop, hypnotized by the screen as it came on.

Embarrassed that she'd forgotten he couldn't drink or eat, she wondered what he'd lived on all those years at his shack. "So, at your shelter, did you eat and drink like you were alive?"

"Yes. I lived off the land. Ate fish and berries. Drank tea. Max was able to eat and drink as well, which was a strange phenomenon, being as we knew we were dead, yet we weren't. We merely existed." He seemed uncomfortable talking about it and focused on her computer.

She didn't want to push him, so she dropped the subject. "You've probably never seen one of these?"

His right brow rose, and his eyes held a ya-think expression.

"This is a laptop computer. Not the best but not the worst either. I'm going to use it to help us make a plan." She stood and removed her favorite diving picture of friendly sea otters from the wall above the dining room table and took it to her bedroom. Coming back, she said, "We can use this wall space to tape pictures and give us a visual that might help us figure out where we need to go and who we need to talk to." She hurried to the kitchen and grabbed tape from a drawer.

Returning, she settled on the chair in front of her computer, but instead of typing she turned to Jonathan, who stood beside her. "Before we get started, I need to tell you something."

Jonathan's gaze was still glued to the screen.

It was probably better he wasn't looking at her. She cleared her throat. "Yesterday, I was trying to get a lot of things done. And this was before the flashlight summoned you, so I was juggling a lot on my own, and I really didn't know if I believed your story about being a ghost and everything. Anyway, I told Professor Takahashi about you."

He turned his full attention to her. "Why?"

She felt like a traitor and had to make this right. "I didn't know what to think about you, and I had so much on my plate; plus, the professor has access to a much larger database than I do."

"Database? I haven't a clue what that is." Worry puckered his forehead. "Wait a minute. Did you say she? Your professor is a woman?" Jonathan seemed surprised.

Gloryanna realized in the forties, not many women held such positions. "Yes, Jonathan. In this day and age, women have made great strides in the workplace."

"Good. I've often thought women were underutilized in my generation. I just hope they don't go to war and fight." He said it as if he couldn't imagine a woman in a battlefield.

"They already do." Now was not the time to debate who should fight in war. "We're doctors, lawyers, CEOs, and even hold key positions in politics."

"Who takes care of the children?" Jonathan's forehead wrinkled.

"Both parents do."

"Hmm. Imagine having both a father and mother equally caring for a child." He paused.

He'd told her that he was an orphan, so the idea of both parents taking care of their children would sound very nice. She didn't know quite what to say.

"Back to your professor." Jonathan cut into the odd silence between them. "What exactly did you tell her about me?"

"I told her that you said you were a ghost and a sand pounder." Gloryanna's neck ached from tilting her head to look at him standing beside her. She pulled out a chair for him to sit on and patted the seat. "But I'm not sure if she believed me. She took a lot of notes. Anyway, I think I should give her a call. She may have some information that could help us." She pulled her cell phone from her purse. "This is a cell phone."

"Your mother had one, and so did the officer."

She explained how the phone worked, answered his questions, then tapped in Professor Takahashi's number.

It rang only a couple of times before the professor answered. "Gloryanna, I'm glad you called. There's not a lot of information on 'Coasties'—that's what they called the beach patrol provided by the Coast Guard. Most of what I found has to do with the Eastern coastline. They had ten districts and approximately 24,000 officers and men. They covered over 3,700 miles. That's both coasts. In the west, they launched a Coast Guard Beach Patrol, which they called sand pounders. Those who served usually had horses, which makes sense because of the distance they were responsible for. They also used dogs."

Gloryanna looked at Max on the couch. He raised his head like he knew he was being talked about.

"The sand pounders worked in pairs so that if they came upon a suspect, one could hold them while the other one went for help. I found a report that a diver off the coast of Oregon found a cave that had lots of empty drums with Nazi signs on them. He even found iron posts in concrete, which could have been evidence of submarine provisions."

"I'd never heard that the Nazis were on the West Coast." Gloryanna was amazed. "I knew their U-boats did a lot of damage in the Atlantic, but here in the Pacific?"

"Upsetting, isn't it?" The professor grew quiet, then said, "There were numerous cases of the Japanese shelling Oregon and California coastlines."

Gloryanna hadn't realized that this project might make the professor uncomfortable. "I'm sorry. I hope this isn't difficult for you."

"Why would it be?"

"Well, because you have Japanese heritage." How could she have been so thoughtless?

"My dear, the war was a very long time ago. And need I remind you, I'm an American."

Now Gloryanna felt even more foolish. "Still, I'm sorry."

"No need to be. Back to what I found. Along the Olympic Peninsula, the sand pounders had a rough time. They had to carry in most of their supplies. A mule packed in a hundred-pound cookstove to make life more bearable. Did your ghost have one in his shelter?"

"Yes." Gloryanna looked at Jonathan. It felt odd that the professor referred to him as "her ghost." She didn't see him as merely a ghost anymore. He was her friend, her friend with whom she'd shared tender moments beside her truck and in the forest just before he'd disappeared. Okay, her very good friend.

"That's probably the stove they were talking about." The professor took a breath. "I found another story that took place south of Cape Flattery. The LaPush Beach Patrol came upon debris and the body of a woman in a lifeboat. They kept searching, but the coast there is very rugged, and they had to search from the cliffs above. Soon, they found the *SS Lamut* and Soviet seamen clinging to jagged rocks and fighting the surge. And this next part is just plain amazing. The patrol tried to rescue them from the cliffs above, but their rope wasn't long enough, so they tied their shoelaces and bandages from first-aid kits to the end of it. The patrol hung that improvised rope over the ledge, and the Soviet sailors had to climb hand-over-hand until they reached safety. Your sand pounders saved fifty-two lives."

"Wow." Gloryanna glanced at Jonathan, wondering if he'd been part of that rescue.

The professor cleared her throat. "Do you think that conning tower you saw could have been part of the *SS Lamut*?"

"Maybe." Gloryanna thought of her grandfather and his claim that he'd been on a submarine that had sunk, but he wasn't Russian, so he couldn't have been on that one.

What was she thinking? Her mother had to be right, and Grandpa had mistaken reality with some movie he'd watched. Focusing on her conversation with the professor, she said, "But so many divers have already been down there. Surely someone would have discovered the wreckage before now."

"Not necessarily. Most divers avoid the vortex current. And with storms and the way the tides come and go, new discoveries are always being made. Too bad you lost your camera. We could have had a closer look," Professor Takahashi said.

A swell of guilt and remorse grew within Gloryanna. She couldn't do anything about losing the camera. Maybe Jonathan could find the thing and levitate it out of the ocean. She wished she would have thought of that while they'd been at his shelter, but she had been too worried about her own safety to even ask. And there was no telling when they'd return or if the camera would be displaced with the movement of the water. She had to stay focused on the conversation she was having with the professor. "This is all very fascinating, but did you find information about Jonathan Dawson?" She glanced at him sitting beside her and wondered what he must be thinking.

"I'm sorry. I haven't. And I'm afraid I won't be able to do more research for you. The dean is after me to help with graduation. You weren't planning to visit your sand pounder and collect your gear until after that, were you? It's the day after tomorrow."

"I hadn't really thought about when I was going. My grandfather hasn't been well."

"I'm so sorry." Professor Takahashi grew quiet and then added, "You are coming to graduation, right?"

"Definitely." But to be truthful, Gloryanna wasn't sure. Yes, she'd worked hard to earn her degree, but being there for a ceremony paled in comparison to being with her grandfather should he need her. And by the way he'd reacted to seeing Jonathan last night, he very well might.

"Good." A noise sounded like the professor had closed her laptop or snapped her briefcase closed. "Why don't we plan to go to your sand pounder's place next weekend? In the meantime, sit tight. We'll get this figured out together."

Before Gloryanna could say thank you, the professor hung up.

"Did you hear what she said?" Gloryanna looked at the handsome man-ghost, who had grown abnormally quiet.

"That would have been impolite, wouldn't it?" He leaned back, and the right side of his mouth quirked up.

"You did, didn't you? Impolite, my eye." She shook her head. "Then you know the bad news is she didn't find any information regarding you personally."

"Do you trust this woman?" His half smile disappeared.

"Yes. Why shouldn't I?" From the conversation she'd just had with Professor Takahashi, she couldn't understand why he would ask.

"I don't know. It's just . . . I'm probably off my game, being this far away from the shack and in a new environment. Congratulations, though, on graduating. I didn't realize how very young you are." He stared at her.

Feeling self-conscious, she rubbed her forehead and gave a halfhearted shrug. "I'm not, really. I saved money for several years before I started college. I wanted to pay for my education myself."

"How old are you?" Again, he scrutinized her.

"Twenty-sixish," she eked out. Why was she being all shy about her age to Jonathan? "And how old are you?"

He looked up at the ceiling. "In ghost or human years?"

She hadn't thought of it that way. "Well, give me both. At your shack, I guessed that you were twenty-nine or thirty. That would be human years, right?"

"Yes, and it's thirtyish."

Gloryanna couldn't help but chuckle because he'd added the *ish* like she had. "What about ghost years?"

"Eighty. And if you combined the two, that would be one hundred and ten." He scowled. "I don't like the sound of that. Let's use human years."

"Human it is."

"And Max was four." He glanced at his dog, who stared at both of them like they were ludicrous.

Gloryanna had to get down to business. "Okay, as you heard, Professor Takahashi suggested I sit tight for a while."

"Are you going to?"

"On that, yes, but let's turn our focus to you. There are other ways to find things out." She intertwined her fingers, then stretched them before posing over the laptop keyboard. "Okay. Can you tell me anything about your teammate? I think you called him Frank."

Jonathan rubbed his chin. "He was always talking about finding gold in Nevada."

"Nevada? I guess it is a major gold-mining area. Or did he mean by gambling?"

"I only half listened to him. Probably gambling." Jonathan nodded. "Before the war, he spent his life surfing in California."

"That's good to know. If we had a surname, that would help a ton." She opened a search engine on her laptop.

"I think it started with a *B*." He thought a moment. "I feel like an idiot." He shifted in his seat. "Who forgets their teammate's name?"

"It seems you do. But don't be so hard on yourself. You are a hundred and ten." She swiped at her mouth to hide a smile.

"Hey! No need to get mean." Though his words were a little defensive, he had a twinkle in his eyes.

Maybe she was pushing too much. "Just think about it for a bit."

"Since I'm already dead, perhaps we should dwell on who could want to harm you." Jonathan studied her. "I don't want you to end up like me."

He gazed at her. His eyes searched hers as if he were reaching into her soul. Her breath caught. He'd looked at her the same way he had when they'd stood in the forest. Did he have feelings for her? Romantic feelings?

Of course not. He was a ghost.

She needed to concentrate on who could possibly want to kill her. Whoever it was, they might harm her family too. She needed to stay on topic and not let her mind wonder. "Okay." She tapped the Word icon. An empty text file opened on her screen. The curser blinked, ready for her to type.

Jonathan rubbed his hands together. "There's that Ralph person, whose camera you lost."

"Speaking of the camera. When we go back to your beach, do you think you could find the camera and levitate it out of the ocean like you did me?"

"I can only home in on living beings because of their spirits. To raise tangible objects, I need to see them." He pursed his lips and shrugged. "Sorry. And I know you don't think your dear friend could be so evil as to sabotage your tank, but he has to be a suspect. It was his responsibility to fill it."

"But he told me Skip filled my tank before the dive."

"Okay, put both of them down."

Gloryanna typed Ralph's name, then clicked on the search engine and pulled up a picture of him. She sent the file to the printer, and right away, she heard the machine working in the other room. Then she entered Skip's name, but no image appeared.

"What is going on in there?" Jonathan stared in the direction of her second bedroom that served as her office.

"I'm printing their pictures to put on the wall. I couldn't find one for Skip. But while I'm at it, I'll do Thomas Clifford."

"Times have certainly changed." He shook his head, then seemed to think of something else. "Don't forget your professor."

"Okay, if you insist." Gloryanna found both of their pictures and printed them as well, then she went to the spare bedroom, collected the images, and brought them back. Putting tape on each one, she stuck them to the wall.

She and Jonathan stared at the three pictures gazing down on them. To think that one of them could have tried to kill her was absurd. "I spoke to each of them yesterday and didn't get the feeling that they meant to harm me."

"A killer is good at hiding intentions." Jonathan stared at the pictures. "Why not start with him?" He pointed to Ralph. "What do you know about this man?"

"I've known him at least ten years. He not only services my scuba gear, but he is also my employer." She paused a moment, thinking of her work. One night when business had been slow, she'd taken a picture of both Skip and Minnie. Skip needed to be on the wall. Finding the shot on her cell, she sent it to her printer.

Jonathan watched her in amazement.

She shrugged as she left to retrieve the picture. She added it to the wall with the others. "Minnie isn't a suspect. She has nothing to do with the scuba part of Ralph's business."

Jonathan gave her a sideways glance. "Don't be so sure. We need to question everyone."

"But they are good people. In fact, Ralph is a very pro-save-the-ocean type of individual, which I totally agree with. Did you know the main threat to the oceans is the fishing industry?"

Jonathan shook his head and seemed interested.

"It's true. Ralph told me there was a study. Most people condemn using plastic straws and bags, thinking that's the main cause of ocean pollution, but in the UK, they found a beached whale, and do you know what was in its bloated stomach?"

Again, he shook his head.

"Old fishing lines and nets. Most fishing companies just drop them into the ocean when they're finished with them."

"There should be a law against that." Jonathan seemed disgusted.

"There is, but it's tough to enforce." She took a breath. "Some officials go out to sea to monitor but don't make it back." Frustration flooded her. "And others mysteriously die, especially if they've reported a company for negligence."

She rushed to her office to retrieve a book Ralph had given her. Opening to the page she wanted, she showed it to Jonathan. "This is Minamata Bay, Japan. In the late 1950s, it became contaminated with mercury from a nearby factory. The mercury was biotransformed by bacteria in the water into methylmercury. The fish became contaminated, and over two thousand people died, and thousands developed crippling injuries.

Jonathan glanced at it. "How sad."

"I know. Many marine biologists are working very hard to help keep our oceans clean. But it's a huge task because sixty-six percent of global seafood consumption comes from the oceans with high levels of mercury." Gloryanna shut the book, unable to bear it. "Ralph helps support the Sea Savers, who are doing all they can to help. They've had some success."

"Does Ralph go with them?" Jonathan stared at the man's picture.

"Well, no." She set the book on the table.

"Why?" Jonathan folded his arms. "If he's such a believer in preserving the ocean, I would think he would go out there."

She didn't like the doubtful tone in Jonathan's voice. "Well . . . he's afraid of the ocean. But he donates a lot of money to the cause."

"Afraid of the ocean yet *he* services scuba gear." He looked at her. "Have you ever been curious as to why?"

"No." But now she wondered.

"Perhaps you should look into that." Jonathan's right brow quirked up. "And his other employees."

"Really?"

He nodded.

"Okay, I will. But Ralph's paradoxes are part of his charm." Gloryanna hated to agree that Jonathan might be right.

"We should probably make a list of things we need to research for each person. Like, for Ralph, he's pro-save-the-oceans, he's afraid of the sea, and he services scuba gear. Is he married? Does he have children?"

Gloryanna typed what Jonathan had said. "He's single, but now that you mention it, I don't know much about his home life or if he has children somewhere."

Jonathan hoisted a shoulder. "That's why we should list it. It might be easier to just tape a page by each picture, and you could write these down. We'll need two pages for this one." He pointed to Skip and Minnie's images.

"You're right." Gloryanna went to her office and grabbed some paper and a marker. She listed all the things Jonathan had said for Ralph and taped it under his image. She put a blank page on each side of Skip and Minnie's photo. "I'm ashamed to say it, but even though I've worked with them, I don't know much about them."

"That's okay. That's the reason we're doing this to learn what we don't know and fill in the blanks. Now, what about him?" Jonathan pointed to Thomas.

She taped a page under his face and one under the professor, then grabbed the marker. "He's rich." She wrote that on Thomas's page. "He's going for his master's in marine biology, like I am." She added that. "And he was an ex-boyfriend of mine and has been my rival in college." After making those notes, she stepped back.

"And he loves you," Jonathan added.

"He didn't say that. He said he has feelings for me." Such a note seemed absurd to her.

"But that's what he meant." Jonathan stared at her like he wasn't going to let this go.

"Look, he only told me that because I went missing, and he felt . . . I don't know. Guilty. He felt guilty because . . ." She stared at his picture. "Because maybe he did something to my tank and regretted it."

"That's possible. So, list it."

Giving in, Gloryanna scribbled the information on his page.

"Okay, moving on to Professor Takahashi." Jonathan threaded his fingers together as he gazed at her picture. "She took you diving."

Gloryanna noted that on her page.

"She had access to your tank."

Gloryanna added that.

"And you told her about me."

She nodded and made another notation.

"In your conversation, she said something about a shipwreck?" Jonathan tapped his chin.

After Gloryanna wrote "shipwreck," she put the cap on the marker and backed up, staring at the wall of suspects and their lists.

Jonathan moved to her side.

"I don't know if putting up pictures and writing things for each person really helps that much." She had her doubts, but at least it was a good visual of possibilities.

"I think you should list the attempts on your life. We don't need to put them beside anyone yet, but we should make note of them." The serious tone of his voice showed how felt strongly about this.

"Okay." She jotted down her tank losing oxygen, the gas stove incident, and her brakes. She taped it under the pictures. "Does that help?"

"I think so." Jonathan moved to the wall. "This Ralph guy loves the ocean. Thomas loves you and wants to be a marine biologist. And the professor—she knows of a shipwreck."

"None of that means any of them would want me dead." The last two words stung. "What do we do?"

"We need more information, so I say we talk with each one."

"I already have."

"But I wasn't with you. This time, I will be. Why don't we start here?" He pointed to Thomas.

"Why him?"

Jonathan dipped his head and gave her a you-know-why look. The love thing.

"Seriously?" Gloryanna dropped the marker on the table.

"Yes, *seriously*." Jonathan moved beside her. "We need to find out why, if you broke up years ago, he would bare his soul to you now. If we find that out, we might learn what he's trying to cover up."

"He's just confused. While he dove searching for me, he probably mistook concern for a friend as something more. He was only trying to be honest." Which, in retrospect, was an improvement for Thomas.

"And you believe him?"

"Honestly, I don't know." The old hurts and anger she'd thought she was over stung once again. "You're right." Gloryanna became energized. "He probably told me that because he's hiding something."

"Where does your boyfriend live?"

"He's not my boyfriend!" Gloryanna tried to tamp down the surge of anger. "That's not funny."

"Yeah, it is." He smiled and nodded with a teasing glint in his eye.

Was Jonathan giving her a bad time about Thomas because he himself was jealous of her and Thomas's past? Or did he do it to see if she really did have feelings for her old flame?

Unable to figure out Jonathan's true motivation with his teasing, she stayed the course. "Not even."

"Just a titch?" He put his index finger and thumb together.

Maybe it was seeing him try so hard to make her say yes, or maybe she just enjoyed this silly word play with this devilishly handsome man-ghost, but she chuckled a little and said, "No."

"A smidge." Jonathan leaned his head in a way that made her want to give in.

"Maybe a hair," she muttered.

"All right." He rubbed his palms together. "Now we're making progress. Where does your boyfriend live?"

She ignored the *boyfriend* part, or they'd be here all day. "Thomas lives off campus."

"So, you know." Jonathan sounded victorious.

"Certainly I do." She rolled her eyes. "We dated. But like I said, that was long ago. And since that time, I've only been there once with a group. We had to meet at his place to study for a final." She hated that she had to tell him that. "Four other people were there. And I was never alone with him."

"Did I ask if you had been?" His smile faded.

"Well, no."

"Are you afraid to be alone with him?" No teasing. Only a serious note in his voice.

"No," Gloryanna quickly said, then stopped. "Should I be?"

"I don't know. Should you?" He squinted at her.

"Stop it." Gloryanna had had enough of this silly game.

"Stop what?"

"Implying that I might be afraid to be alone with him because I have feelings for him, which I don't. Well, not in the way you think. The only feeling I have for him is mistrust." There. She'd laid it all out on the table. At least, she thought so.

"And that is precisely why we start with him. Where is his off-campus abode?" Jonathan headed for the door.

"It's near the college, about five miles away." She grabbed her purse.

"I suppose we're traveling on the bike again." Jonathan's enthusiasm seemed to wane.

"It's the only wheels we have. But like I said, he's not far. Maybe fifteen minutes on the freeway."

"Freeway?"

"We were on the freeway earlier when the brakes failed in my truck." She stopped.

Max got off the couch and moved beside Jonathan.

"We could take the bus, if you'd rather." She'd said it as an alternative but hoped he'd say no.

"Yes." He nodded and glanced down on his dog. "That would be a more preferrable way to travel."

"I don't know though . . ." She paused.

"What?"

"I don't think they allow ghosts on public transit." She chuckled.

"And how would you know?" he countered. A smile tugged at the corners of his mouth. "I'll bet you've been riding with a lot of ghosts and were none the wiser." He passed her.

"Okay. But think of this with more people around us, the more likely the chances will be that someone else will see you. Are you sure you want to risk that?" She waited at the door near the table where she'd placed the helmet she'd worn.

Jonathan's teeth clenched, a defeated look on his face. "All right, we'll go on that contraption you call a motorbike, but could you go a little slower? Trying to keep up with you is exhausting."

"Then I'll stick to side streets." She grabbed the helmet, and they walked out. She locked the door behind her and led the way to the underground parking. "The trip will take longer, but we can go as slow as you want, Grandpa." She couldn't help but throw in the jab.

"I am not your—" His face lit up like he got what she meant. "I understand. You made a joke about my would-be age?"

"No, about your sense of adventure." She looped her purse strap over her head so it crossed her body, then pulled the helmet on. For the second time today, she got on the Harley and started the engine. The motor rumbled to life. The seat cushion behind her moved, and she knew Jonathan and Max were ready. With a fleeting smile on her lips and trepidation in her heart, she pulled out and headed to the last place on earth she wanted to go.

CHAPTER ELEVEN

Max seemed all legs as Jonathan tried his best to hold him and remain focused on keeping up with the motorcycle. A mighty feat. Luckily, the wind blew right through them, which helped. Plus, he managed to feed off the strength coming from Gloryanna.

Their journey seemed never-ending as she maneuvered the bike in and out of traffic, but she finally pulled to a stop in front of the Shadow Ridge Apartments. He marveled at the stately glass building. He'd never seen such a structure, and he wondered how it had been built. But more importantly, he wondered why someone would want to live in such a fishbowl.

He and Max moved from the bike, then Gloryanna set the brake and pulled off her helmet, placing it beneath her arm. "This is it. Come on."

Following her into the building, he was surprised to find a doorman in his late fifties, with graying hair, dressed in a red blazer and tie, sitting behind a counter.

"Yes, miss?" The man gave her a poker-face look.

"I'm here to see Thomas Clifford."

Right away, he glanced at a screen that looked something like the one Gloryanna had used. She'd called it a laptop. "Mr. Clifford didn't say he expected a guest."

"That's because he didn't know we were coming."

He looked around her. "We?"

He couldn't see Jonathan or Max.

"Oh, I meant he didn't know *I* was coming." Gloryanna's hand shook as she nervously smoothed her wild hair behind her ears. She smiled and focused on the doorman and his name tag on the lapel of his blazer. "Mr. Sylvester, I've been going to college with him, and I'm used to coming with the group at night. That's why I said *we*. We study with him. You probably don't work the night shift."

The doorman nodded. "And your name is?"

"G . . . abriella Smith."

He reared back. "Wait a minute." He rubbed his shaved chin. "I remember you. Years ago, you used to come here with Mr. Clifford all the time. It's nice to see you again. Sorry I didn't remember your name. And I'm also sorry to tell you Mr. Clifford isn't home at the moment. I believe he said he was meeting his father and would be gone for several hours."

"He'll be okay with us—I mean me, just me—waiting for him." Her cheeks blushed red as she hurried to the elevator and pressed the Up button.

Jonathan and Max followed her.

"But, Ms. Smith, do you still have a key?"

Her chin descended in a reluctant nod. "Thanks for your help."

The elevator opened, and they got on. The doors slid shut.

Jonathan watched her stare at the needle above the door, showing that they were moving up. She obviously didn't want to talk about what just transpired, but he did. Even though he knew she was upset with herself, Jonathan had to point out the problem. "Do you really think it's wise to break into his home?"

She folded her arms. "No, but I'm desperate. And I don't think he's going to come out and tell me he's trying to kill me either. So, if we go in and have a look without him there, we might find more than if he were. Besides, we aren't going to steal anything, just have a look around."

"I suppose you're right." He decided not to dwell on it. "By the way, nice job covering up. You think fast on your feet."

"You mean, other than almost telling him my real name and saying *we* instead of *me*?" Her cheeks were still red. "It's only a matter of time before he realizes I gave him a fake name."

"If luck is on our side, we'll be long gone." He hoped that made her feel better, but her pretty face pulled into a frown.

The elevator opened on the top floor. They exited to a gray hallway with walnut-stained wainscoting halfway up the walls and black lighting on some sort of track system above.

"There are two penthouses." Gloryanna led the way to a door. "His is on the right. It overlooks the town of Bellingham." She waited by the entrance.

"I thought you had a key." Jonathan expected that she would mine in her purse for it. "Which only feeds into the boyfriend argument, I might add. Especially since the doorman still remembers you."

"I lied about the key." Her eyebrows rose. "But I don't need one. I have you." Her eyes sparkled as she ignored his boyfriend remark. "And you don't need one."

He supposed she was right. He didn't know why he hadn't thought of it before. Without further delay, Jonathan and Max stepped through the wooden door and entered a lavishly decorated modern apartment. Floor-to-ceiling windows were bordered with bare concrete interior walls, where industrial bookcases held a few books but mostly plants. Max sniffed around the open floor plan, where a modern charcoal-colored sofa divided the room for a lounge area. Behind it stretched a dining set. The six moss-green seats complemented the wooden table. The exterior walls were glass.

A knock came from behind, reminding Jonathan to let Gloryanna in. Using his mind-over-matter ability, he tripped the lock and opened the door. He could have done that before coming in, but he'd wanted to make sure Thomas really wasn't there. A bit of energy drained from him. As soon as he moved closer to Gloryanna, it would return.

"It's about time." She closed and locked the door behind her. Walking past the gray kitchen that sprawled across the entire width of the room, with a long cooking and dining island placed in front, she crossed the diagonally laid, natural, wood-grained flooring to the living area and set her helmet on the coffee table that looked like a large cube. Glancing around, she said, "In case you were ever curious, this is how a rich kid lives while going to college."

"I find the gray a bit depressing." Jonathan much preferred his shack with nature surrounding him instead of this glass and concrete. Wanting to stay on task, he added, "Where should we begin?"

"There obviously isn't anything that appears suspicious in here." She motioned around the room, where nothing was out of place, then headed down a hall. "Maybe in his bedroom. That's where his laptop will be."

He followed her, passing a geometric-lined wall.

They stepped into the master suite of dark blues, browns, and grays that continued the posh theme. However, the bed was unmade, and clothes, papers, and books were strewn about, making it look as if a storm had blown through. Max sniffed at empty beverage cans lying on the floor. In the corner rested a scuba tank and gear.

Jonathan nodded. "So this is where he truly lives."

"It's probably the only area where he doesn't allow the maid to clean, which means we may find something." She went to his desk, where his laptop rested. Stacks of books and paper waited beside it.

While Gloryanna turned on the computer, Jonathan checked out the man's closet concealed by a barn door. Poking his head in, he saw a couple of tailor-made suits, some white, long-sleeved shirts and T-shirts, some jeans, and some jackets. In the shoe rack rested various shoes sneakers, wingtips, and tasseled loafers. Dress shoes. All the clothing of a rich college kid. Against the back wall of the closet rested another scuba tank and gear.

Jonathan pulled away and noticed the laptop's screen blink. Gloryanna typed on the keyboard. "It's password protected, which doesn't surprise me."

"Password? You mean it has a code?"

She bobbed her head.

"Do you know what it is?"

"No." She glared at the computer. That was when her eyes caught on something Max was sniffing. She rose and went to a pile of clothes. Picking up a pair of trousers and a shirt, she said, "Look."

Jonathan didn't know what she was getting at, though the clothes seemed nothing like what occupied the closet.

She held the shirt out. On it was a logo of some type. "This is the uniform the gas company has their employees wear." She took a deep breath and shook her head. "Wearing this, he could have gone to my house, and no one would have questioned him. The person who did something to our stove had to have been Thomas."

"Wait." Jonathan hated to put a damper on what she'd said, but it wouldn't hurt to look for more. They needed to find as much evidence as possible. "Just because he wears a uniform, it doesn't mean he'd walk into your home or that he was the one who did it. Don't forget, whoever it was may have also cut the brake line of your truck. Plus, you already asked your mother if someone from the gas company stopped by yesterday afternoon and she said no."

She grudgingly nodded. "True. I could ask her if she noticed if someone from the gas company was in the area." She pulled her cell phone from her purse and pressed the screen. "But she would have said something about it when I told her there was a leak. Rats. I'd hang up, but she's going to see my number on her phone and worry that something is wrong."

Jonathan marveled at the device in her hand, impressed with the giant leap modes of communication had made while he'd been stuck in a time bubble.

Max lay on a pile of clothes, perched where he could keep an eye on them.

"Hi, Mom." She inhaled deeply. "I'm curious, did you happen to notice yesterday if someone from the gas company was working near your place?"

Jonathan eavesdropped on their conversation.

"Not that I recall," her mother said. "I called the gas company after you left. They're going to send someone to check things out."

"Okay." Gloryanna sank onto the chair in front of the desk. "How's Grandpa?"

Clever girl, putting something else in her mother's mind so she wouldn't dwell on why Gloryanna had asked about the gas company.

"Your grandpa ate most of his breakfast, did ten minutes of exercises, and showered. He's sleeping now." Her mother sounded tired.

"Did he mention anything about last night?" Gloryanna looked at Jonathan. She must still be worried about the old man's reaction to seeing him and Max.

"Well . . ." Her mother's voice grew sad. "His dementia is worse. He keeps going on about a harbinger and his canine minion, and that the entire family is in danger."

The old codger was right in that the entire family was in danger, but it wasn't from Jonathan. Jonathan was stumped as to why the elderly fellow had seen him. He still felt that perhaps the man may have had glimpses of the spirit world because he was close to leaving mortality. That made sense. And yet, not.

"Well, I'm glad he's resting now. I'll be back home in time to spell you tonight. You get some rest too, Mom." Gloryanna ended the call. A sadness had befallen her. "I'm sure you heard what she said."

Jonathan nodded and stared at the uniform. "But there must be some reason Thomas has these clothes."

"I know. It doesn't make sense. As you can plainly see, he doesn't need to work." She thought a moment. "And another thing for our list. I don't understand why he's competing with me for the grant to earn his master's degree."

"Perhaps his father has fallen on hard times." Jonathan took a guess, though he agreed that something wasn't right about that.

"Nah. Mr. Clifford was listed as number one on Washington's top ten wealthiest people." She turned and looked at Thomas's laptop. "From what the guard said, Thomas is going to be gone awhile. Let me try to guess his password. There might be something on his hard drive that we could use." She typed, but the screen only changed to ask if she'd forgotten the password and if she'd like to create a new one.

"Why not make another code word?"

"Because if I were to do that, the program would send him a text or email letting him know. And we don't want that. Just give me a minute." She went back to work.

Jonathan glanced around the room and noticed some framed pictures on Thomas's dresser. He moved closer to have a better look. An older couple smiled for the camera. Must be his parents. Another picture was of Thomas himself standing on a sailboat.

Jonathan studied the man. Tall, muscular, and, by the expression on his face, very self-assured. A strong negative feeling he hadn't felt in a long time rippled through Jonathan. Dislike? Jealousy? Or envy? Yes, all three.

This man could live a life with Gloryanna. He could be the father of her children. He could always put his arms around her and could kiss her deeply, passionately. A loathing filled Jonathan. Did this man have any idea how lucky he was? He must, or why would he live in such a palatial apartment? With money like this, why would he compete for a grant? Nothing added up. The man was a paradox. Could this Thomas person be the one trying to kill her?

Why didn't Gloryanna like Thomas? She, too, must have some instinctual feelings about him. Granted, not the same as Jonathan did. There had to be a good reason though.

On the surface, Thomas appeared to be what every single woman could ever want in a husband good looking, rich, and—specific to Gloryanna—liked marine biology. Though, unlike her place, his apartment didn't have diving pictures hanging on the walls, which Jonathan found quite interesting.

A man with such a passion for the ocean should have some evidence of his chosen field. In fact, other than in this room, the place hardly had any personal touches and could have belonged to anyone. And then Jonathan's gaze caught on another picture on the dresser.

This was a candid shot of Gloryanna alone on a boat, wind blowing through her unruly tresses as she peered over the ocean. She had been deep in thought and oblivious that she'd drawn anyone's attention. This must have been taken when they were dating or during a diving class. Jonathan highly doubted she would have gone alone with Thomas after they'd broken up.

He debated drawing her attention to what he'd found. It would only upset her, but she had a right to know. Still, he was reluctant because this picture proved that Thomas's feelings for her were sincere. Jonathan couldn't let his dislike for the man cloud his good judgment. She had to know. "Gloryanna, I think you need to see something."

"Might as well. I'm not having much luck cracking his password." She rose and came over.

As soon as she saw her picture, her brows rammed together and her face pinched. She grabbed it. "Where did he get this?"

Relieved that she seemed repulsed, he said, "I assure you, I don't know."

She turned it over and flipped the latches, holding the picture in the frame. "You can't take it." He stopped her.

"And why not?" Anger reddened her cheeks. "He shouldn't have it. I mean, people should ask your permission before taking a picture of you and framing it. It gives me the willies." She shivered.

"But if you take it, he'll know that you've been here—or at least that someone has been here. It won't be long before he figures it out." Though Jonathan hated that the man had her picture, they needed to be rational.

"It's like he's stalking me." She huffed.

Max started to bark, warning that something was wrong.

The sound of a door opening and closing came from the other room.

Terror captured Gloryanna's face. "He's back," she whispered as she hurried to the laptop and closed it. "What are we going to do?"

Footsteps headed toward the bedroom and then stopped. "Is someone there?" came a bass voice.

"How do you suppose he knows?" she whispered.

"Maybe the guard told him. You hide. I'll take care of him," Jonathan said. He couldn't wait to do a number on this man. Max came to Jonathan like he was ready to do battle to save their fair maiden.

She scrambled to the closet and slid the barn door closed just as Thomas walked in wearing a suit and carrying the helmet Gloryanna had left on the coffee table. Maybe the doorman had told him they were here, but if not, the helmet was definitely a clue.

He set the helmet on his unmade bed, dropped his keys on the nightstand, and loosened his necktie. He stared at the helmet, deep in thought.

He looked up, and his gaze hit the pictures on his dresser. Gloryanna had neglected to put hers back exactly where it had been. He went over and moved the frame to its proper spot. His brows puckered together as he noticed that his rumpled gas uniform on the floor had been moved as well. Taking off his suit jacket, he headed toward the closet. This was not good, not good at all.

Jonathan needed to somehow get him to leave the apartment. Or at the very least, leave this room so Gloryanna could get out safely while he was distracted. Jonathan thought of just the thing. Using his gift, he willed the hot-water faucet to turn on in the master bathroom's shower.

It worked. The pulsing water drew his attention.

"Who's in there?" Thomas tossed his suit jacket on the bed. "Candace, is that you?" He disappeared into the bathroom.

Though weak, Jonathan opened the closet.

Gloryanna stared with frightened eyes, and then relief found her as she recognized him.

Thrilled that he'd saved her for the moment, Jonathan had to get her going. "It's not over yet. You need to get out of here." He peered through the walls, watching Thomas reach through the shower, avoid the steaming hot water, and shut off the faucet. He straightened and looked around the bathroom.

Gloryanna had to leave. Now. Jonathan turned to her, but she wasn't standing where he'd thought she'd be. She came from the dresser area, snatched the helmet off the bed, and dashed from the room. Good. She knew what needed to be done. Jonathan wanted to make sure she wasn't followed, so he stayed behind, but he motioned for Max to go with her.

Thomas must have heard her open the door because he came rushing out of the bathroom, his white dress shirt wet from his encounter with the shower.

Jonathan had to stop him. Dodging ahead, he slammed the bedroom door, causing Thomas to run into it. Then Jonathan grabbed the doorknob so Thomas couldn't open the door. The knob twisted and turned. It took most of Jonathan's willpower to hold firm. A loud thud came on the door. Thomas must have kicked it.

Then the doorknob moved again. This time, when Jonathan tried to stop him, he couldn't. Most of his energy had been zapped. He hoped he'd given Gloryanna enough time to leave the building.

He scrambled ahead of the man, moved through the apartment entrance door, and got to the elevator before Thomas. With his last bit of energy, he pushed the down button.

"Hold the elevator!" Thomas yelled.

But the doors closed, and the elevator moved downward. Jonathan supposed he could have gone through the outer walls and floated to Gloryanna, but with his strength so depleted, he didn't want to take the chance of not reaching her.

It seemed to take forever, but finally, the elevator opened on the first floor. Jonathan hurried out, bypassing people speaking with the doorman, and fled the building.

Gloryanna waited at the curb on the motorcycle, helmet on her head, revving the engine. Max stood beside her, wagging his tail upon seeing his master. As Jonathan neared Gloryanna, he felt some of his energy return. Getting on behind her, he motioned for Max to jump onboard just before she peeled out and just before Thomas raced from the building, yelling for her to stop.

CHAPTER TWELVE

GLORYANNA SPED DOWN THE ROAD with Jonathan and Max in tow. The last time she'd been that scared was when the vortex current had taken her. And just like then, Jonathan had rescued her. She'd come dangerously close to Thomas catching her in his condo. She hated to think what he would have said if he had.

She and Jonathan had gone there to talk with him, not to illegally enter his home. She should have listened to Jonathan. But luckily, Thomas hadn't seen her until she'd been on the Harley and had the helmet on. He wouldn't know if the intruder had been male or female.

But he'd surely talk with the doorman. Even though she'd given him an alias, he'd seen her multiple times before. He'd tell Thomas that Gabriella Smith had been there. Thomas probably couldn't remember all the names of the women he'd had in his condo, so that was good. But if the doorman told him what she looked like, Thomas would know it was her. Add that to the real problem. On the spur of the moment, Gloryanna had stolen the picture he had of her and slipped it into her purse.

What a stupid thing to do. And Jonathan had warned her. But she just couldn't stand that Thomas had a picture of her. He'd eventually see that the picture was missing and know she'd been there.

Speeding through traffic, she worried that he would follow. Glancing at the little rearview mirror on the handlebar, she couldn't see his dark-blue Land Rover, but that didn't mean much. As a precaution, she didn't drive straight to her condo. Instead, she drove down the coastline until she was fairly certain she wasn't being tailed, then took side streets back to her home.

Greatly relieved to pull into her underground parking, she shut off the engine and set the kickstand. She felt Jonathan and Max move away, so she climbed off the bike and tugged the helmet from her head. Their images weren't as clear as before. "Are you two all right?"

"Between running interference so you could get away safely and trying to keep up with you while you darted in and out of traffic, I'm not quite myself." His voice wasn't as strong either.

"Let's get you up to the condo where we can relax." Carrying the helmet, she led the way.

Once inside, her eyes were immediately drawn to the wall with all the pictures of their suspects. "We need to stand something in front of this in case Thomas stops by."

She tried to think of what to do. The folding privacy panels she had in her bedroom. Her father had made them for her to put in front of her window, even though she had curtains. He was such a worrier and looked after his only child. Right now, she was glad. "I'll be right back."

She rushed to her room, set her purse on the bed, and pulled the panels to the dining area. She leaned them against the opposite wall. "If Thomas shows up, I'll pull these in front of the pictures and he won't see what we've been working on."

Jonathan gave an agreeing nod, his image still faint.

"I should probably change clothes too. I'll be right back." As she quickly took off her jeans and shirt and tugged on leggings and a sweatshirt with the university's logo on the front, she worried about Jonathan. He'd really exerted himself running interference for her.

Last night, he'd grown dim when he'd helped her move Grandpa from the floor. But Jonathan had seemed to recover okay from that, claiming he'd needed to be near her to recharge. Well, he hadn't said those exact words, but that was what he'd meant. If his energy returned by staying near her, why was he still so weak after being with her on the motorcycle?

Feeling she could never solve the mysteries surrounding Jonathan, she quickly refreshed herself in the bathroom and stared into the mirror. She looked awful, with hair poking in all directions. Her mascara and eyeliner had migrated to her cheeks and were making her look like a goth. She washed her face and quickly redid her makeup. Then she grabbed her hair pick and worked through the tangles before she twisted her locks up to the nape of her neck, where she secured them with a hair band.

She headed into the dining area and found Jonathan resting on a chair, Max sitting on the floor next to his feet. Jonathan stared at the wall where she'd taped the suspects with the lists of concerns near their pictures.

"Thomas is definitely a person of interest." Jonathan stared at his image. "But I'm still not convinced he's the one who tried to kill you."

"Why? What else do we need? He had the gas company's uniform and, for some reason I can't fathom, my picture on his dresser." She was mystified that Jonathan still had misgivings.

"The picture makes me wonder. It wasn't a creepy I-have-to-have-her photo. Before visiting his place, I said there are two reasons a person kills love or money. Thomas has both." Jonathan focused on her. "But something is off. We're missing the true reason why he would want you dead."

The subject of why Thomas would do anything felt overwhelming. "I don't know. Why do husbands kill their wives? Crazy people don't exactly act rationally."

"You should add 'has gas uniform and picture of you' to Thomas's list."

She did what he said.

"What about Ralph and that Skip guy who filled your tank?" He focused on their pictures.

"I can almost guarantee they were working last night." She felt pretty confident that she was right about that.

"But what if one of them slipped away for a while? Don't you think we should at least question them?"

"Maybe, but first I need to buy Ralph a new camera. And that's not cheap." She typed in the camera brand on her laptop and hit Return. A row of pretty cameras flashed onto the screen along with their expensive price tags.

"Holy smokes." Jonathan stared at them. "I should have bought stock in photographic cameras. It's incredible what they charge."

"Yes, but these can go underwater. Plus, they're digital, with tons of pixels."

"Pixels?"

"Yes." She tried to think how best to explain this to a man from the forties. Starting with the basics, she said, "A digital picture has pixels. The word *pixel* combines the word *picture* with the word *element*, and pixels are the smallest bit of information in an image."

Jonathan reared back and gave her a wary look. "How many pixels create a good picture?" His gaze went to the faces she'd taped to the wall.

"Those you're looking at are only two to three hundred ppi, which means pixels per inch. We don't need the best pictures for what we're doing. But when I dive and take shots, I want megapixels so I have a sharper picture."

"Megapixels?"

"Hold on." She went to her room and pulled her cell phone from her purse. Returning, she looked for something to take a picture of. The wall where they'd put the photos and lists beside them would be a good shot. She tapped the phone screen a couple of times. A flash lit the room for a second.

"What are you doing?" Jonathan stared at her and then her cell.

"I wanted to show you a picture with megapixels. My phone has twelve." She gave it to him.

His eyes grew large as clam shells. "This is amazing."

"It is, isn't it? It's like we're living *Star Trek*."

"Star what?" He squinted at her.

"You've never heard of *Star Trek*, have you?"

He slowly shook his head.

"You know, it's not important. And I only brought up the pixels of a camera because I need to buy Ralph a better one than what he had." She scanned the cameras on her laptop screen. "It needs to have full manual controls. And the housing should take macro and wide angles. Low shutter and long battery life." She read about several and checked their prices, then settled on one that cost over a thousand dollars. But it would be on her card; she could pay it off with time. She clicked Buy Now. "It probably won't get here for a few days."

"What do you mean, 'get here'? You don't have to go to the store to buy it?"

"No. I bought it using my computer, and it will be shipped to me, or, rather, to my parents' house. I'm not here much during the day, so I have everything shipped to them because someone is always home."

"Again, I find myself amazed at the world you live in." He shook his head.

She stepped into her small kitchen and grabbed the Lucky Charms off the top of the refrigerator. She opened the box and returned, mining out a handful and eating one morsel at a time.

"What is that you're eating?" He stared at it like a curious cat.

"Cereal."

"More like candy. Eggs and bacon is a better meal. Wait . . ." He froze as he seemed to concentrate. "Bacon. Frank Bacon." He wagged his head like that didn't make sense.

What in the world was he talking about? "Are you remembering your sand pounder partner's name?"

"I think so." He tapped his fingers to his forehead. "Bacon's not quite it. Becken. No, Becker." And then he stopped and looked at her with confidence. "My teammate's name was Frank Becker." Relief covered his chiseled, ghostly face, which had grown steadily clearer. His strength must be returning.

"All right." She brushed cereal crumbs off her fingers and typed the name in the search bar. Rotating dots whirled around and around until, finally, a picture of a man appeared.

"That's him!" Jonathan pointed.

"He looks like that 1950s actor Troy Donahue."

Jonathan shot her a baffled stare.

She waved her hand back and forth. "I saw Troy Donahue, not Frank, on the late, late movie one night as I crammed for an exam."

"You went to a theater to study?" Again, that quizzical look framed his handsome face.

"No. I watched it on TV." She paused a moment. "You did have televisions in the forties, right?"

"I'd heard of them but had never seen one."

She got up, grabbed the remote, and clicked on the TV that hung on the wall in the living room. The news came on the screen.

"I thought that contraption was a rather odd art piece." Jonathan marveled at the device as though he'd discovered a sunken treasure.

On the flat-screen, a reporter stood outside what looked like Thomas's apartment building that they'd just left. A frisson streaked over her skin, and she pressed her finger on the remote to turn up the volume.

"No one knows why someone would shoot the Clifford heir, but the security guard said a woman riding a motorcycle visited him earlier." Gloryanna froze. Questions whirled in her mind. Was Thomas dead? Was she now a suspect? What was happening? She could hardly breathe.

"Calm down"—Jonathan had come out of his stupor over the television—"and listen."

The reporter went on. "The paramedics took Thomas Clifford to Mercy Hospital, but there are no reports on his condition at this time."

The scene changed to paramedics wheeling an unconscious Thomas on a gurney to a waiting ambulance.

"What . . . ? I . . ." Feeling dizzy, Gloryanna sat on the couch. "He was fine when we left him. I mean, he chased us."

"Yes, I was there." Jonathan sat beside her. "But we had nothing to do with this. Remember that."

Gloryanna frantically retraced what they'd done, then stopped at when they'd first gone into the building. "Even though I gave the guard an alias, he recognized me and could figure out my name. It's only a matter of time before the police come knocking on my door. What am I going to tell them?"

"The truth." Jonathan seemed unshaken. "Always the truth."

"That a ghost and I broke into Thomas's apartment, and when he got home, we hightailed it out of there?"

"No. That you went to visit him, but when you left, he was fine." Jonathan stared at her, expectation in his gaze—an expectation for her to be strong and do the right thing.

Gloryanna's cell phone rang. She pulled it from her hip pocket. "It's Mom. She's probably heard about Thomas on the news." She swiped her finger across the phone's screen. "Hi, Mom." She forced a cheerfulness in her voice. "What's up?"

"Did you hear about Thomas Clifford?"

"I just saw a little about it on TV. Do you know what happened?" Gloryanna hoped her mother could fill in some blanks.

"I don't know, sweetheart. But when I heard a woman visited him who rode a motorcycle, I thought I'd better check on you." There was no accusation in her voice, only caring.

"I went to talk with Thomas about the dive, but he wasn't there at first. And then when he arrived, I left. I couldn't face him." She'd left out that with Jonathan's help, she'd gone inside Thomas's apartment and searched it.

"Honey, I think you need to talk to the police and tell them what you told me."

Her mother was right. But did Gloryanna have the courage to do what she said?

Max started barking.

"Are you still there?" Mom asked.

"Yes." She motioned for Jonathan to take care of his dog. Still talking with her mother, she said, "And I know that's exactly what I need to do. It's just—" How could she tell her mother everything she'd learned about Thomas? That he could have posed as a man from the gas company and made their stove leak. That for some reason, Thomas had a framed picture of her on his dresser. Or that Jonathan, a ghost, had helped her escape from Thomas's apartment. None were good options.

Max's barks grew more intense. Jonathan had moved to the sliding glass doors that looked out on guest parking. He motioned that she needed to take a look.

"You're right, Mom. I'll give them a call." She stepped beside him, and her heart plummeted. A patrol car.

A knock came at the door.

"Someone's here, Mom. I've got to run."

She shut off her cell and wished with all her heart that she really could *run*.

CHAPTER THIRTEEN

Jonathan stared at Gloryanna. Fear emanated from her. He couldn't blame her, but he'd stay by her side through whatever happened.

She quickly moved the folding panel in front of the wall, then gave Jonathan a long, dreadful look.

Knocking came again, harder.

"It will be okay." Jonathan tried to comfort her. "You have nothing to hide." Except for the pictures on the wall. But he didn't say that out loud.

"You're right." She squared her shoulders, went to the door, and opened it.

"Ma'am, I'm Officer Baker." The muscular, tan man nodded. "And this is my partner, Officer Tinsdale." The woman, whose uniform looked a bit too tight, dipped her head. Her bun pulled at her eyes, slanting them slightly. Baker continued. "We'd like to talk with you, if you have a minute, or you could come down to the police station with us if you'd rather."

Gloryanna stepped back. "Come in."

Baker nearly walked through Jonathan as he entered. Jonathan quickly moved and was grateful that neither officer had seen him.

"Could I get you a drink or something to eat?" Gloryanna motioned toward her couch, offering them a seat. Baker sat while Tinsdale stayed by the door, looking around and doing a sight search. The folding panel caught her attention. Gloryanna must have noticed, because she pulled one of the dining chairs over and offered her a seat.

Tinsdale shook her head and remained standing.

Gloryanna sat on the chair.

Jonathan wished he could take the pictures down, but his energy had been too depleted; plus, if they saw pictures floating in the air, that would not be good. Better to wait this out.

Max went to Gloryanna and sat on his haunches.

"No, thank you, ma'am," Baker said. "Let me get right to the point. Do you know Thomas Clifford?"

"Yes. I've had classes with him at the university." Good, she let them know they were in college together, which helped pave the way for why she had been at his place.

"Mr. Clifford was shot earlier today." Baker watched her every movement.

"I saw a report on the TV about the shooting. Is he going to be all right?" Another plus, that she acknowledged she knew something had happened to Thomas.

Baker ignored her question. "Did you visit him today?"

The doorman must have remembered her real name and told them. Jonathan moved closer to her and placed his hand on her shoulder, hoping that somehow, she'd feel his touch. He wanted her to know he was beside her.

She leaned toward him. She must feel something.

Taking a breath and maintaining a calm appearance, she said, "I stopped by his place earlier, but we didn't talk."

Baker nodded. "The doorman said you ran from the building, and shortly after, Mr. Clifford raced after you, but you drove away. Would you mind telling us what that was about?"

Jonathan had to hand it to the doorman; he'd been observant. But at least with this witness, the police knew Gloryanna hadn't shot Thomas.

She clasped her hands together. "I'm afraid we had an argument. A couple of days ago, Thomas and I went diving with our professor. I was separated from them, and he was still upset about that. I didn't want to stick around to hear him lecture me."

She'd fielded that question well. Jonathan was proud of her.

"That's right. I thought I recognized the name. You're the woman who went missing from a dive and then turned up in the Olympic primitives." Baker jotted down notes on his pad. Jonathan had been so worried about Gloryanna that he'd forgotten about Tinsdale.

She had gone to the folding panels and was zeroed in on their wall of taped photos, especially Thomas's. "Ma'am, what is this about?"

Gloryanna turned, and for a split second, Jonathan caught fear in her eyes.

He'd hesitated speaking to her while the officers were in the room, but he had to speak up now. She needed his help. "Don't let her rattle you. You've got this."

She briefly looked at him, gave him a slight nod, but then turned her full attention to the woman. "Oh, that's just research."

Tinsdale moved the folding panel and stepped closer to the wall, reading the lists they'd made with each photo. "Research for what?"

"Draw her away," Jonathan coached.

Gloryanna rose, and a smile came to her face. "I'm working on an article I need to write." She went to the officer and stepped between her and the wall. "I'm trying to win a grant that would help me earn my master's degree. That's why Professor Takahashi, Thomas, and I went diving. We were doing research, but then I got caught in the vortex current." Gloryanna tried to guide the officer away, but the woman wasn't budging.

Max rose and, using his ghostly power, herded Tinsdale one reluctant step at a time away from the wall. She seemed confused as to why her feet were moving, but still, she moved, though against her will. Thank goodness for Max. Jonathan hadn't realized the dog had such an ability.

Gloryanna followed and, without missing a beat, said, "And since the incident, I've been trying to remember what exactly happened. I got all mixed-up about what took place before. I'm just trying to refresh my memory."

Everything she'd said was the truth. And she'd done it with such calm and grace when Jonathan knew very well she was dying inside.

Before Tinsdale sat on the couch next to Officer Baker, she asked, "You said there were three of you on the dive, but who is Jonathan?" She pointed to the list next to Professor Takahashi's photo, where his name was written.

Gloryanna glanced at Jonathan.

He shrugged. "Tell the truth."

Taking a deep breath, she turned back to the officers and said, "He's the man who rescued me."

Both stared, waiting for her to go on.

But instead of saying more about Jonathan, Gloryanna sat on her chair again and said, "I'm so sorry about what happened to Thomas."

Good, she was distracting them with another topic, though her choice left a lot to be desired.

"Ma'am." Baker scooted to the edge of the couch. "Do you own a firearm?"

That wasn't part of the plan. Why would he ask that? They'd already stated that Thomas had been fine when she'd left. Fine enough to chase after her. How would Gloryanna reply?

"No." She merely looked at them.

"You're sure?" Tinsdale added.

"You're free to look if you want." Brave confidence seemed to take hold of Gloryanna. And while it was admirable for her to give them permission to search her residence, it could prove to be a grave mistake. Any little thing they found could be taken as evidence.

Maybe they believed she'd returned to Thomas's apartment, snuck in the back way, and shot him. As absurd as the thought was, Jonathan knew it was entirely possible and highly likely.

Both officers stood and began their search.

Fear filled Gloryanna's eyes. She must have realized her error. Jonathan believed she had nothing to worry about and probably had nothing to hide, yet there was that possibility they'd find something.

Baker went to the kitchen, while Tinsdale disappeared into Gloryanna's office.

Jonathan pointed to Baker, directing Gloryanna to follow him. Jonathan trailed Tinsdale. The portly woman poked around the printer, then opened the desk drawer, picking through papers and generally making a mess. Wanting to hurry her along, Jonathan pushed a book from a shelf. It fell to the floor next to the officer and startled her.

She picked it up, read the spine, and set it back on the shelf, then she left the office. Good. Jonathan hoped she'd join her partner in the kitchen. She walked past, heading to Gloryanna's bedroom.

Jonathan hadn't been in there yet, so as he followed the officer, he looked around. Across from the daybed, which was neatly made and nearly filled with decorative pillows, sat a huge flat-screen TV, much bigger than the one in the living area. Beneath the TV were shelves filled with what looked like very thin books. The shelf above the TV displayed seashells. Her walls were adorned with more pictures of underwater sea life, probably shots she'd taken herself during her many dives.

Jonathan turned his attention to Tinsdale now. She'd found Gloryanna's purse. The woman glanced at the doorway, then back at the bag. It was clear she was tempted to open it and look inside. Gloryanna needed to get in here. Fast.

Jonathan moved from the room. Gloryanna and Baker were leaving the kitchen, so Jonathan caught her attention. "You need to come in here. Quick."

She uttered, "Excuse me," and hurried to her bedroom just as Tinsdale picked up the purse.

"Can I help you?" Gloryanna took her bag from the woman.

"Do you mind if I have a look inside?"

Gloryanna glanced at Jonathan, hesitated a moment, but said, "Not at all."

She dumped the contents of Gloryanna's purse onto her bed a wallet, a package of tissues, hand sanitizer, a pack of gum, Rolos, the keys to her father's motorcycle, a comb, Jonathan's flashlight, and the framed picture of herself that had been in Thomas's apartment. That explained the look Gloryanna had given him. She didn't want him to see that she'd gone against what he'd told her and had taken the picture.

Tinsdale picked it up. "Why were you carrying a framed picture of yourself?"

"I planned to give it to my parents." She didn't bat an eye as she said her first lie to the officer.

Jonathan had learned the hard way how dangerous that could be and that one lie led to another and then another. Lying had been his favorite sport in the orphanage, but every time, he'd get caught and punished with banishment to the cellar—that creepy, dirty, cold place where he'd huddle in the corner and cry. Oh, he'd played tough for the matron, but his scars of punishment ran deep, competing with scars of not having a mother and father. He had just wanted someone to love him, to actually care. And though Gloryanna was in no danger of such harsh punishment, she could have more severe consequences should the truth come out. So much more.

Her eyes were drawn to Jonathan as she tried to act guiltless and honest.

Tinsdale placed the picture back on the bed with the purse. Without saying a word, she left the bedroom. Gloryanna followed and avoided Jonathan's stare.

Officer Baker waited by the entrance, where he opened the door. "Ma'am, I strongly advise you to not leave town for the next few days."

"Why? You don't think I shot Thomas, do you?" Gloryanna squinted at them.

"Until a case is closed, everyone is a suspect," Tinsdale said as she left.

"Have a nice day." Officer Baker followed his partner out, closing the door behind him.

Gloryanna stood there a minute, staring at the door. When she finally turned around to face Jonathan, she said, "I can explain about the picture."

Jonathan could hardly wait.

CHAPTER FOURTEEN

GLORYANNA HATED THAT JONATHAN HAD found out she'd stolen the picture. "Look, I couldn't stand that he had a photo of me. It felt wrong to leave it. Do you know that some cultures believe having your picture taken steals part of your soul?" She didn't wait for him to answer her rhetorical question. "There was even a study done on it at a university. The camera snatches light from people's aura—their soul."

"Your university did this study?" Jonathan leaned toward her.

"No." Gloryanna didn't want to tell him but then decided it didn't matter. "The University of Arakab. The head of their paranormal sciences department did the research." She wasn't going to back down. "You, of all people—" She stopped as she stared at his ghostly image. "Well, you, being a ghost, should understand that."

"In fact, I do. But still, you shouldn't have—"

"I know. I shouldn't have taken the picture." She wished she could rewind life to put the stupid thing back. "When it comes to Thomas, I don't think logically. But he had no right to take that picture without my knowledge. No right to frame it. No right to look at it." She shuddered as she fought against the feeling of being violated.

"Why are you arguing? I agree with you." Jonathan leaned his head to the side. "But if Thomas survives, he will go home and find that your picture is missing, if he doesn't know already. And I'm sure you've thought of this, but he probably still has the picture on his phone. You showed me how easy that is to do."

A swear word rode on the tip of her tongue. She went to her room, retrieved the picture from her bed, then stormed to the kitchen and dropped the hideous thing into the garbage. "I wish I'd never seen it."

Jonathan rubbed his chin, then shrugged. "You do realize the police will talk with your parents?"

She unfolded her arms, wondering where he was going with this.

"And the police very well might look for the picture you said you were taking to them and ask about it when they don't see it." Jonathan just looked at her, waiting.

"I'll say I haven't given it to them yet. They'll understand that because they saw it here with me." There. She'd bested him at his Sherlock Holmes deductions. Besides, he had no idea if the police would do any of that, but the way Jonathan said it made her think he knew something she didn't.

"Look, I learned in my short life to always cover the trail I made if I planned to do things someone in authority might not like." He shrugged. "I'm not proud of it, but growing up in an orphanage, I could lie with the best of them. Mrs. Allred, the owner, always found out. *Always*. I'm just trying to help you cover your trail."

Gloryanna knew he'd lived in an orphanage, but he hadn't expounded on it. This was the first glimpse she'd had into his youth. She'd been so worried about herself that she hadn't given Jonathan a second thought.

Well, other than that he was a ghost. From their first meeting, he'd done everything he could to help her saved her life from the current, showed her the right trail through the forest, and even ran interference with Thomas. All he asked of her was to tell the truth and to help him figure out what had happened to him, which she planned to do if the drama in her life would ever calm down.

She swiped a hand over her face and gave a deep, repentant sigh before she returned to the kitchen and pulled the picture from the garbage. Like a guilty child, she took it to her room and put it back in her purse, then returned to Jonathan in the dining area. "If I give it to my parents and by some weird chance Thomas sees it there—not that he'd ever go to their place, but hey, he tampered with their stove, so, yeah, he could—then he might think they took it. At the very least, he'll know I did."

Jonathan must have had more energy because he moved the chair she'd sat on while talking with Officer Baker and placed it with the dining room table. "That's a risk you need to take. Or maybe you should just tell Thomas what you did."

"Only as a last resort." Gloryanna could feel a headache coming on. "I screwed up."

"Yes, you did." He sat on the chair he'd brought to the table.

She took a seat in front of her laptop. "I'm sorry."

She reached to pet the dog, but her hand went through. Rattled for a moment, she said, "Thanks for your support, Max." She looked at Jonathan and didn't know what to say.

"Hey, I'm on your side," he reminded her. "But you need to listen to me, or what good am I to you?"

"You're right. Again, I'm sorry." To show that she was sincere, she tapped on the laptop. It sprang to life, revealing the image of Frank Becker that looked so much like a young Troy Donahue. They'd been talking about him before she'd turned on the TV and discovered what had happened to Thomas, before the officers had invaded her home and her sense of well-being. "Remember what we were discussing?" She pointed to the screen.

Jonathan looked at it and gave a nod. "That's him, all right."

"Let's see what else we can find about your teammate."

Jonathan stared at his old friend.

She clicked on a line she hoped would give more personal information about the man. "This gives his birthdate but no death." She moved the cursor and found an article about him living in a care center. "This article was dated three years ago. Looks like he won a bowling tournament at the age of a hundred and two."

"That means he's a hundred and five now, if he's still alive that is." Jonathan stared at the screen, reading ahead. "And he lives in an assisted living center. What's that?"

"It's a fancy term for *rest home*." Gloryanna read the address. "The place isn't far from here. What are the odds?" she marveled.

"I wonder if he ever made it to Nevada." Jonathan stared at his friend's face on the screen.

She quickly jotted down the address and asked her phone for directions while digging her earbuds out of her purse.

"Why are you talking to your phone?"

"Because it's going to tell us how to get there. Feel up to another ride?" She looped her purse strap over her head.

"I rather thought you'd had enough adventure for one day." He seemed reluctant. She couldn't blame him after what they'd been through.

She glanced at the clock on the wall. "We have just enough time to check it out, and then I need to return to my parents. Mom asked me to stay with Grandpa again tonight."

With great reluctance, he called Max to him, and they both followed her.

As she climbed onto the motorcycle, she glanced at Jonathan. His puckered face reminded her of a child being forced to take his medicine. Oh, what she'd put him and Max through last night and today. Wanting to give him more incentive, she said, "You know, this trip might bring you two the answers you've been looking for."

Jonathan said nothing. She tugged on the helmet and started the engine for the third time today. What would she have done without her father's motorcycle?

Jonathan and the dog settled behind her, so she pulled out.

Traffic was more congested than it had been earlier, which made sense because it was rush hour. She stuck to side streets and avoided the freeway, which took a bit longer, but she followed the directions on her phone and soon found it.

She pulled into visitors' parking and turned off the engine, then shoved the helmet off and turned to talk with Jonathan. Anyone who saw her would wonder what she was doing, but she didn't care. "This is it." She nodded toward the sprawling building. A circular drive curved to the front under a portico. An elaborate sign read Mount Olympus Care Center.

Jonathan and Max moved away from the Harley. "It's a mansion." Jonathan stared at the building that looked more like an elaborate country club with turrets and bay windows galore.

"This is one of the better ones. Not many people can afford to live in a place like this." She thought of her grandfather. "Mom, with all her connections in the healthcare industry, couldn't find one Grandpa could afford. She said it can cost between five and ten thousand a month."

Jonathan reared back. "How in the world could Frank afford this?"

"Maybe he found that gold you told me he was always talking about." She got off the bike. "Shall we go in?"

Jonathan didn't move.

"What's the matter?" She looked around, wondering if he'd seen something she'd missed.

"I don't know. I want to see him, but I don't."

"Well, he won't see you, and nobody will even notice you're here, if that's what you're worried about." She tried to understand why he suddenly had cold feet.

"No. That's not my concern." He stared at the building.

"What is?"

"I don't actually know." He shook his head as if he could shake off his worry. Then he straightened, looked forward, and said, "Let's go."

They started toward the entrance beneath the portico. Immaculate flower beds filled with early summer blooms of pinks, reds, and blues spread around a pretty bubbling fountain.

Gloryanna stepped on the doormat before the threshold, and the glass doors slid open. Highly polished floors in a black-and-white checkerboard pattern led to a reception desk. A grumpy-faced woman in a well-tailored suit sat on the other side. She looked over the top of her reading glasses at their intrusion. "May I help you?"

"Yes." Gloryanna gave her a smile, hoping to warm the woman's frosty greeting. If this was how she greeted everyone, the place had a PR problem. But maybe they didn't care because only the very rich could stay here anyway. And the woman could probably tell by Gloryanna's unruly hair and leggings that she didn't have a lot of money. "I'm looking for Frank Becker."

The woman typed on her keyboard and waited. "Yes. He's in the Regency section. Looks like he has another visitor at the moment. It might be better if you wait until after she leaves. In fact, you might want to return this evening when he's rested. What time can I tell him to expect you?"

"I'm not sure. I might have to wait until tomorrow." Gloryanna knew Jonathan was disappointed. "I kinda wanted to surprise him, so please don't tell him I was here."

"I don't know who you are, so that's not a problem." The woman went back to what she'd been reading.

Gloryanna hurried away, with Jonathan and Max trying to keep up.

Once she was outside and heading toward the motorcycle, Jonathan said, "I wonder who his visitor could be."

"Maybe his children. He probably married and had a family after the war." She walked toward her father's Harley. But when they reached it, she didn't get on. "Why don't you go in? They won't see you. You could slip into his room to see if something trips your memory about your old partner. I'll wait here."

"Good idea." He started to retrace his steps but stopped. "Did she say a room number?"

"No, but she said he was in the Regency section, so that will at least take you in the general direction."

Gloryanna saw someone leave the building. A woman with long black hair. Something seemed familiar about her. Gloryanna looked a little closer. It couldn't be . . . Professor Takahashi? "Wait, Jonathan!"

He came back to her.

The professor didn't notice them but went straight to her Jaguar and got in. Knowing the woman would soon pass right by her, Gloryanna quickly put her helmet on to hide her identity.

The Jag rolled by and pulled away from visitors' parking. As soon as the car was out of sight, Gloryanna tugged off the helmet. So many questions spun in her mind that she couldn't form a cohesive thought.

"Was that someone you know?" Jonathan stood beside her.

"Yes. Professor Takahashi. I wonder if she has family here."

"Oh. I thought I'd seen her before. It must have been from the picture you printed."

Max started barking.

"Something isn't right." Gloryanna set the helmet on the bike.

"No, something is very wrong." Jonathan started for the center. "Come on. We're going back in."

This time, she wasn't stopping to quibble with the receptionist. This time, she was marching right by her.

As she neared, she heard an alarm blaring. She glanced at Jonathan. He heard it too.

Together they stepped into the palatial building. The receptionist wasn't at her desk. This was perfect. While everyone was busy with whatever the alarm was about, Gloryanna, Jonathan, and Max could find Frank.

She saw a sign giving directions to different sections of the center. Regency was to the left. They headed that way but soon found a crowd of concerned elderly residents, some in wheelchairs and some leaning on walkers, gathered around the door of a room. Some poor soul was having trouble.

As Gloryanna worked her way through the crowd, she glanced at the sign by the room number that showed the resident. To her utter astonishment, it read "Frank Becker."

CHAPTER FIFTEEN

JONATHAN READ FRANK'S NAME ON the small sign by the door at the same time Gloryanna must have. But unlike her, he and Max floated over the people standing in the doorway and headed into his old partner's apartment.

They passed the lavishly furnished living area adorned with golds and creams a camel-backed couch with two brocade wing chairs in front and between them an ornate coffee table. But Jonathan didn't stop to admire the furniture. Voices were coming from down the hall and to the right. He headed toward them.

Two nurses stood on one side of the bed. A man in a lab coat, who was probably the resident doctor, and another nurse waited on the other side. The man held round pads the size of a bar of soap attached to tubing that connected to a machine.

Frank's clothing had been torn from his chest, and red marks marred his white age-spotted skin. One close to the sternum and collar bone and the other on his left side just below his heart. A nurse pumped Frank's chest while another nurse held some sort of breathing device over his nose, squeezing a large collapsible bulb that must shoot air into his nostrils.

A type of radar showed a straight line across the screen.

"Again!" the doctor yelled, holding the pads so the nurse near the monitor could squirt some goo on them. Once she was done, the doctor rubbed the flat surfaces together to smear the gunk evenly over the disks. "Press the dial to 360."

The nurse near the machine tapped a button. A beeping sound seemed to be ticking off time or possibly gauging the current's increase, and then a red light came on under the word *shock*.

"Stand back," the doctor yelled as he placed the pads over the red marks on Frank's chest. The nurse pressed the red light. The doctor pushed down the pads, and Frank's entire body jolted.

All eyes turned to the radar as jagged lines replaced the straight one.

The medical staff gave a collective sigh of relief.

The doctor set the pads on the cart. The nurse near Frank's head leaned over and said, "Mr. Becker, can you hear me?"

He moaned and blinked. Seeing the nurse, a slight smile came to his lips. He looked around at the others, but then he stopped as his gaze rested on Jonathan.

"No!" Terror seemed to seize him. "Why are you here? I had to do it!"

Surprised that his old friend could see him, Jonathan floated closer.

Frank then looked at Max. "It can't be. Not both of you!" He struggled to get out of bed.

"Mr. Becker, lie still." The doctor blocked his path. "You've just had a major heart attack."

Frank pushed him away, and then he gasped, clutched his chest, and fell back on the bed unconscious.

His jagged beats on the radar collapsed and formed one straight line.

"What is going on?" The doctor grabbed the pads again. "We had him back. What happened?"

The team set to work.

Jonathan knew their fight was futile. He waited, expecting to see Frank's spirit leave his body as he passed from his mortal form. But nothing happened.

The medical team worked feverishly to coax life back into him, but no matter what they did, it was no use. Frank Becker seemed to have died.

And it was Jonathan's fault. He tried to understand what had happened. Why had Frank been able to see him? Why had he become so frightened? What had he meant when he'd said he'd had to do it? And why had he tried to escape? But an even bigger question was, Where had his spirit gone? By all rights, Jonathan should have been able to see him leave his body.

Maybe Frank had gone to a different level.

Deep, depressing sadness befell Jonathan. Did most people who died skip this stage that he and Max were stuck in? It seemed so.

Turning his back on the medical team futilely fighting to save Frank's life, Jonathan left the posh apartment and scanned the anxious elderly crowd, searching for Gloryanna. Worried looks claimed their faces—worry for their friend and worry for themselves because they knew someday, sooner than they wanted, death would visit them.

He finally spied Gloryanna standing at the back. She saw him and waved.

As he neared, she asked, "What happened?"

An elderly woman with salt-and-pepper-colored hair, manicured red nails, and a hopeless look on her well-preserved face stood beside Gloryanna and said, "I'm not sure, hon. But it's never good when the medical crash team hurries to a room. Did you know Frank?"

Gloryanna appeared startled that the lady had answered her but then clearly realized the woman couldn't see Jonathan and thought Gloryanna had been talking to her. Gloryanna said, "Not personally. I knew someone who knew him."

"Not that vixen who visited him earlier, I hope." The woman's head shook as if she had Parkinson's.

"Vixen?" Gloryanna questioned.

The elderly woman's ruby-red lips pulled into a frown as she patted Gloryanna's arm. "Oh dear, I'm sorry. It's just that every time that Japanese woman visits him, he gets all riled up."

She must be referring to Gloryanna's Professor Takahashi, whom they'd seen leave the center earlier. Jonathan glanced at Gloryanna. Her face had paled, yet she continued to give the elderly woman her full attention.

"Does she come often?" At least Gloryanna was giving a good try to find out what she could.

"Once a month, like clockwork. Frank is a ladies' man. He's taken out nearly every woman in the care center at least once or twice. But when the Empress—that's what some of us call her—stops in, he won't come out of his room for hours." The elderly woman's blue-veined hand turned white as she tightened her grip on her cane.

Why in the world would Gloryanna's professor be visiting Frank? And why would her being here upset him?

"Do you know why she visits him?" Gloryanna kept digging.

"Like I said, Frank is a ladies' man." A slight smile crossed her face.

Gloryanna patted her arm. "Are you one of his ladies?"

"Why, yes. I'm his favorite." And then her well-preserved face puckered, and tears came to her glassy green eyes. "I hope he's not dead." Her bottom lip trembled. "He's over a hundred, you know."

Gloryanna glanced at Jonathan.

He shook his head.

She closed her eyes for a second, then opened them and put her arm around the elderly woman's slumped shoulders. "He lived a good long life. I shouldn't have pried."

With a shaky hand, the woman pulled out a hanky that had been tucked up the sleeve of her sweater. "You're fine, but maybe another time we can talk about him." She shuffled away, dabbing tears from her cheeks.

Gloryanna nodded toward the exit.

Jonathan got her meaning. She wanted to leave, so he followed her. Once they reached the motorcycle, he told her what had happened and that when Frank had revived and seen him, he'd collapsed and died on the spot.

An ambulance and two fire trucks screamed past them and parked under the portico. Paramedics jumped from the vehicles and yanked out a gurney.

Gloryanna put on the helmet. "Let's leave." She got on the bike, and Jonathan and Max got situated behind her.

As she drove away, Jonathan realized his best hope at finding what had happened to him had probably died along with Frank.

CHAPTER SIXTEEN

WEAVING IN AND OUT OF traffic, Gloryanna went over and over her conversation with the elderly lady. She'd said that Professor Takahashi had known Frank. That was disturbing. And the woman had also said the professor had visited him often for quite some time. Now the man was dead.

What a cruel blow it had been for Jonathan to have Frank die before they could talk, especially because the man had seen both Jonathan and Max and had become so upset that he'd died. Why hadn't Frank been happy to see Jonathan? Why hadn't he been thrilled to have the opportunity to talk with his old buddy?

She braked at the stoplight and felt Jonathan adjust behind her, probably wrangling with Max. The light changed to green, and she revved the motor as they started on their way again. Instead of going to her parents' house like she'd planned, she decided to return to her condo for a little while. They needed to regroup. She drove to her place and parked in her covered parking space.

She tugged off the helmet and led the way up the stairs. She mined her keys from her cross-body purse and stopped. Something didn't feel right, which was stupid. But after the day she'd been through, she decided to follow her instincts. "Do you think someone could be waiting in there?"

"I'll check it out." Jonathan passed through her door.

It seemed an eternity until he came back. He gave her a nod. "No one else is here."

"Good. Did you notice if anything has been disturbed?" Yes, she was being paranoid, but better paranoid than dead.

"Not that I could tell." Jonathan gave a skeptical shrug. "But I'm not very familiar with your home."

He was right. She needed to check for herself. She shoved her key into the lock and went in.

As she scanned the living room, she set her helmet on the couch, then walked through her office and bedroom. Everything looked undisturbed. She went to the dining area. Her laptop rested on the table, and next to it waited the box of Lucky Charms she'd been munching on. She checked on Herman, her goldfish. He swam about his tank as usual. "All is exactly as we left it earlier." She glanced at the wall of suspects. "Even them."

Gloryanna's headache had grown worse. She headed to the kitchen. "Just a minute."

She grabbed a bottle of ibuprofen from the cupboard and pulled out the pitcher of water she kept chilled in the fridge.

Max barked at her.

She nearly dropped the glass in her hand. "Give me a second, and I'll check things out."

She threw a pill into her mouth, and as she brought the glass to her lips, she saw strange tiny white particles in the water. She quickly set the glass down and spit the pill in the sink, not wanting to dry swallow it. She grabbed the water pitcher. It had tiny particles too. "What do you suppose that is?"

Jonathan moved to her side and stared at the white specks. "I'm not an expert, but it could be poison."

"Poison?" She did a double take at the water. The pounding in her head increased. The room swirled. Gloryanna grabbed the counter.

If the water had been poisoned, she'd once again come close to dying. She glanced at Max. Nearly overwhelmed with gratitude, she got down on her knees in front of the dog. "Thank you. If you hadn't warned me, I might not have noticed anything in the water." How she wished she could put her arms around the German shepherd's neck and give him a hug.

Rising up on shaky legs, she said, "This is enough already. I'm calling the police. They could test the water and might even find someone else's fingerprints on the pitcher."

Jonathan's face creased with concern. "Under any other circumstance, that would be the best thing to do. But that police officer who helped with your truck?"

Why was he bringing that up? She slowly uttered, "Yes?"

"He wrote down that you may need a psychiatric evaluation." Jonathan gave an affirming nod. "If you call this in, that could come up, and our chance to catch whoever did this could vanish."

Shocked at first and then angry, she said, "Why would he write that?"

"Think about it. You went missing for a couple of days, then crashed your truck. Maybe he thinks you're suicidal." He gave a hesitant shrug.

Her headache throbbed. Pressing her palm on her forehead, she said, "Okay, then. I'll just leave it here on the counter. We may need it for evidence later."

"Now you're thinking." Jonathan's brows knitted together. "Who could have done this?"

"We were here earlier, so it must have happened after we left." She glanced around her condo. This time everything looked . . . suspicious. Wary of her surroundings, she said, "Let's go to my parents' place. I can't stand being here."

She grabbed her helmet, and out they went. The sooner they got away, the better.

As she drove, she tried her best not to dwell on what had happened. It would only make her emotional, and she didn't want to go there. She turned down the street that would take them to her parents' home.

A white Jaguar, just like Professor Takahashi's black one, passed them going the opposite direction. Again, Gloryanna wondered about the professor's relationship with Frank and how they knew each other. Obviously, he meant a great deal to the professor. Gloryanna should call her and tell her the sad news of Frank's passing.

Gloryanna's parents' place came up on her left. She pulled into the driveway in front of the freestanding garage and pressed the opener so she could pull in and park.

Like the times before when she'd reached their destination, she felt Jonathan and Max move away. She secured the bike, dismounted, and removed the helmet from her head. Looking at Jonathan, she said, "I've been wondering how Professor Takahashi and Frank knew each other?"

"I assure you I have no idea. It's been eight decades since I last saw him." Jonathan paused a moment. "But Frank must have found his gold. His apartment and its furnishings were quite elaborate." Looking directly at Gloryanna, he said, "Don't you find it rather odd that after your professor left Frank, he died?"

"Yes, I do."

"What if she caused Frank's heart attack?" Jonathan stared at her. "And what if after she left there, she went to your place?"

"To poison me?"

He winced. "Sounds crazy, right?"

Gloryanna didn't want to think it could be true. "I don't know anymore. If we're talking suspects, earlier in the day, when Thomas came to my place, he spent time in the kitchen. He could have done something then."

Jonathan's eyes widened, but then he looked at Max. "If that's the case, I think Max would have warned us."

"Good point. But Max was in strange surroundings, and I didn't get into the fridge." Now she was just making excuses. Her thoughts went back to the professor. Gloryanna didn't like that her mentor and friend could have had something to do with Frank's death. "Actually, Frank died when he saw *you*." Feeling like she'd rubbed salt in Jonathan's wound, she said, "But his heart had already been weakened before that. Remember, the receptionist told us when we first got there that he would probably need to rest before we saw him, so he'd been very ill. Besides, he was at least a hundred and five."

She set the helmet on the workbench and hung the key to the motorbike on the same peg she'd taken it from earlier in the day. Her father would be none the wiser that she'd used his beloved Harley.

She headed for the back door.

"I know you're fond of your professor," Jonathan said behind her.

"Darn right, I am. She has helped me earn my degree, and even now, she's trying to help me earn my master's." She stopped and pressed the large button next to the exit. The rumble of the huge door rolling down echoed through the garage.

"I know you don't want to think the worst of her." Jonathan paused a moment. "But you need to step away from your loyalty and study the facts."

"I don't want to." Gloryanna worried that if she did, she might discover something she didn't like. "What I need to do is call the professor and tell her what happened to her friend." She reached for the doorknob.

"You can't." Jonathan's worried voice stopped her.

"Why?"

"Because then she'll know that you were there too." Jonathan's eyes studied hers.

"So? Why cover up that we were there?"

"I don't know. It's just a feeling." Jonathan looked down at the concrete floor. "Don't let misplaced devotion for the woman hide the fact that your life is at stake." He glanced up at her. "And maybe your family's as well."

She grabbed the doorknob, wanting to escape from the truth that was trying to break through. She and her family were in danger. A tidal wave of emotions crashed over her. "I know. And I'm scared." She stood there wondering what to do or where to turn.

Jonathan's hand found hers, and a wisp of loving energy rode up her arm and filled her being. He stood behind her, and she could swear his arms cradled her, filling her with warmth.

"You can face this," he said into her hair.

She gazed at the glass window of the back door and saw her reflection but couldn't see Jonathan's even though she knew he was there. She looked back at herself. Her curly out-of-control hair poked in every direction. The girl staring at her was weak and frightened.

But Jonathan saw something else in her.

She wanted to be the person he believed her to be. If something bad was going to happen, she wanted to go down fighting, not cowering in the corner, afraid of what she would find. She needed to put on her big-girl pants and suck it up. As much as she didn't want to, she had to think about what Jonathan had said. He was here to help and guide her. She'd seen flashes of his face as she'd fought for air on her dive. For some reason, fate had brought them together, and she needed to listen to him.

Filled with new resolve, she said, "Okay. You're right. It is odd that he became so ill right after Professor Takahashi left him." She opened the door and stepped outside.

"There you go." The worry lines on Jonathan's brow softened.

"And I see what you mean." The wind blew a lock of her hair into her face. She smoothed it behind her ear. "If the professor has known Frank for some time, there's a very good possibility that he told her about you, so why—when I sat in her office yesterday, telling her how you saved me from the vortex— why did she not say something about knowing your teammate?"

"I find that very curious too." Jonathan gave a nod like now she was onto something.

She pulled at her bottom lip, thinking. "Why did she pretend not to know anything about the sand pounders and their mission to guard the coast when I asked for her help to research them? If she knew Frank, she had to know all about your division." Gloryanna was on a roll. She could feel it in her bones. "And when I called her this morning, she acted as if she'd just discovered all that information. Why the charade?" Her hands fisted. "Still, the pieces don't fit together. I wish we could have stayed at the condo so we could add all these questions to the professor's list."

"I feel as frustrated as you do." His dark eyes studied hers. "I'm so sorry I don't have the answers. This is much bigger than I even imagined."

"It's not your fault. You weren't with me when I was sucked into the current. And if it weren't for you, I'd be dead." Another thought jarred her mind. "The professor took Thomas and me diving so we could get information to write our articles in hopes of earning that grant. But now I wonder if she had ulterior motives."

"Such as . . ." Jonathan stepped back.

"I don't know. It's not as if she knew the vortex would take me." She thought a moment.

"Do you think she was the one who did something to your tank?" He'd verbalized what Gloryanna had held off saying.

The kitchen door opened. "I thought that was you." Her mother stepped out already dressed in her scrubs, ready to go to work. "Who are you talking to?" She waited on the step.

Taking a deep breath and swiping her hand over her face, Gloryanna looked at Jonathan.

She had wasted her chance to discuss with him what had happened. But once her mother left for work, they could pick up where they'd left off.

Her mind felt fractured with sharp, cruel edges of information. And now she'd have to put it all on hold and pull herself together so she could have a casual conversation with her mom like nothing was wrong.

Whatever was going on with Takahashi and Frank was much bigger than Gloryanna had ever imagined, and for some reason, she was smack-dab in the middle of it.

"Sweetie?" Her mother stared at her and came down the back steps.

Jonathan leaned toward Gloryanna. "You can face her."

That was what she needed to hear. She plastered on a smile. "Yes, Mom."

"Who were you talking to?" Her mother glanced around.

"Myself." She tried to make light of it.

Her mother looped her arm through Gloryanna's. "Don't get upset."

"About what? Has something happened to Grandpa?" Gloryanna's heart quickened.

"Oh, no. He's fine. But I just heard on the news that Ralph Wagner, your boss at the Fish Tail, was arrested for shooting Thomas."

CHAPTER SEVENTEEN

JONATHAN COULDN'T IMAGINE RALPH SHOOTING Thomas. Not after the way Gloryanna had glowingly talked about him. But then again, Jonathan didn't know Ralph. Or his two employees, Skip and Minnie, who were also suspects.

Gloryanna stood there, frozen.

"Sweetheart, I'm sorry to just blurt it out, but it's all over the news. Come in and see for yourself." Her mother led the way into the kitchen and over to the alcove, where a flat-screen TV looked down on the couch Gloryanna had slept on last night. Jonathan hadn't noticed the television before.

Gloryanna said nothing as she sat on the cushions, her eyes glued to the images on the screen. Jonathan positioned himself behind the couch near her.

Staring at the TV, he recognized Ralph from the photo on the wall. He looked like a sixty-year-old beachcomber, except for the handcuffs on his wrists. And the police officer leading him into the courthouse was none other than Tinsdale.

Seeing Tinsdale must have spurred Gloryanna's memory, because she pulled the framed photo out of her purse and handed it to her mother. "I thought you might like to have this."

Her mother took it. A smile brightened her face as she gazed at her daughter's image. "Thank you." She put it on the coffee table. "That's very thoughtful."

"Tell her where you got it," Jonathan coached.

Gloryanna gave a sharp shake of her head.

"Trust me." Jonathan moved to the side of her, where she could see him. He wasn't letting up. "You need to tell her everything for her own protection and yours. You don't want something to happen to her, do you?"

Gloryanna stared at him.

He could tell by the downward slant of her eyelids and the slump of her shoulders that she was near her tipping point. But he had to keep at her. "Plus, you might need her help."

Gloryanna shook her head.

He folded his arms and stared at her, trying to will her to do what he'd asked, but he didn't have control over her. She had to choose.

Another way to approach this came to him. He thought of the orphanage and how alone he'd been through his trials. "I wished so many times I had a mother I could confide in. You're never too old to ask your mom for help."

Gloryanna stared at him, and an appreciation emanated from her gaze. She dipped her head, gave a deep sigh, then turned to her mother. "Actually, Mom, it wasn't thoughtful of me at all. I want to tell you something, but I don't know exactly how to go about it."

Her mother turned off the TV and sat next to Gloryanna on the couch. "You know you can tell me anything."

"Yes." Gloryanna closed her eyes. "I stole that picture from Thomas's apartment."

"Why?" Her mother leaned back against the couch cushions, her face caught in confusion. "And when?"

"It was after Jonathan, Max, and I left here this morning." Gloryanna bit her bottom lip.

"Jonathan and Max?" Her mother placed her palm to her forehead, and she inhaled. "Honey, when you left, you were alone."

"No, I wasn't. And just a little while ago, when you asked who I was talking to before we came in, I was talking to Jonathan."

Gloryanna's mother studied her more closely. "I think you'd better start at the beginning."

Over her mother's head, Gloryanna gave Jonathan a here-goes-nothing-and-if-this-backfires-it's-all-your-fault look. "Jonathan saved me from the vortex. He and his dog, Max, are here right now in this very room."

Her mother glanced around. Upon seeing nothing unusual, she zeroed in on her daughter. "No one else is here. Only you and me and Grandpa upstairs."

"Mom, I know you don't believe in the hereafter, but it is real. I know because I should have died in that vortex, but I didn't. Max, Jonathan's German shepherd, let Jonathan know I was in trouble. And Jonathan saved me. He wasn't in the water. He stood on the shore and somehow willed me to safety."

Her mother didn't so much as blink; in fact, there was no reaction on her face. No twitch. Or anything else.

"Do you want me to levitate something? That would convince her." He'd do whatever he could to help.

Gloryanna shook her head. Then looked at her mother. "You okay, Mom?"

"Oh, I'm fine. It's you I'm worried about." She took Gloryanna's right hand in hers. "Tell me more. What happened when you met Jonathan? And leave nothing out."

"I hate to pull you into this, Mom, but I think we're going to need your help."

"By 'we,' you mean you and Jonathan and his dog, Max?"

"Yes."

Her mother drew in a deep breath and stood. She pulled her cell phone from her pocket. "Before you get started, I want to check on your grandfather, and then I'm going to call the hospital and let them know I won't be in tonight."

Gloryanna nodded.

Her mother hurried up the stairs.

"Well, she could be calling the men in white lab coats to come take me away." Gloryanna glared at Jonathan. "I shouldn't have given in to you. And I don't want you levitating anything. I want her to believe me, have faith in what I say. If you floated something in the air—"

"It's an easy way to convince her." Jonathan didn't understand her hesitation or the dynamics between mother and daughter, but they must be dealing with some trust issue.

"Nothing has ever been easy between us. Not when she's trying to get me to stop diving altogether."

"You're doing the right thing." Jonathan sat by Gloryanna on the couch. Max jumped up on the other side of him. They were in this together. "I'll say this though you need to have a little more faith in your mother."

"Did you see the way she looked at me, as if I'd grown two heads?" Gloryanna exhaled.

"Give her time to digest what you've said. I gave you as much time as I could." He'd tried to make her feel at home in his shack and had waited until he couldn't hide the truth anymore before he'd told her that he and Max were ghosts. And after he'd told her, he hadn't flown things in the air to convince her. She'd had to believe him on her own.

"You're right. But why does it feel wrong?" She shivered and folded her arms. "And . . ." She pointed to the TV. "I can't believe Ralph shot Thomas. It doesn't make sense. I mean, I just thought they were casual acquaintances. What in the world would make him do such a thing?"

Jonathan wasn't sure. "Did Ralph service his scuba tank?"

"Yes. We all go there."

"Maybe he filled Thomas's while Skip filled yours and got them mixed up. I just feel that something's not right there," Jonathan thought out loud.

Gloryanna sat up straight. "That's a stretch. Why would he want to harm Thomas?"

"Good question. For that matter, why would anyone want to harm you?" He pondered a moment. "The professor knows Ralph, too, right?" Jonathan didn't know where this was going, but some kind of picture was forming.

"All of us know him. We go to his supply shop before and after every dive." She said it like it was no big deal.

"Okay, sweetheart." Her mother came down the stairs, still holding her cell phone in her hand. Her kind eyes rested on her daughter as she set her phone on the coffee table and sat in the rocker adjacent from the couch. "Grandpa is watching *Twenty Thousand Leagues under the Sea*. He should be good for a while."

"You didn't tell him what we were talking about, did you?"

"No." Her mother grimaced. "But I'm beginning to wonder if he saw your ghost as well. That would explain why he was so upset last night."

"He did." Gloryanna took a deep breath. "I should have told you before, but I couldn't. I feel horrible that I let you think Grandpa was hallucinating. But I just didn't know how to tell you."

"Are the ghosts here now?" Her mother scanned the room.

"Yes, they are. They're sitting on the couch next to me." She motioned beside her.

Her mother looked, but she never made eye contact with him, so Jonathan knew she didn't see them.

Gloryanna told her mother how Jonathan had taken her to his shack, given her clothes to change into, even fixed her some tea and stoked the fire so she could warm up.

"That explains the strange clothes you were wearing. Wait a minute. A ghost doesn't need clothes. And how could he stoke a fire and fix tea?" The little worry lines at the corners of her mom's eyes became more pronounced.

"I know. That's why I didn't believe him and thought he was just some delusional homeless man." She gave him a timid, apologetic glance.

Was she worried that he'd be offended? To alleviate her concern, he said, "I suspected that was what you thought, so don't worry about me."

She seemed to relax and turned back to her mother. "Just let me finish telling you everything, and maybe you'll understand." Gloryanna told her how she'd insisted on finding help and how Jonathan and Max had gone with her for a bit.

"You mean he left you alone in the forest when night was coming on?" Her mother clasped her hands together.

"I don't think he wanted to." Gloryanna stole a quick, fortifying breath. "Just before he disappeared, he touched me."

Her mother reared back in the rocker, making it creak. "The ghost touched you?"

Gloryanna dipped her head in concession. "I know it sounds strange, like, how could a ghost touch me? But he did. And when he did, the most awesome, magical feeling overcame me. It was warm, peaceful. Hard to explain." She drew a deep breath. "This isn't coming out right."

"You're doing better than you think." Caring filled her mother's eyes. "Go on."

Gloryanna looked at Jonathan. Her brows pinched together.

He wanted to reassure her. "She needs to know. It's okay."

Gloryanna gazed deep into his eyes. "Really?"

Her concern for him made Jonathan want to take her in his arms, but to actually hold her could spur a different consequence. Something he couldn't even envision. "Yes. Trust her."

"He's talking to you, isn't he?" Her mother calmly waited for Gloryanna to confirm she was right.

"Yes, he is."

"What did he say?"

Gloryanna let out a long lungful of air. "He wants me to trust you."

Her mother clenched her teeth, stole a breath, and said, "Okay, then. I don't mean to sound doubtful; I just want to know, How does a ghost touching you work, exactly?" Her mother leaned an elbow on the arm of the rocker, studying Gloryanna and taking in her every twitch.

"Remember, I told you that at his shack, he seemed mortal."

"No, you didn't."

"Oh, well, I meant to."

Her mother rubbed her temples. "Okay, let's put aside where he is mortal and where he isn't." She drew in more air. "What happened after he touched you?"

Jonathan was impressed by the woman and how patient she was being with her daughter. Gloryanna had said her mother didn't believe in the afterlife, yet she was taking all this information in good stride. But she couldn't very well dismiss her daughter's claim when she was starting to wonder if her own father had seen the same thing.

"I was upset because I thought he was trying to kiss me, but he wasn't. He was merely trying to make a point."

"That's what they all say," her mother interjected, but then winced and said, "Continue."

"From the first time he saw me walking toward him on the beach, he said a shadow of darkness followed me." Gloryanna took a deep breath.

"What kind of darkness?"

Gloryanna looked at Jonathan.

He nodded for her to go on.

"A foreboding darkness, which I immediately dismissed because I thought he was"—she glanced at him—"a bit crazy. Anyway, after he touched me, I headed down the trail into the meadow. He tried to follow, but he was transported back to the shack."

Her mother slapped her leg and rolled her eyes.

"I know it sounds absurd, and if someone else were telling me this, I'd think the same thing you probably are. When he first disappeared, I believed he was hiding from me and playing some kind of sick game. I was terrified. But when nothing happened and I kept walking, I started to wonder if maybe he'd told me the truth. But I wasn't totally convinced." Gloryanna leaned back against the couch.

"Did you tell this to the man who found you in the woods?"

"Mr. White?" Gloryanna squinted at her.

"Yes." Her mother waited patiently for her to answer.

"Kind of." Gloryanna explained her meeting with Mr. White and how he'd told her about the stories he'd heard about the Olympic forest being haunted, but that no one had seen a ghost. "I didn't tell him that I saw a ghost; he just came to that conclusion. Here's the curious thing Jonathan said I was the first person who had actually seen him."

Jonathan realized that over the last few days, two others had seen him as well her grandfather and Frank. Though Gloryanna and her grandfather were related, they had nothing in common with Frank.

"Why do you think that is?" her mother asked.

"Jonathan believes it's because I'm the only person who can help him and Max move on from this world."

Jonathan was proud of her. She'd shown great courage confiding in her mother. Now mother and daughter sat there staring at each other. Neither one spoke, just waited.

Her mother broke the stalemate. "You said he was transported back to his shack?"

Naturally, she would have a lot of questions. Jonathan would have been disappointed if she hadn't. He just hoped that in the end, she'd trust her daughter enough to help her.

"Yes. That's what I said. I believe he couldn't leave the area in mortal form because he died there, was possibly murdered close to the shack, and until he remembers what happened, he and his dog are stuck in limbo." Gloryanna rubbed her chin.

Murdered? He'd never considered murder in all these years. Could that really have happened? The only other person at the shack had been Frank. Jonathan thought of Frank's last words. That he didn't want to do it. Could his friend, his teammate, have killed him?

"But his spirit came here." Disbelief filled her mother's words. "And he doesn't know how he died? Or how his dog died?" Her mother rubbed her forehead while staring at her daughter.

Jonathan wanted to tell Gloryanna what Frank had said, but he was still trying to wrap his mind around it, still trying to digest it.

"Yes." Gloryanna took a breath. "You know how it is with some accident victims and how they can't remember what happened before their accidents?"

Her mother thought a moment and nodded like she wanted to know more.

"I think that's what happened to Jonathan. He must have been so shocked that it wiped out his memory of the horrible event." Gloryanna said it with confidence, which made Jonathan think she could be right.

Giving a deep sigh, her mother asked, "Okay, I have to go back a little. So, if he's supposed to be stuck at the shack, why is he here now?" She gazed at the space beside her daughter where Gloryanna had told her Jonathan and Max sat, then back to her daughter.

Gloryanna dug in her purse and pulled out the Eveready flashlight. "When I was showing this to Grandpa, I accidentally turned on the SOS option, and when I turned it off, Jonathan and Max were here."

Her mother took the flashlight and studied it. "I've never seen one like this."

"Before I turned it on, I was showing it to Grandpa, and he said it's like the ones they used during the war."

Her mother swiped her hand over her face. "Add this to what Dad said about Jonathan and his dog . . ."

"You believe me?" Gloryanna seemed to hold her breath.

"I shouldn't, but let's just say I'm open to believing you." She nodded. "Tell me about what the three of you did today."

Jonathan expected her to tell her mother about the attempts on her life. But instead, Gloryanna told her about the pictures of Thomas, Ralph, Skip, Minnie, and the professor and also the list of concerns about each of them. Then she told her about their visit to Thomas's apartment. Maybe she didn't want her mother to be worried about her, or she was waiting until the end. He needed to be patient and see.

Her mother said nothing, totally enthralled with her daughter's story. When Gloryanna got to the part when the police officers visited her condo, she said, "I'm sorry I fibbed and told them I got the picture for you and Dad."

Her mother picked it up off the coffee table. "Where do you suppose Thomas took this picture?"

"We've gone on dives with other students a lot. By the length of my hair, it must have been last year. It gives me the creeps that he printed and even framed it. He's only ever been rude and annoying to me since we broke up, hardly ever had a kind word to say."

"He's been your foil."

"My what?"

"Your nemesis and the reason you've studied so hard." Her mother nodded like she was onto something. "Have you ever thought that maybe he treated you like that because he likes you? Maybe even admires you?"

"Don't say that." Gloryanna shuddered. "I mean . . . that's so backward. And I'm a little confused about him. Don't get me wrong, I'm mad that he took my picture without my knowing and had it on his bedroom dresser, but something else isn't right here." She told her about finding the gas uniform in his apartment. "It's not like he needs the money."

He expected that Gloryanna would tell her that they suspected Thomas of doing something to the gas line, which could easily lead to her saying that he may have put poison in her water, since he had been in her kitchen. But she did neither.

"Sweetheart, his father owns the local gas company."

"He does?" Gloryanna rubbed the side of her head. "Why didn't I know that?"

"I don't know. But maybe his father wants him to learn the business from the ground up." She shrugged.

Gloryanna looked at Jonathan.

"She could be right," he said. "It makes more sense than him wearing the uniform to gain access to your home to do something to your stove." His hunch about her mother being a help to them was paying off.

"I guess so," Gloryanna muttered.

"And the stove is old and needs repaired. I don't think anything sinister is going on in regard to that. I called a repairman who should be here Friday to look it over. Maybe he can tell us more. In the meantime, we need to double-check some things." Her mother got up and went to the desk in the kitchen to grab a pad and pen. "I think we should make a list to add to what you have at your condo. Pity you couldn't set it up here."

"Seriously, Mom?" She seemed surprised and, at the same time, relieved that her mother believed her.

"Yes." Her mother wrote down to check into Seymore Clifford.

Gloryanna slapped her forehead. "Wait. I took a picture of my wall with my phone."

Her mother paused a moment.

"I was explaining to Jonathan about pixels in cameras, and to show him how they worked, I took a shot of the wall." She tapped on her phone, then pressed the screen with both her thumb and finger.

Jonathan watched as the picture magically grew larger, making it so they could read the lists that Gloryanna had made for each suspect. She showed it to her mom.

Her mother copied down the information. "What is this?" She pointed to the list of attempts on Gloryanna's life.

"Well . . ." Gloryanna squirmed.

"Tell her and don't leave anything out." Maybe this moment was why he had felt so strongly that she should add the attempts to the wall, so her mother would see them now.

"I wrote down how many times I've nearly been killed in the last couple of days." Her eyes avoided her mother's.

Her mother's face paled as she put her arm around Gloryanna's shoulders.

"You need to add another one too," Jonathan reminded her.

"And . . ." Gloryanna stole a deep breath. "Before coming here, we stopped at the condo. As I was about to drink from my water pitcher, Max barked a warning. Jonathan and I think someone put poison in my water."

Her mother shot to her feet. "We need to call the police."

"No, Mom." Gloryanna glared at Jonathan. "We can't. After the incident with my truck, and with my going missing for a couple of days before that, the police think I need to be analyzed. There isn't time. But I saved the water."

Her mother rubbed the back of her neck. It was clear that she was worried for her daughter and wrestled with what to do. Taking a deep, cleansing breath, she said, "I'll drop going to the police if you promise me that Jonathan and his dog will stay with you all the time. They've kept you safe so far."

Gloryanna looked at Jonathan, and he nodded.

"I promise," she said. Her faith in him warmed his spirit.

"Good." Her mother wrung her hands together and studied the list again. "Okay, then. We need to add the water to the list. And I think we need to add to Ralph's list that he shot Thomas."

Jonathan felt great relief that Gloryanna's mom was on board with what they wanted—no, needed—to do. He tried to think of what else they should discuss. "And don't forget we need to make note that we saw your professor leave Frank's care center, and that Frank is now dead." Jonathan still couldn't believe how frightened Frank had become at seeing him and Max, so much so that he'd died.

"You're right," Gloryanna said.

"What, honey?" her mother asked as she wrote on her paper.

"Jonathan reminded me that I still have more to tell you."

"More?" Her mother set down the pen and gave Gloryanna her full attention. Gloryanna told her they'd visited Frank.

"You've been very busy." Her mother folded her arms.

Gloryanna nodded, and then told her about seeing Professor Takahashi leaving the care center. That made her mother's eyes widen. Gloryanna told her that Frank had gone into cardiac arrest, and just when it looked like he was going to make it, he'd glanced up and seen Jonathan and Max and coded right then and there and never regained consciousness again. "He died, Mom."

"Oh my! What have you gotten yourself into, sweetheart?" Her worried mother leaned forward and took Gloryanna's hands in her own. This was why Jonathan had wanted her to tell her mom. Gloryanna needed her support. The kind of support Jonathan couldn't give her.

Her mother looked at the paper. "At the top here, you have 'scuba tank ran out of air.' What exactly happened during your dive?"

Jonathan believed Gloryanna had purposely skipped telling her parents about the tank so they wouldn't worry, but now she'd have to tell.

"I ran out of air just before the vortex took me." Gloryanna paused. "I've never thought of this before, but the vortex saved my life." The color left her cheeks. "When I think of everything that has happened, I'm a bit overwhelmed."

"I'm glad you told me." Her mother studied Gloryanna's face.

"Telling you was Jonathan's idea."

Her mother glanced around the room. "Thank you, Jonathan, for convincing her."

"You're welcome." He wished she could hear him.

"He said, 'You're welcome.'"

Her mother picked up the pen and pad of paper. She flipped to the list for the professor and added that Takahashi knew Frank and had visited him, and he had suffered a heart attack but had died when he'd seen Jonathan. She glanced at Gloryanna. "So, you think whoever is trying to kill you could be one of these people?" She held up her notepad.

"It looks that way."

They sat in silence for a moment. Then her mother said, "What if Ralph thought your tank was Thomas's and didn't fill it like he should have?"

"Jonathan wondered the same thing."

Her mother looked at the couch where Jonathan sat. "I'm glad we're on the same page."

Jonathan admired the woman's leap of faith in believing he was there.

She looked back at her daughter. "Ralph obviously had a score to settle with him." Her mother's brows rose. "And you had no idea there was any angst between the two men?"

"No." Gloryanna shook her head, but she seemed preoccupied, thinking.

Gloryanna's mother was onto something. Jonathan added, "We need to see Ralph, Skip, and Minnie and question them."

Gloryanna leaned her elbow on the armrest of the couch. "We could talk to his employees, but Ralph's in prison."

"I assume Jonathan said you need to talk with Ralph," her mother said. "He should make bail by tomorrow. You could talk to him then."

"But graduation is tomorrow. I guess I could swing by the Fish Tail on my way, and I could talk with Professor Takahashi at the ceremony." Though Gloryanna had been reluctant to suspect the woman, Jonathan was relieved to see that Gloryanna was not going to let her loyalty stop her from finding the truth.

"As much as I hate to even suggest this"—her mother set the pad and pen on the coffee table—"I think you should visit Thomas in the hospital tonight."

"Mom, he's one of the main suspects." Gloryanna pointed to the paper her mother had written on. "He was in my kitchen this morning."

Her brows knitted together. "I really think you should speak with him. Thomas is in Intensive Care. I don't think he'll be a threat. But Jonathan will be with you. He'll keep you safe." Her mother folded her arms.

Jonathan tapped down a stirring of jealousy and was about to object when Gloryanna beat him to it.

"True, but . . ."

"I remember how Thomas looked at you when you brought him over to meet us. A guy doesn't fake that special gleam in his eyes. I really don't think he'd poison the woman he loves." Her mother stared at her.

"You don't know the whole story." She might as well tell her now. "He was dating other girls at the same time he was seeing me."

Her mother's brows rose. "Well, that puts him in the cad category with or without the gleam. Did you have an agreement that your relationship was exclusive?"

Gloryanna looked down at her hands. "No."

"Ah, honey. I've found you have to pretty much spell things out for some men. Your dad and I had a similar misunderstanding." About to say more, her mom stopped herself and shrugged a shoulder. "Suffice it to say, we all make stupid mistakes. Maybe Thomas has regrets from his past. Besides, you won't be talking about your relationship. You'll be asking him what he remembers before the three of you went on that dive. I think that's imperative."

"You're right." Gloryanna dipped her head.

"However, before you go, you should maybe change your clothes, refresh your makeup, and comb your hair." Her mother smiled slightly. "Won't hurt to look your best." She rose and grabbed her purse from the stool it had been slung on and took out her keys. "And take my car. If I have an emergency with Grandpa, I'll call the paramedics."

"I hate to say it, but your mother is right." Jonathan had tried to stay out of the exchange about Thomas, but he had to call it like he saw it. "If his feelings for you are genuine, it wouldn't hurt to talk to him, and he might tell us something that would be helpful."

Gloryanna took the keys. "Thanks, Mom."

"While you're gone, I'll do a little digging into the professor on the internet. And please"—her mother looked around the room—"make certain Jonathan and Max go with you. I'll worry if you're alone."

He chuckled. Though Gloryanna's mother claimed she didn't believe in the afterlife, when it came to helping her daughter, she was opening her heart to new possibilities.

CHAPTER EIGHTEEN

GLORYANNA HAD BEEN TOTALLY AMAZED at how well her mother had accepted everything. And her mom had been helpful. Her point that Thomas might remember something that had happened before the dive gave Gloryanna one more lead to follow. But as she pulled into the parking lot to Mercy Hospital, her courage to face Thomas waned.

"You can do this." Jonathan sat in the front seat with her. Max occupied the back.

"I don't know. I don't feel like I can." She pulled down the visor and checked her makeup in the mirror. "But I'm very glad you'll be with me."

Max growled and barked.

"Something's wrong." She peered out the window, glancing at cars spotlighted by streetlights, but could see nothing unusual.

Jonathan pointed to the entrance. "Looks like we have company."

The press had camped out near the doors. Of course they would with one of Washington's wealthiest sons having been shot.

"We can use the employee entrance." Gloryanna took her mother's lanyard that hung from the rearview mirror, her photo on one side and passcode that opened doors on the other.

They got out, and dodging in between parked cars to stay away from the press, they made their way to the back door. Several employees sat on a bench nearby, smoking.

Walking toward them and trying to act normal, Gloryanna softly said to Jonathan, "I've never liked the smell of cigarette smoke."

"I don't either. That's why I smoke a pipe, but coming here, I haven't missed it."

She glanced at Jonathan one last time before reaching the others. He stared at her with admiration, which calmed the fear inside her, and for the first time, she wondered if she'd seen flashes of him before she'd passed out on the dive to help calm her and prepare her for what would follow. She hadn't put the two things together before, but now, it made sense.

Jonathan wasn't the cause of how she felt. He'd been part of the cure, and she was extremely happy that he was with her.

She walked by the employees, giving them a nod of hello in passing. They did the same and kept talking. She pulled out the lanyard, swiped her mother's ID, and stepped inside.

Glad to have cleared not only the hurdle of the press out front but also of getting past the employees gave her a bit of confidence.

She paused, glancing up and down the sterile-looking hallway.

"What's wrong?" Jonathan came to her side.

"I'm a little discombobulated. I've never come in using that door, and things are backward." She saw a sign that read ICU Second Floor and arrows pointing to another hall. "Mom said he'd be in Intensive Care for a day or so." She headed in the direction the arrows pointed and came to an elevator. She pushed the button, and the elevator doors slid open. They got on and rode to the second floor, where they found another sign with arrows directing them to the ICU.

They rounded the bend and saw a security guard stationed in front of the ICU door, and Gloryanna's steps faltered.

"Not to worry." Jonathan stared at the man.

At that moment, a nurse came out of the unit, carrying a tray of half-eaten food.

Gloryanna watched as Jonathan concentrated on the tray, and all at once, it flew from the nurse's hands and dumped its contents onto the guard.

"I'm so sorry." The nurse scrambled to clean the mess. "I don't know what happened. One minute I was fine, and then it was like the tray had a mind of its own."

The guard grumbled as he wiped mash potatoes off his shirt. His uniform was soaked. "It's okay, ma'am. I've had worse things thrown at me." But he made no move to leave his post.

Jonathan glanced at Gloryanna with a frown. She chuckled. Obviously, this was going to be harder than he'd thought.

The nurse had picked up the dishes and garbage, and as she rose, Jonathan zeroed in on her, and she fell into the guard. The tray and its contents once again spilled all over him.

"Oh my." The nurse's face flushed bright red. "I must have tripped on your shoe. I'm so sorry."

The guard bent down this time and helped her retrieve the mess. "Are you all right, ma'am?"

"I'm beginning to wonder." She looked as puzzled as he did. "Since I was taking my dinner break, I thought I'd return a patient's tray to the cafeteria."

"Maybe I should walk with you to make sure you get there."

"Oh, no. I'm fine." She gripped the tray so hard her knuckles turned white. "Really, I am." She hurried away, not looking back. She turned the corner, passed Gloryanna, and got on the elevator.

As the doors closed, Gloryanna said to Jonathan, "Did you see how upset you made her?"

He nudged a rueful shrug. "Yes, and I still didn't succeed in getting the guard to leave his post. I'll have to get creative. Be ready. I won't be able to keep him occupied for long."

Gloryanna wondered what Jonathan had up his ghostly sleeve.

The steel door at the end of the hallway that led to an emergency staircase flew open and banged against the doorstop. Wind and bits of debris blew down the hall. The guard looked around as if expecting someone else to rush by and close it, but when no one came, he hurried to take care of it.

"Max, keep him busy if you can," Jonathan told the dog.

The German shepherd followed the guard.

Gloryanna knew this was her chance. She hurried to the door, swiped her mother's ID over the lock, and turned the handle. She and Jonathan slipped in just as the guard closed the exit door and turned around.

The ICU nurses' station was close to the door. Only one nurse sat behind the counter, watching monitors. The others must have been busy with patients. Gloryanna walked to the desk.

The stern-faced nurse in green scrubs and hair in a twist on top of her head half glanced up. "Who are you here to see?"

"Thomas Clifford."

"Are you family?" she asked, her eyes on a monitor.

"No."

"Sorry, only family is allowed." She stopped. "Are you Gloryanna?"

Surprised, she nodded.

"When he was first brought in, he was asking for you." She looked around. "I think it might do him a world of good to see you. He's in the second room on your right." She smiled as if she enjoyed playing Cupid.

As much as she wanted to, Gloryanna didn't correct her. "Thanks. That's very thoughtful." She headed down the hall before the nurse changed her mind.

Jonathan followed.

She slowed as she reached the second room. Max rejoined them, and Jonathan stroked the animal's head. His tail wagged.

"Both of you behave yourselves while we're in there." She didn't wait for an agreement but pushed open the door. Jonathan and the dog tracked her steps.

In the private room, a curtain had been pulled around his bed, which struck Gloryanna as odd, but maybe the nurse did that so her coming and going wouldn't disturb him.

Not wanting anyone to overhear the conversation she planned to have with Thomas, she closed the door, then stepped to the other side of the curtain.

A peacefulness framed Thomas's slumbering face. A five o'clock shadow covered his cheeks, solid chin, and upper lip. A huge white bandage wrapped around his left shoulder, making his hospital gown hang at an odd angle. An IV drip was attached to his arm.

She didn't want to wake him, but she didn't have much time. "Thomas."

His brown-topaz eyes blinked open, then stared at her as if she were an apparition. "Gloryanna?"

"Yes. I heard you were shot and thought I should come see you." She struggled to find the right words. She didn't want to give him false hope about her feelings, but if needed, she'd play on his emotions to learn what had happened between him and Ralph.

"Did you break into my apartment?" Though his eyes were drooping from the drugs, his mind was still alert. As usual, he'd skipped over the nice-to-see-you bit and gotten right to the point. He'd used the same tactic in class.

"I didn't break in." That was the truth. She hadn't. Jonathan had opened the door for her.

"So, how did you—?"

"Your door was open," she said, not letting him finish. Again, the truth because of Jonathan's help. "I didn't think you'd want me lurking in the hall. People might talk."

"My only neighbor is in China right now; besides, that wouldn't have been a problem. After I questioned Sylvester and figured out that my mystery visitor was you and not some Gabriella Smith I don't know, I decided to pay you a visit instead of calling because I knew that when you saw my name on the caller ID, you wouldn't answer." He pushed the button on the railing of his bed, and the head of the bed rose to a sitting position. "So, why did you come to see me at my place today? It wasn't just to steal the picture I had of you, was it?" He gazed at her, sincerity in his eyes.

"You have a picture of me?" She feigned innocence. "I never gave you one." That felt right. Make him fess up about the candid shot.

"You know what picture. You stole it before you drove off on the Harley." He didn't sound angry or even upset. In fact, he looked in control, which infuriated her even more.

"I'm here for two reasons. When you went into my kitchen, you got a glass of water. Did you put something in the pitcher before putting it back in my fridge?"

His head reared back. "No. What happened?"

She didn't answer him. By his genuine reaction, she didn't think he'd done it. "I don't want to go into it now. Shortly after I left your apartment, you had another visitor. Why did Ralph shoot you?" She hoped that would stop him asking more questions about the water.

Jonathan shook his head like she'd made a huge mistake. She ignored him the best she could and focused on Thomas.

"That's the million-dollar question. Why did Ralph Wagner shoot me?" Again, Thomas was hedging, playing games.

"And there you go. Answering a question with another question. Can't you, for once in your life, be straight with me?"

"I was straight with you at your condo, remember?" All playfulness left his face, replaced with a solemn genuineness she'd rarely seen from him.

"Was that when he told you he had feelings for you?" Jonathan butted in.

She'd almost forgotten that he and Max were there. "Yes."

"So, you agree with me." Surprise gentled Thomas's face.

She glared at Jonathan to keep him quiet.

Jonathan hunched his shoulders. "I was having trouble keeping up. But I know now. Carry on."

Trying her best to disregard Jonathan so she could concentrate on Thomas and learn more about the shooting, she said, "Thomas, I do remember, but I thought you said all of that because you felt guilty." She could ask him again right now in front of Jonathan if he'd done something to her scuba gear. Thomas was vulnerable, and he might slip and tell the truth. "And maybe you felt guilty because you did something to my tank?"

He raised his head from his pillow. "Did you tell Ralph that I did?"

"Did he say that to you?" Immense culpability rained down on her.

"No, but why else would he come at me in my parking garage, waving a gun and saying he'd come to set things right?"

"And that's when he shot you?"

He nodded. "Sort of. I tried to talk reason with him and get the gun out of his hands. He was having none of it. I think he'd been drinking."

"Ralph never drinks." That was not the man she knew.

"Believe me." Thomas's eyes widened. "He was either drunk or stoned. He made all sorts of accusations, saying I was a spoiled rich kid and it wasn't right that you almost died. He said that I must have done something to your tank. I told him he didn't know what he was saying and that he was a washed-up beach bum who was scared of the water. He aimed the gun at me. I tried to wrestle it away from him. One thing led to another, and the weapon went off."

She fought to recall what exactly she'd said to Ralph. "I told him my tank ran out of air, and I wondered if something happened to the oxygen line. But I never told him that I thought you had done something to it."

He eased back on his pillow.

"By the way, did you?"

"Did I what?" He glared at her.

"Did you do something to my tank?" She had to ask again and give him another chance to fess up. She clenched her teeth and looked past Thomas to Jonathan, who had moved to the other side of the bed.

"First, you claim I put something in your water pitcher, and now you think I did something to your tank? Do you really think I would try to kill you?" Thomas's voice softened.

"There were only six people who had access to my tank me, Ralph, Skip, Minnie, you, and the professor. I don't know what to think."

Pain creased Thomas's face. He rubbed his forehead. "Cross me off your list. I would never hurt you. I . . . I love you."

Taken by surprise, Gloryanna fell speechless. This was worse than when he'd told her he had feelings for her. There'd been a time years ago when she'd yearned to hear him say those very words. But all that had changed when she'd seen him with another woman. She gulped.

Thomas stared at her. "Aren't you going to say something? Anything?"

"I . . ."

"I've never said that to anyone." He looked up at her. "You may not believe me, but I'm telling the truth."

"Ask him who Candace is," Jonathan cut into the awkward moment.

"What?" She looked at Jonathan.

"I said, I've never told that to anyone," Thomas repeated.

"I'm not talking to you. I'm talking to Jonathan." She waited for him to say something.

"Who's Jonathan?" Thomas looked where she did, but obviously, he couldn't see him.

Jonathan folded his arms as he stared at Thomas. "At his apartment, when he first heard the shower go on, he called for Candace, remember?"

She vaguely did. Turning back to Thomas, she said, "You called for Candace when you heard your shower. She must be someone close to you. A special roommate with certain privileges?" And though she'd said it to dig at him, she kinda felt bad, which was ridiculous. It wasn't like he was being disloyal to her or anyone else, for that matter.

"She's a flight attendant. When she's in town, we get together. It's nothing serious. We both know it." Thomas took a deep breath and held it a second. "Look, Gloryanna. Until you went missing, I didn't realize how much you meant to me. I've always had a soft spot for you. You have to have known that on some level." He waited for her to acknowledge what he'd said.

She thought about what her mother had told her. Had she been right?

"Have you known?" Jonathan butted in again.

Looking at Jonathan and then at Thomas, she said, "I've kind of wondered." The truth hurt sometimes. Most times. She looked at Jonathan and couldn't help but think of his touch on the trail and the unexpected sensations that had coursed through her body. She'd never felt that when Thomas had touched her.

"Good." Thomas reached and took her hand, pulling her attention away from the man, the ghost, she had true feelings for.

Dragging her hand from Thomas's, she said, "Look, there's something you should know." She couldn't tell him about Jonathan, could she? She gazed at him. He shook his head as if he'd read her mind. So, she decided not to tell Thomas and went a different way. "I'm in trouble. Someone is trying to kill me, and I don't know who or why."

"Whoa!" Thomas took her hand again and squeezed. "Believe me, I didn't do anything to your tank or anything to your water pitcher."

"Did you cut the brakes on my truck? Or do something to the gas line at my parents' house?"

"No!"

"I saw your uniform on the floor of your bedroom."

Thomas shook his head. "My father wants me to forget marine biology and join the company. He insists I learn the ropes, says he'll quit funding my education if I don't. So, yes, I work at his gas company. And that's why I wanted to try to get the grant. He's not going to pay for my master's degree."

That explained a lot. But she was far from satisfied. "If you didn't do those things, who did? And if it wasn't you, that leaves only four other people Ralph, Skip, Minnie, and Professor Takahashi. They are the only ones who had access to my tank."

"Ralph wanted to shoot me because he thought I was responsible for what happened to you, so I don't think it was him." Thomas took a deep breath. "Skip—I don't know about that guy. He seems a bit sketchy to me. Have you had a misunderstanding with him or something?"

"No." She rarely even spoke with him.

"He has access to your address since you both work for Ralph. It would be easy to look at your employee file. He's one to look into. And Minnie, she's over the grill and wouldn't know how to sabotage an oxygen tank." Thomas had a point.

"It's always the one you least expect." Jonathan scowled. He must not have liked the way Thomas had glossed over possible suspects. "We still need to check into Minnie. And Ralph could have shot Thomas to cover his tracks."

"You could be right." She'd always dismissed the notion that Ralph could be to blame, but now she didn't know.

"Good. I'm glad you think so." Thomas must have thought she'd answered him. He continued. "You know, I saw something strange on the ocean floor when I was searching for you."

"What?"

"It looked like some type of conning tower." He scrunched his face like that was impossible even though he'd seen it.

"I saw it too. I was going to take a picture, but then the camera broke loose from my wrist. As I swam after it, my tank ran out of air. And all at once, the current got me."

Thomas stared at her. "Did you tell Ralph or the professor you saw it?"

"Yes. Ralph didn't say much, and Professor Takahashi thought it might be part of the SS Lamut, a Russian sub that sank." She'd also had a conversation a little over a week ago with Takahashi about her grandfather's delusions of serving on a submarine that had sunk just off the coast. But she hadn't told Ralph about Grandpa and the sub. "Did you tell them about the tower?"

"Yes. Both of them. And look where I am now." Thomas pulled off his blanket and sheet and tried to get up.

"What do you think you're doing?" Gloryanna tugged his covers back over him.

"Whoever tried to kill you could be after me too. I'm not staying in bed." He tried to rise again but grabbed his shoulder and sank back to his pillow.

"Look, Ralph is in jail, so if it was him, you're fine. And if it wasn't, there's a guard stationed outside the ICU. He won't let anyone in. And the nurse told me that only family could see you."

"But you're here. How did you manage to get by both the guard and the nurse?" His brows rose.

She looked at Jonathan, the guy who always seemed to beat the drum about telling the truth. "The nurse heard you say my name. She thinks we're an item or something."

Thomas smiled. "And the guard? How did you get by him?"

She didn't want to tell him about Jonathan. It would complicate an already very complicated situation. She shot a look at Jonathan. He gazed at her, waiting. He had been a stickler for telling the truth. Maybe she needed to take a leap of faith and try it. "Jonathan and his dog helped me."

CHAPTER NINETEEN

RARELY ASTONISHED, JONATHAN DIDN'T KNOW what to think. Why had Gloryanna told Thomas about him and Max? It made no sense. "What are you doing? Don't we have enough trouble without telling him about me?"

"You're always wanting me to tell the truth," Gloryanna defended. "Besides, if Thomas tried to kill me, he needs to know that I have a ghost and his dog on my side."

"Ghost! Seriously?" Thomas winced, favoring his shoulder while peering around the room. "And I did not try to kill you."

Gloryanna gave an indifferent shrug of her shoulder. "So you say. But if you had tried, would you tell me?"

His eyes tightened at the corners. "What would be my motive?"

"The grant."

"You've gone so far over the edge that I can barely see you." Thomas glowered. "If I had sabotaged your tank, why would I nearly kill myself trying to find you? And may I point out that *I'm* the one lying in a hospital bed. Not you. I mean, what more can I do to prove I'm innocent?"

Gloryanna rubbed her forehead, not saying anything.

"Are you going to answer him?" Jonathan asked. She'd dug herself a pretty deep hole. He wanted to see how she was going to get out of it.

"Do you believe him?" She stared at Jonathan.

Thomas squinted in the direction she looked and shook his head.

"Now you're asking me what I think?" Jonathan asked.

"Yes." She waited.

Jonathan studied Thomas, who glared with concern at Gloryanna. "I believe him. He's got that look about him."

"What look?" Her face scrunched as she did a double take of Thomas, who reared back against his pillow, staring at her.

"A caring look." Jonathan couldn't bring himself to say a *loving* look. But that was what it was. "I think in his own way, he's devoted to you. And before this is over, we may need his help. Tell him."

Giving her head a subtle nod, she focused on Thomas. "I believe you."

Thomas let out a deep sigh. "Okay, now that that's settled, tell me about the ghost you seem to be talking to."

Gloryanna sat on the edge of the chair beside the bed. "Jonathan was a soldier, a sand pounder, actually, assigned to patrol the beach. Max was his German shepherd."

Deep furrows creased Thomas's forehead. "Are you saying he's the ghost? Him and his dog?"

"Yes. They died sometime during World War II."

"Sometime?" Thomas's face pinched.

"Jonathan doesn't know for sure. Someone murdered him and his dog." She wrung her hands together. "But they saved me from the vortex current."

"I'm beginning to think this is all some colossal hallucination and you're not really here." Thomas closed his eyes.

Gloryanna touched his arm. "It's not. And I am here."

Thomas's eyes opened, and he stared at her. "You really expect me to believe a ghost and his dog saved you?"

"Look, I understand why you're reluctant to believe me. I mean, it took me a while to believe it." She bit at her bottom lip and looked at Jonathan.

He gave her a lone nod.

Thomas put his hand on top of hers. "I want to believe you. Explain some more. What was a sand pounder? And why was he patrolling the beach?"

"During World War II, sand pounders watched our beaches. They used dogs and even horses." She checked with Jonathan. "Did you have a horse?"

"No. The terrain made it too difficult for them. Plus, it was hard enough to get supplies for us to survive, let alone take care of a big animal like a horse. On flatter beaches, closer to towns, that's where equines helped."

Thomas patted Gloryanna. "Are you talking to him?"

"Yes."

Max began pacing back and forth.

"You might hurry this along," Jonathan said. "I think someone is coming."

Gloryanna focused on Thomas. "We don't have much time."

"How do you know?" Thomas anxiously stared at the hem of the curtain in front of the door, where he could see the feet of anyone who might enter.

"Jonathan told me to hurry up. Plus, Max, his German shepherd, is anxious."

"The dog is here too?" Thomas squinted as if trying to see the animal.

"Yes."

He focused on the space by the curtain.

"Eyes on me." She moved her hand in front of him.

Thomas brought his gaze to her.

"Let's set aside the topic of Jonathan and his dog. I don't have time to convince you. And I don't know why Ralph tried to kill you or why someone is trying to kill me, but I think it has to do with that dive we went on." Her face froze for a moment. "You said you saw the conning tower. What if under the tower is a shipwreck that has never been found before?"

"What would that have to do with it? And didn't you say Takahashi thinks it could be debris from the *SS Lamut*?"

"Yes. But what if it isn't?"

"Most all sunken ships have been identified in that area." Thomas shook his head. "We probably stumbled on one of those."

"That's what I thought at first, but Professor Takahashi also told me new discoveries are being made all the time because of the tides; plus, most divers avoid the vortex current above where we saw the tower. And you know as well as I do that only 5 percent of the ocean has actually been seen." Gloryanna shook her head. A lock of hair escaped her bun and hung down the shallows of her neck.

Jonathan could see by the determined expression on her face what she planned to do. He had to stop her. "You're not going back there. You can't take the risk. Besides, before you even found the tower, someone tampered with your tank."

"I know. Which doesn't make sense at all. But the dive is where all this started. I have to go." She glared at him.

Thomas rose off his pillow. "You have to go where?"

"I have to go back to see for myself." Gloryanna paused. "I promised my parents I wouldn't dive there again, but I can see no other way."

Jonathan envied Gloryanna's courage. He glanced at Thomas, who stared at her with genuine worry in his eyes. The man definitely loved her. And by the way she studied him, Jonathan could see she'd once had feelings for the guy. But then she tore her gaze from Thomas and looked at Jonathan.

In the deep recesses of her eyes, he saw love. But Jonathan couldn't be the man she loved. He was a ghost. His arms yearned to reach out and hold her, cradle her to him. He wanted to tell her everything would be all right—but he couldn't.

Her lips curved into a don't-worry smile. Breaking the spell, she turned to Thomas. "I'm so sorry you were shot. And I'm sorry I accused you of trying to kill me." She started to move away.

"Wait a minute." Thomas grabbed her arm. "Tell me you're not thinking of diving solo?"

"I have to. There's something down there that someone doesn't want the world to know about. And they think you and I know." She pulled away from him. "Can I use your scuba gear?"

Jonathan couldn't believe that she planned to go through with this.

"The tank is empty." Thomas let go of her arm, holding his bandaged wound. "What am I saying? You can't dive alone."

"See, even he thinks it's not a good idea," Jonathan said.

Gloryanna ignored Jonathan and said to Thomas, "You have another tank in your bedroom closet. I saw it when I hid from you. Besides, I've been working on solo diving. I'll be fine." Her brows rammed together, waiting for him to answer her.

He closed his eyes and shook his head. "You'll need my key to get in, and I'm not sure where it is. My pants have to be around here somewhere."

"I don't need the key. I have Jonathan."

"The ghost?" Thomas glanced around the room.

"Yes. He helped me before; he can do it again."

Thomas's chin descended in reluctant agreement.

Jonathan relished her confidence in him and also that she'd said that to Thomas.

"Oh, and take my father's boat," Thomas said. "Professor Takahashi and I docked it at Neah Bay Marina. Those keys are on my dresser."

She leaned over and gave Thomas a kiss on his forehead.

At that moment, the nurse who had allowed Gloryanna to see Thomas came in holding a syringe. "Sorry to interrupt. So glad your girlfriend found you. You make a cute couple. It's time for your next dose." The nurse injected the pain medication into the tubing of Thomas's IV.

"I should be going." Gloryanna headed for the door.

"Please call to let me know what you find out." Thomas's eyelids were already droopy.

Jonathan almost felt sorry for him. Almost. He and Max followed Gloryanna from the room. "So . . . you expect me to break into Thomas's apartment again? What if I say I won't?"

She didn't stop to argue as Jonathan had expected, so he followed her.

"Yes, you will." She hurried out of intensive care.

A new guard had replaced the one they'd contended with earlier. He said nothing, just gave her a nod.

"I can't take part in helping you go against common sense. Thomas capitulated too easily. You shouldn't dive alone." They all stopped at the elevator. She pressed the Down button.

"Well, I'm not diving alone." She said it with great conviction.

"Who's going with you?" He couldn't wait to hear this.

The elevator doors opened, and the nurse who had spilled the tray of food on the other guard stepped off. Her hands were empty. She paid Gloryanna no mind and hurried away.

They got on the elevator, and as the doors closed, Gloryanna said, "I'm not diving alone because you're coming with me."

***

Gloryanna pulled up to the Shadow Ridge Apartments, where Thomas lived, and parked her mother's SUV. Jonathan had said nothing since they'd left the hospital elevator, but that didn't mean she couldn't guess what was on his mind. Besides, his judgmental glare spoke volumes. She turned in her seat to look at him. "So, what are you thinking?"

"That you assume a lot." He cast his gaze out the window at the posh apartment building.

She glanced in the back seat, where Max waited. "Is he always like this when he doesn't get his way?"

The dog looked at her, then at Jonathan.

"Don't drag him into this." Jonathan's voice was edged with annoyance as he turned toward her.

Gloryanna's head throbbed, and she rubbed her temple. "Can't you see? I have to dive. I don't know what else to do. I can't ask Professor Takahashi to come with me. There's graduation tomorrow. Besides, after what happened to Frank, I don't know if I can trust her. That's a major red flag." Her stomach growled.

"Not to change the subject, but when was the last time you ate?" Concern framed his face.

She thought a moment. "I ate some Lucky Charms at the condo, whenever that was."

He gave a tight-lipped huff. "No wonder you're not making sense. You need sustenance."

"What I need are answers." Her stomach growled again, traitor that it was. "But food would be nice."

Jonathan peered at the apartment building. "Let's get this over with and get you home so you can eat."

Gloryanna got out and locked the car. Jonathan and Max joined her as she walked into the lobby.

A different doorman sat at the desk. He was older and shorter than Sylvester. "Can I help you, miss?"

"Mr. Clifford told me to pick up his scuba tanks." No reason not to tell the truth.

The guard gave her a concerned look. "I hope this doesn't mean he's diving in his condition."

"No worries there."

"Good." He gave an approving nod.

She crossed the distance to the elevator and stepped on. In no time, the doors opened to Thomas's floor. Concentrating on what she needed to do, she didn't look where she was going and bumped her arm against the fire alarm near Thomas's apartment. That was going to leave a bruise.

"You okay?" Jonathan asked.

"Yeah. I wasn't paying attention." She motioned for Jonathan to go in.

He walked through the door and disarmed the lock to let her in.

Gloryanna went straight to the bedroom and Thomas's closet, where she pulled out his spare steel tank. She cupped one hand in front of the valve and turned it on for a second. Air leaked into her hand, and she smelled it. No impurities. She looked at the O ring. It wasn't torn and appeared to be ready to use. She found the hydrostatic date stamped on the tank. Good, it had been tested a year ago. She secured the buoyance compensator device to the tank and made sure the valve was turned to where her hair was.

"What are you doing?" Jonathan stared at her. "You're not diving yet."

"I want to make sure we have all the equipment we need before leaving." She grabbed the octopus—a basic regulator—and attached it to the tank. Then she turned it on to check the pressure and found the tank was just shy of 3,000. "That will be plenty of air for the dive."

She grabbed the mouthpiece and tested it too. It worked fine. She inflated the BCD. The jacket held air. She quickly checked the dump valves and found them ready to go. Securing the octopus in place, she turned to see what Jonathan was doing. She'd been totally absorbed in making sure everything was working and had forgotten him for a bit.

He stood at the dresser, gazing at the pictures of Thomas's family. She could feel another lecture coming on about her stealing her picture. But that was the least of her worries, especially since Thomas already knew. Her priority was getting what she needed for the dive. She also snagged Thomas's dry suit, mask, and diving light from the closet. She'd left hers at Jonathan's shack.

The boat keys were on his dresser, as he'd said. She set her load on the unmade bed and went to the dresser, stopping next to Jonathan. "Are you okay?"

"I just wonder if my life would have been different if I'd been part of a family like that." His voice sounded wistful.

Feeling like a heel for not being more empathetic toward him, she said, "It must have been tough growing up in an orphanage."

He bobbed his head. "Don't get me wrong, I had friends. But no adult really took an interest in me. Thomas is very lucky."

Gloryanna realized that she, too, was lucky. She'd grown up with parents who loved and worried about her. Jonathan hadn't had that. "You mentioned that you were orphaned at a very young age."

"The woman who owned the orphanage, Mrs. Allred, told me my father died in the Battle of Cantigny in the Great War. He was part of the Twenty-Eighth Infantry Regiment and helped secure the village from the Germans, but he was mortally wounded in the attack. He died a war hero."

"What about your mother?"

"She was pregnant with me at the time of my father's death and moved home with her elderly parents. She caught the Spanish Flu in 1920, just as the pandemic was drawing to a close. It took both her and her mother. My grandfather was devastated and unable to keep up with a two-year-old, so he gave away all parental rights. My mother was an only child, and my grandfather never knew my dad, so the state turned me over to Mrs. Allred." He paused a moment. "She had her hands full with over fifty children of various ages to care for."

Gloryanna's heart ached for him and the tragedy he'd gone through as a small child. "The woman ran the place by herself?" She couldn't imagine.

"Oh, no. She hired nurses and teachers. But Mrs. Allred was the boss, and she let everyone know it." His face grew solemn.

She caught herself before telling him how DNA testing had helped many people find their relatives. In Jonathan's case, that wouldn't be a comfort. And since he was dead, he wouldn't be able to test. "You know, I've often heard that when people die, one of their dead relatives is on the other side to greet them. I guess that didn't happen for you."

Jonathan reached down and rubbed the top of Max's head. "Nope. Only Max." He then stroked his short beard. "If only I could remember how we died or if we were murdered. I have a feeling Max and I were together and that's why we're stuck in this limbo state."

"That makes sense." She thought of Frank. "Seems so strange that you didn't see Frank's spirit when he died."

"I thought so too."

She'd been about to pat his arm, then stopped. Her gaze went to where her picture had been.

Jonathan's eyes were drawn to where she looked. "Even though you were angry that Thomas took a candid picture of you without your knowing—"

"It borders on stalking." An old ember of anger flared within her.

"Let me finish. You willingly went with him and your friends boating. Anyway, he must have deep feelings for you to have framed it and put it here in a place of honor with his family."

She'd never thought of it that way. In the last couple of days, her bitterness had begun to peel away. "Four years ago, I would have been flattered to think such a thing."

Jonathan gave her a nod. "Where did you two meet?"

"On campus at a coffee cart. I was running late that morning and was desperate for a cup of joe." As she spoke, the memory reeled through her mind. "I only had spare change to pay. I was juggling my books in my arms, trying to get money out of my pants pocket. When I finally did, I reached to pay the vendor and dropped the money. A bunch of people in the line behind me groaned. Embarrassed, holding my books under one arm and trying to retrieve the coins from the ground, I hurried as fast as I could, and suddenly, this handsome guy picked up the money. He gave it to me, then handed the vendor his credit card and said, 'I've got this, fair lady.'"

"He actually called you fair lady?" Jonathan squinted.

"Yes, he did."

"And you fell for the gallant act?" He shook his head.

"I did. We dated for a few months, and I thought we were getting serious. And then one day, when I was hurrying to class, I spotted him with his arm around another woman, using that same smile he'd given me when he'd paid for my coffee. I ignored it, but when I saw him a day later in a restaurant, making out with that same girl, well, that was it."

"The scoundrel. Did you confront him?" By the little lines that creased Jonathan's forehead, he understood why she'd been upset.

"Not then. We had dinner together that night. I remember sitting across the table from him at Pedro's Pizza Palace. We'd ordered our food and were waiting. Took me a while to work up my courage, but finally, I asked him about the girl I'd seen him with. At first, he acted like he didn't know what I was talking about. And then he got defensive, saying we'd never agreed to be exclusive."

Even now, Gloryanna felt tears stinging her eyes. "And he was right, but it showed me that I thought more of him than he did of me, so I broke it off." She'd been crushed, but at least they'd dated for only a few months. No good would come from reliving the past. She took a deep breath and glanced around the room. "I can't believe I'm in his apartment and borrowing his equipment."

"Life can be surprising." Jonathan went to the picture window that overlooked Bellingham.

His longing for life set his rugged face in a thoughtful expression, reminding her of when she'd looked at him through the binoculars at his shack and how handsome he'd been. Wanting to know more about him, she said, "When you were walking with me in the forest, you mentioned a girl named Mary Ann."

"Mary Ann found someone else. It's that simple." He turned away from the window. "Maybe we should get on our way."

Sharing time was obviously over. She picked up the keys from the dresser. "These have to be the keys to Thomas's father's boat."

Jonathan said nothing; he merely clenched his jaw.

"I know you don't approve of me diving, and I'm even breaking a promise I made to my parents, but I feel that if I'm going to find out why someone is trying to kill me, I have to do this. Something is very wrong."

Her cell rang. Looking at her phone, she said, "It's Mom." She motioned to him that she had to take the call. "What's going on? Is Grandpa okay?"

"He's fine," her mother said. "I wanted to know how it went with Thomas."

She told her what happened but skipped her plan to dive. Her mother would only worry and lecture her, and right now, Gloryanna had her hands full.

"I ordered your favorites from Dragon Wong's Diner," her mother said. "It should be here in about a half hour."

At the mere mention of her favorite takeout food, Gloryanna's stomach growled. "Thanks, Mom. I shouldn't be too much longer." She ended the call.

Jonathan folded his arms and smiled at her. "So, Chinese food puts the wind in your sails."

"Yes, it does. And we'd better get going." She pocketed the keys and picked the scuba gear up off the bed. "What was your favorite food?"

"During my years at the shack, I've become quite fond of steamed crab."

She stopped, thinking about his shack, the furnishings he'd made, the records he had, and the simplicity of his life there.

And then he'd touched her on the trail, and something that would have been so minor between humans had been pushed to a different plane for her with Jonathan. The warmth and tingling that had breathed over her was something she'd never forget. She never wanted to.

He and Max waited for her at Thomas's bedroom door. "Are you coming?" Jonathan asked.

He had no idea what she'd been thinking, and for that, she was glad. She smiled.

"What?" His brows came together.

"I'm just hoping that in the next few days, we can go back to your shack." She didn't elaborate and quickly walked past him.

"To collect your gear?" He followed her through the living area and past the kitchen, heading for the exit.

"Yes, and other reasons."

At that moment, the sound of a key sliding into the door sounded. Someone was coming in. It couldn't be Thomas. He was connected to an IV in the hospital.

Gloryanna turned and dashed back to the bedroom just as the door opened.

CHAPTER TWENTY

JONATHAN WATCHED GLORYANNA DIVE INTO Thomas's closet once again. She secured the door just as a distinguished-looking man with graying sideburns and a tailor-made suit entered with an elegant woman in a designer dress. Jonathan recognized them from their pictures—Thomas's parents.

"I wonder where the doorman was," Thomas's father said, leading his wife to their son's bedroom.

"Probably on a break. Where do you suppose Thomas would put it?" The woman looked around at the untidy room, but she stopped when she saw his scuba gear in the corner and the bundle Gloryanna had left behind. "Why does he have to have so much diving gear?"

"In his mind, he always has to have a backup. I think he'd put the keys on the dresser where he empties his pants pockets." The man nearly walked through Jonathan as he made his way to the dresser.

Max growled.

"It's okay, boy." Jonathan stroked the dog and stayed closer to the wall, out of their way as he watched them.

The man stopped, staring at the empty abalone shell as if he'd known that that was where his son kept his keys, but they were gone. "I don't know why Professor Takahashi wants to borrow the boat. Thomas must have left the key in his pocket." He picked up a pair of jeans and checked them. "I'm just glad the professor sees it my way now and will quit talking to him about that grant. Of all things."

"But you told him you wouldn't pay for his college anymore. What did you expect him to do? Thomas is as strong-willed as his father." She took the pants from her husband and folded them.

"The last time the professor and the kids used the boat, someone nearly died." He grabbed another pair, searching them as well.

"Not just someone. The girl Thomas has been pining over for years." Thomas's mom walked to the scuba gear in the corner.

His father dropped the pants onto the bed and went back to the dresser, checking there again. "Didn't he used to have her picture here on his dresser?" His father glanced at the photos. "What was her name?"

"Glory something or other. I think she's the reason he's so set on earning his master's degree. Do you really believe that crazy man blamed Thomas for what happened to her and tried to kill him?" She didn't wait for an answer. "When I think how close we came to losing our son, I just . . ."

Her husband went to her and took her in his arms. "But he's fine. He's only in ICU as a precaution and because I'm a huge donor to the hospital."

Jonathan could tell they loved each other very much. And they loved their son. He envied Thomas. He had parents and a good education and was set for life in a well-paying job—all things Jonathan never had or could have even dreamed of when he'd been alive.

The woman cuddled her husband and said into his chest, "I know." She sniffed and stepped away. "I couldn't stand it if something happened to him. I just wish he'd settle down." Her eyes went to the scuba gear again. "I wonder if we're doing the right thing, expecting him to give up his dreams to work with you."

The man scoffed. "He doesn't know what he wants until I tell him."

"Seymore, you don't mean that." She started making the bed, like any caring mother would.

Seymore helped by picking up the pillows. "I know, but it's what my father did. And aren't we grateful? It's given us a good life. Thomas needs to face facts. He needs to continue the legacy of the gas company. His sister can't, married to that Russian ballet dancer. Good night! What was she thinking?"

"Love makes people do strange things." His wife shrugged. "At least she's happy."

Strange things . . . Her words resonated with Jonathan. Strange things, like a ghost falling for a human he could never have a mortal life with.

He'd fallen in love with Gloryanna, which, in and of itself, was very strange since he was a ghost. Living a life with her would have made him very happy. They could still have something of a life together now. He could almost picture them in his shack above the cliffs. That was the only place where they could be kind of a couple.

Would she be giving up too much for him? She'd be close to her family and could visit them whenever she wanted. And if Jonathan and Gloryanna had a life together, they could take care of the beach. But they could never be a "real" couple.

Max whined, reminding him that he and the dog were held hostage between life and death. He looked down at his faithful companion. The dog was right. They needed to get out of this limbo that had trapped them.

Thomas's mom straightened a wrinkle in the comforter, then started picking up her son's clothes and heading toward the closet. If she opened the door, she'd find Gloryanna. Jonathan had to do something.

He willed the TV to turn on in the living area and upped the volume.

"What in the world?" Thomas's father walked to the door and motioned for his wife to stay behind him. She dropped the clothes on the bed and anxiously stood behind Seymore as he peeked into the living area. Upon seeing no one, they left the bedroom.

With Max watching the couple, Jonathan checked on Gloryanna in the closet.

"How long do you think they'll be here?" she whispered.

"I'm hoping they'll leave soon."

Max barked.

"Stay here." Jonathan left before she agreed.

He joined Max in the other room as the woman walked from the living area to the kitchen. "Who do you suppose turned it on?"

Her husband grabbed the remote from the coffee table and clicked the TV off. "No one else is here. There's probably a short in the remote or TV. I'll have a repairman check it out."

She seemed to accept the explanation and came over to her husband. "I wish Thomas would find a nice girl and settle down."

Her husband set the remote back on the coffee table and pulled her into his arms. "Like I did? Do you still think I'm a nice man? 'Cause, sometimes I wonder."

She gave him a slow kiss that made Jonathan turn away. But then he couldn't help himself and looked at them again.

The woman pulled back. "We also came here to pick up Thomas's suit just in case he's able to attend graduation tomorrow, remember?" The woman walked toward the bedroom.

Jonathan needed to do something to get them out of the apartment. Something big, like the fire alarm Gloryanna had bumped into near Thomas's door. Using his gift, Jonathan tripped it.

A loud blaring noise rang out.

"What is that?" The woman put her hands over her ears.

"The fire alarm," her husband yelled and grabbed her hand. "Come on. I'll buy Thomas a new suit in the morning." They headed for the door.

Relieved, Jonathan returned to the closet and Gloryanna. Leaning close to her ear, he said as loudly as he dared, "They're leaving."

She picked up the gear. "Is that horrible noise the fire alarm?"

"Yes. I had to use drastic measures to get them to go." Feeling weak from exerting his gift, Jonathan stayed close to Gloryanna as she made her way through the apartment to the door.

He checked the hallway. Empty. Nearly yelling to be heard over the noise, he said, "They're gone."

She left the apartment, heading for the elevator.

"I hate to say this, but maybe you should use the stairs." The emergency exit was down the hall.

"I'm not packing this gear down twenty flights." She pressed the button. They waited and waited. She pressed it again. "What do you suppose the hang-up is?"

"Could be all the residents evacuating because of the alarm." He couldn't help but think he'd made a mistake in tripping it. "We could be here awhile."

Gloryanna looked past him at the emergency exit and gave a heavy sigh.

He couldn't stand to think of her lugging the tank and all the scuba gear by herself. "Let me levitate the tank." Though he already felt weak, he had to try to help her. Concentrating on it, he floated the tank out of her arms and toward the emergency exit.

"Thank you." She bundled up the rest of the gear. "You're beginning to fade like you did when you helped me with Grandpa." She followed him down the hall.

Max had beaten them to the door and was barking.

"What's with him?" Gloryanna asked as she tried to keep up with Jonathan.

"Could be the alarm bothering him." Jonathan had to remain focused on the tank.

Reaching the emergency exit before Jonathan, Gloryanna leaned against the push bar with her hip. The door swung open, and standing there on the other side was Professor Takahashi.

CHAPTER TWENTY-ONE

"Professor!" Gloryanna quickly blocked the woman's view so she couldn't see the scuba tank floating in midair. It thudded to the floor, but with the fire alarm blaring, the sound wasn't noticeable unless she was listening for it.

"What are you doing here?" the professor yelled over the noise.

Taken by surprise, Gloryanna didn't know what to say.

"Max tried to warn us," Jonathan said, his image faded. "Tell her Thomas wanted you to collect his gear."

Gloryanna nodded and yelled, "Thomas wanted me to take his gear in to be looked at. Why are *you* here?"

Professor Takahashi glared at her. "He's not planning to dive already, is he?" She'd ignored the question, answering with one of her own.

"No," Gloryanna yelled back. She tried to think of a reason. "He just wants it to be ready when he does."

"I see. Well, let me help you." Professor Takahashi grabbed the tank off the floor and waited for Gloryanna. She bundled all the other gear against her again.

Jonathan motioned for Gloryanna to go ahead. He and Max would follow behind. That made Gloryanna feel a little better, knowing they'd keep an eye on the professor. But Jonathan had grown transparent. Max wasn't much better. Would they be able to stop Takahashi if she tried to do something?

With each step, Gloryanna grew painfully aware that Professor Takahashi had the perfect opportunity to slam the tank against her head. No one else was in the stairwell. If she had been the one behind her scuba tank failing, the faulty gas line to the stove, her brakes failing, and the poison in her pitcher, surely this was the perfect opportunity to kill Gloryanna.

She was letting fear get the best of her. Nervous, she shouted, "I thought you were busy with graduation." She stopped and looked back at Takahashi.

The professor shook her head. "I can barely hear you. I'll tell you when we get away from this noise."

Gloryanna's heart thudded against her ribs like an icebreaker pounding a path in the frozen arctic. The scuba gear in her arms slipped, causing her to trip. She grabbed the railing and glanced behind.

Takahashi stared at her while patiently holding the tank in her arms.

She must think I'm an idiot.

As they reached the nineteenth floor, more people joined them. Relieved, Gloryanna's fear of the professor receded a little. About midway down, the alarm quit ringing. But they still didn't talk and made good time with the others to the ground floor. Surrounded by people taking the stairs, Gloryanna followed them out the door. The cool night air felt refreshing. A drizzle of rain had started to fall.

Some people dashed away to find shelter. Other residents were huddled under the canopy at the entrance. The doorman came out, letting them back inside.

Gloryanna and the professor dove into the rain and hurried across the parking lot.

Takahashi trailed after her. "This weather does not bode well for graduation tomorrow. Looks like we may need to go to plan B and have it in the auditorium instead of the football stadium."

Gloryanna's mind was reeling, trying to grasp a plan of action, but nothing came quickly enough. Against her better judgment, Gloryanna led her to her mother's SUV.

"I need to get going and call the dean about changing locations." Professor Takahashi leaned the tank against the vehicle and hurried to her Jaguar.

Relief sprinkled over Gloryanna along with the rain.

Still holding the scuba gear, she looked at Jonathan. "Why do you suppose she was here?" Doing her best to tolerate the weather, she pulled her mother's key fob from her pocket and pushed the button to unlock the door.

"That is the question, and only she knows why." Jonathan stared at the handle, and the door opened.

"Thank you." Gloryanna dropped the gear in the back seat. "I don't know what to think about the professor. I should have questioned her about the dive, but to be honest, I was a little afraid of her. She was acting so weird. I hope Mom was able to find more information about the professor's background."

Gloryanna hefted the tank into the car and slammed the door shut. Then she got in the driver's seat and waited for Jonathan and Max to join her. Jonathan's image was even more transparent. He'd used his gift too much. "You don't look so good. I better get us home." She started the engine.

As she drove away, she caught a glimpse of Thomas's parents dashing to their Mercedes. She couldn't help remembering the couple's conversation while she'd hidden in the closet. They'd said Thomas called her Glory and that they wished he'd settle down. They'd also said he'd been trying to get the grant for the master's degree because his father refused to give him any more tuition money, confirming what Thomas had told her at the hospital.

Maybe Thomas truly had changed. Maybe he could earn her trust again. But not right now. Right now, she only wanted to get home, get warm, and eat something.

***

Sitting next to Gloryanna on the ride to her parents' helped recharge Jonathan, but he still wasn't back to normal by the time she pulled into the garage in back of their house.

True to her word, her mother had a late supper on the table when they arrived. She was on the phone when they entered, so she held her hand over the mouthpiece and said, "This is your father. Go ahead and eat." And then she continued listening and walked into another room.

Gloryanna pulled her wet hair behind her ears. "I've got to get out of these clothes. I'll be right back." She ran upstairs.

Though Jonathan had no need to eat, he could still smell. The aroma from the two bags of Chinese takeout made him wish he could at least taste. He was tempted to follow her mother into the other room to listen, but he decided against it. She was only talking to her husband, and Jonathan saw no need to eavesdrop.

Gloryanna returned dressed in dry gray sweats. Her wet, curly hair had been twisted into a bun, yet tiny spirals graced her neck. She moved the takeout bags to the breakfast nook and sat. Then she looked at Jonathan. "You're still pretty faint. I wish I could give you and Max something to eat."

"We're fine." He rubbed Max's ears. "Aren't we, old boy?"

The dog moaned and leaned against Jonathan.

"Come sit with me. That might help you recover more quickly." She scooted over and proceeded to pull containers of food from the bags. She found a set of wooden chopsticks and pulled them apart in preparation to eat.

Her mother returned to the room, stopped, and gave her an odd look as she noticed the space on the bench seat. "Your dad said to say hi. They're finishing up early, and he thinks he'll be back in time to attend your graduation. Is Jonathan with you? Is that why you left a little room?" Her mother slid in across from them in the booth.

"He is. He was amazing." As she ate, Gloryanna told her mother about Thomas's parents almost catching her.

Her mother nodded in all the right places, but when Gloryanna finished, her mom said, "I have to ask, Why did you go to Thomas's apartment in the first place?"

"Aren't you going to eat, Mom?" Gloryanna said.

"Tell her," Jonathan said.

"It's eight o'clock, honey. I've already eaten." She waited.

"Tell her what you plan to do." Jonathan needed her mother to know so she could talk some sense into her daughter.

"Thomas asked me to water his plants." Gloryanna took another mouthful of what looked like chow mein and avoided Jonathan's gaze. He knew that she knew she didn't need to look at him to know he was disappointed in her.

Her mother turned to him. "Jonathan, is she telling me the truth?"

"Mom"—Gloryanna stared at her—"can you see him?"

"No, but you said he was there, right?" Her mother pointed to the space.

"I like your mom." Jonathan's chuckle escaped him.

Gloryanna ignored his comment and said, "Yes, but—"

"And you listen to him, right?" Her mother turned her attention to her daughter now.

"Mom, I listen to you." Gloryanna shoved her container away. "I just don't need the both of you ganging up on me."

"So . . ." Her mother craned her neck. "You weren't telling me everything."

"Your mom is a smart lady." Jonathan leaned back against the booth and folded his arms. "Tell her that you're planning to dive solo. I dare you."

Gloryanna cleared her throat. "Mom."

Gloryanna fidgeted as she attempted to squirm her way past the truth minefield. He knew there was no way she'd tell her mother that after graduation tomorrow, she planned to go to Neah Bay, take Thomas's father's boat out, and dive alone so she could find a shipwreck beneath the conning tower. He also knew she couldn't tell her mother because Gloryanna believed that if she didn't dive, someone else could get hurt. Or worse, killed.

"What, dear?" Her mother smiled in that way he'd seen other mothers do to make their children tell the truth and nothing but.

"Have you ever had to do something that you knew other people wouldn't want you to do so that you could save the people you love?"

Kudos to Gloryanna. She'd masked one truth behind another.

Her mother shook her head. "You lost me, sweetie."

"I don't want to tell you exactly why I went to Thomas's because I have to do something that you may object to, but I have to do it whether you want me to or not." Gloryanna set her elbows on the table.

"Okay." Her mother reached out and took hold of her hands. "Don't tell me. But please know that I'm on your side no matter what."

"Wow," Jonathan said. "Your mother is amazing and at the same time, very gullible."

Gloryanna glanced at him. "Too bad you're not like her."

"What did he say?" Her mother once again looked at the space where he sat.

He wished she could see and hear him.

"He thinks you're amazing, and I agree." Gloryanna motioned for him to move.

Jonathan stood so she could get out.

She closed the container she'd been eating out of and grabbed the others. She went to the refrigerator. Opening one of the french doors, she placed the food inside. "Mom, what did you find out about Professor Takahashi?"

Her mother grimaced. "Not much. Come take a look." She went to the alcove where the couch stood by the fireplace. A laptop, much like the one he'd seen at Gloryanna's, rested on an end table. She opened it and tapped a few keys. Soon, a picture of the professor appeared.

"I can't find any record of her birth or much of her life before she began teaching at the university." She moved her finger down the screen, and large sections of text and more pictures flipped by. "Has she ever mentioned anything in class about what she did before moving here?"

"Not that I can recall. But she is a master at avoiding talking about herself and is pretty private." Gloryanna paused a moment. "Please keep trying." She yawned. "How's Grandpa?"

"Why don't you stop in his room before you turn in. He's doing a lot better than he was this morning. More lucid. In fact, he's been asking for you. When I left him, he was watching that sailing show he likes."

"Sounds good." She gave her mom a hug. "I can hardly wait to lie down."

"Just a minute, honey." Her mother glanced around the room. "Where exactly are Jonathan and his dog going to stay while we're sleeping? He could sleep in the apartment above the garage. It's been empty since we moved Grandpa into the house."

Gloryanna glanced at Jonathan.

He shrugged. "I'll be fine in a chair in the corner of your room." Then he realized what he'd said. "But don't tell her that."

"He says he'll watch over us." Gloryanna snickered. "Don't worry about him."

Jonathan followed Gloryanna to the staircase, but she looked back at her mother sitting in the alcove, working away on the laptop in front of her. Admiration filled Gloryanna's eyes, and he realized the woman was not only Gloryanna's mother but had become her friend as well.

***

Gloryanna went to the bathroom to get ready for bed. She pulled off her sweats and tugged on the cozy long-sleeved T-shirt that used to be her father's. She ran a pick through her locks, washed her face, and brushed her teeth. Leaving the bathroom, she paused outside of Grandpa's door. She needed to check on him. And since Jonathan was in her room, now might be a good time. She didn't want her grandfather to get upset by seeing him. She leaned closer and heard voices and music from his TV, so she tapped on his door.

"Enter if you must." Her grandfather's voice sounded strong, almost normal. She slipped in.

"There's my little Starbuck." He patted the side of his bed. "Come tell an old man what you've been up to." He turned down the volume on the TV.

Relieved that he was in such good spirits, she gave him a hug and settled beside him. Maybe now was a good time to ask him some of the questions she had. If he was feeling good, his clear thinking could last a while. "Grandpa, what do you remember about World War II?"

He frowned and turned the TV off. "That's a heavy subject just before bedtime."

"I know, but I have a friend who is in trouble, and I was hoping I could ask you some questions that might help him." She studied his reactions.

He blinked his wrinkly lidded eyes. "What is it that you'd like to know, my dear?"

"You served in the navy and were stationed in the Pacific, right?"

He tilted his head in a yes.

So far, so good. "Did you ever hear of a division in the Coast Guard called the sand pounders?"

"Certainly." He rubbed his nose. "They patrolled the beaches. A brave lot of men. A lonely job for them."

"Did you ever know any sand pounders personally?" This was a wild question to ask since her grandfather had served on an aircraft carrier. But he may have run into some while on leave.

"One. No, two." A frown came to his face. "A nasty business." He stared at the darkened TV screen. "I couldn't believe what happened. One moment, he stood there, and the next, he was gone." Grandfather's bottom lip quivered. Tears came to his eyes. "I could do nothing to stop it. I tried. Really, I did."

"Grandpa, it's okay." She wished she'd never brought it up. She stroked his arm, drawing his attention to her.

"He's here now, isn't he?" Fear pinched his age-spotted face as he glanced around the room. "I saw him before." He pointed to where Jonathan and Max had first appeared. "Him and his canine minion. They were right there." His finger shook as he pointed.

She took his hand and held it to her cheek. "Look at me, Grandpa."

He tore his gaze from the space. Sheer terror emanated from him as he took deep, labored breaths. "I wanted to help." His eyes reddened. "I shall never forget what happened." He shook his head. Little gray hairs wisped about.

Then he softly said, "I think it's time I tell somebody."

CHAPTER TWENTY-TWO

JONATHAN SAT IN THE COZY armchair beside Gloryanna's bed. She was taking a long time returning from the bathroom. But he'd always heard that women smeared night creams and such on their faces. However, that didn't sound like something Gloryanna would do.

Perhaps she visited her grandfather before retiring. "Think I should check on her?" he asked Max, who was resting on the floor at his feet.

Without waiting, Jonathan moved from her room to the hallway. He stopped in front of the old man's door and pressed an ear to the wood. The elderly man's voice sounded upset. Gloryanna must be having a hard time with him. Jonathan poked his head into the room. She sat on the side of the bed, stroking her grandfather's arm.

"Grandpa, whose partner stepped on his hands?"

"The sand pounder's. His partner met us at the beach. We had to abandon our ship."

Gloryanna's eyes narrowed as she studied him. "Grandpa, your ship never sank. You were on the *USS Enterprise* and helped to win the war, remember?"

Her grandfather shook his head and leaned close to her. "I never served on that vessel. And if it weren't for Frank helping us, we would have been caught."

At the mention of Frank, Jonathan moved into the room, staying out of the elderly man's vision. He had to hear what her grandfather had to say.

"Can you keep a dying man's secret?" Her grandpa stared into Gloryanna's eyes.

Fear seemed to bunch her brows together as she slowly nodded.

"I served on a U-boat."

She shook her head. "Have you been watching old war movies again? You know how you get when you watch those."

"I have to tell someone before I die. I may go to jail, but the truth needs to come out." He took her hands.

"Grandpa, you're not dying." She pulled away from him. "And I'm not going to sit here and listen to you talk like this."

Her grandfather grabbed her arm and pulled her back. "Child, you know deep in your heart I will die soon." His bloodshot eyes stared at her.

She bit at her bottom lip and shook her head.

"Yes, I will, and I need to tell someone my story. I've hidden it long enough." With a trembling hand, he rubbed his whiskery chin.

Jonathan moved closer, catching her eye, but she quickly looked at her grandfather. She must be afraid he might see Jonathan too.

"Our U-boat was on a secret mission. We had important passengers a lieutenant general of the Luftwaffe, two colonels, also of the Luftwaffe—they were rocket experts—and two lieutenant commanders from the Imperial Japanese Navy." He bowed his head and paused a moment, then said, "To the crew's knowledge, our most important cargo was a crate of gold bars Hitler was sending to Japan as a last-ditch effort to gain their support. But there was something else. Something the Luftwaffe commanders didn't want the rest of us to know."

"Did you ever find out what it was?" Her forehead wrinkled as she focused on her grandfather.

"Some thought we were hauling liquid mercury that the Japanese could use in building detonators. Our destination was Osaka and the Riken Laboratory in Tokyo."

"Grandpa, you don't know what you're saying." She felt his forehead, then placed her palm to his withered cheek.

He caught her hand, kissed her knuckles, and said, "I do know." He stared at her. "My mind is clear. I may not be able to remember what happened this morning, but the distant past is very vibrant in my mind. It haunts me."

"Grandpa, you're not even German."

"Yes, my child"—he bowed his head—"I am. In my teens, I was part of the brown shirts. My instructor saw great talent in me, and I trained for several years to become a spy. That's why I have no accent. My first mission was with three other men. We were to cripple the US aluminum and hydroelectric power production. But our mission was scrapped when our U-boat was sighted off the coast of New York."

"Grandpa . . ." Gloryanna stared at him in disbelief.

Jonathan wanted to go to her but knew he had to stay where her grandfather couldn't see him. If he knew Jonathan was here, he might stop telling her what happened.

"It's true. I've wrestled with this burden ever since the harbinger appeared in my room. Him and his dog have come to get me." He leaned his balding head against his pillow.

"No, they haven't, Grandpa." She glanced at Jonathan. "They haven't come to hurt you. They've come to help me."

The elderly man blinked and blinked again.

Gloryanna gave a deep sigh. "Remember, I told you about Jonathan." She looked directly at him, but her grandfather seemed too deep in thought to follow her gaze.

She tried again. "And I showed you his flashlight."

He thought a moment, and then said, "Flashed SOS."

"Yes, it did. And for some reason, by doing that, it summoned Jonathan and Max, his dog, from the shack."

"The shack!" He sat up and wiped his brow. "That's where we hid while Frank and Lieutenant Eginhardt set up the plan."

"Plan?" Again, her face pinched with confusion and worry for the man she dearly loved.

"Yes. Let me explain while I can." His red-rimmed eyes seemed to beg her. "I spent the war on U-boats, so I never saw the ravages of battle up close. On that last mission, we were to transport personnel and materials to Japan. The days of the Reich were ending. Lieutenant Eginhardt told us the enemy would find nothing but rats and mice in Germany, but we should never give up."

"Grandpa, do you see the US as your enemy?" The pleading in Gloryanna's voice tore at Jonathan's heart. The man she'd admired all her life was not who she'd thought he was.

"No, child. I was able to live out my days here. I met my wife, your grandmother, and we had a family. I wanted to protect them from my past and not burden them with my secret, so I hid the truth from those I loved. I was afraid I'd be deported or arrested, so I made up the lie of my serving on an aircraft carrier. Now my days are numbered. I need to tell you the truth so you understand why." He took her hand in his. "My ship narrowly escaped an attack at sea, but the XB submarine was severely damaged. We stayed at Schnorchel depth for days and only surfaced at night for two hours so the lieutenant could send and receive messages from our contact in the US. We limped along, avoiding detection for weeks. But our vessel had been badly damaged. We had to abandon ship. Frank met us on the beach."

"Frank met them?" Jonathan could not contain himself.

Startled to hear another voice, Gloryanna's grandfather turned to see where it had come from. His breathing became labored as he stared at Jonathan—the ghost from his past.

Bits and pieces of memory flew at Jonathan. "I remember. Max and I waited and waited for Frank to return from patrol, but he didn't. We went to search for him."

A deep, penetrating coldness settled on Jonathan. The icy fingers of death wrapped around him, though he was already dead. He fought it off. "I even walked to Purgatory Point to see if he'd fallen."

Her grandfather sank against his pillow. "Frank led us from the beach to the shack, and that's when we saw you and your dog."

As if summoned, Max entered the room and walked up to Jonathan's side.

"Your dog attacked Herrick. I pulled him off. Herrick had a bad temper." His gray brows pinched together. "He'd not hesitate to kill a dog. But the dog bit me, and I let go." Looking at Max, he said, "You charged Herrick. So he kicked you over the cliff. I'm so sorry." With a trembling hand, he covered his mouth.

"Grandpa." Gloryanna scooted closer to him.

"I saw the shock on your face." He looked at Jonathan.

Memories whirlpooled in Jonathan's mind. All at once, he stood at the cliff, staring at a much younger version of Gloryanna's grandfather and the hopeless expression on his face at what had just happened. Jonathan rushed to the ledge and saw Max's lifeless body on the rocks below.

Intense sorrow nearly doubled Jonathan over. He felt the ocean's wind brush his face and heard his heart thudding in his head. Life-affirming energy pulsed through him as if his heart still beat, making him stronger and stronger.

"I thought you would kill us all." Her grandfather motioned for Gloryanna to step back. A gallant attempt to protect her from Jonathan.

Her grandfather's confession could not undo the past. Jonathan and Max were dead, were ghosts, sent here not only to help Gloryanna but themselves too.

And now Jonathan knew why.

Her grandfather held the key. He had all along. Jonathan had to acknowledge what he'd said. "Back then, I would have killed that man for what he did, but Frank got in my way and shoved me off the ledge."

Panic surged through Jonathan like it had when he'd gone over the ledge and he'd clawed at the ground, trying to save himself by grabbing at the grass. Frank had stared down at him. All he'd had to do was reach a hand out and help Jonathan up. But instead, Frank had stepped on his fingers, crushing them into the ground. The soil had given way. And Jonathan had free-fallen to the rocks below.

Strangely, by learning his demise, an inexplicable lightness overcame him. His anger changed to sheer joy. The mystery that had haunted him for decades had finally been solved.

Max pawed against his legs. Jonathan stooped down, giving his beloved friend a hug. "We should be able to move on now."

Yet nothing happened.

Jonathan's gaze met Gloryanna's. She'd just learned the heart-wrenching truth her grandfather had hidden from his family all these years. Great empathy filled her eyes though. Empathy for Jonathan. "Do you see a light at the end of the tunnel?"

He had no idea what she was talking about, but a strong impression settled on him. Everything her grandfather had revealed coalesced into one sphere of knowledge. "No, but I do know why Max and I are here and why the ocean sent you to me."

CHAPTER TWENTY-THREE

"Why?" Gloryanna's grandfather asked, startling both her and Jonathan.

Sitting on the edge of Grandpa's bed, Gloryanna stroked his arm, trying to calm him. After he'd confided his hidden past, she knew he'd played an important role in bringing her and Jonathan together.

Jonathan moved beside her. "It wasn't mere fate that Max alerted me to your dire situation as you fought the vortex." He peered into the depths of her eyes. "Nature was trying to correct a colossal human error endangering not just our little section of the ocean but inevitably the world. What happens here could domino."

"What are you saying?" Her mind reeled. Didn't she have enough to worry about after hearing Grandpa's confession? Now Jonathan was dumping the fate of humankind in her lap?

Jonathan motioned for her to step away from the bed.

She checked Grandpa. He seemed to have dozed off, exhausted. She walked over to Jonathan.

"I need you to listen to me." Jonathan seemed pretty sure of himself.

Something had changed in him. Maybe learning how he'd died had given him more confidence. But it scared her. "I'm trying to understand."

Jonathan leaned close. His ghostly essence shimmered, and his gaze pierced through to her very soul. "If that U-boat sank not far from our shores with a cargo of liquid mercury on board nearly eighty years ago, those canisters could be leaking."

She'd been so busy trying to come to terms with Grandpa's secret life that she'd forgotten that there might have been liquid mercury on the sub. She immediately thought of the sickly-looking anemones she'd seen just before she'd spied the conning tower and before the vortex had grabbed her. She'd wondered if it had been mercury poisoning. Jonathan could be right.

If that liquid mercury were biotransformed into methylmercury in the water, they very well could have a catastrophe on their hands. She thought of Minamata, Japan, and how thousands had died because of methylmercury contaminating sea life. Feeling overwhelmed with the enormity of the problem, she said, "What do we do?"

"I hate to say it, but—" Jonathan stopped, then started again. "Someone needs to go down there and make sure. And since you planned to go anyway . . ."

"Wait a minute. We should get ahold of the Coast Guard or the EPA. They'd know what to do." She really wanted to pass this burden to someone with more authority.

"Do you honestly think they would drop everything to check on a sunken U-boat that a nearly hundred-year-old man who fights bouts of dementia claims is down there?" Jonathan tilted his head.

"I could tell them I saw the tower of what could be a sunken U-boat. They couldn't ignore that." Even as she said it, doubt flooded in.

"Okay." He sat on the armrest of the chair next to the bed. "They might listen to you and fill out a report. But when they learn you're the granddaughter of the man who claimed that a German U-boat sank off the coast of Washington, they will bury that report, even if you tell them about the mercury being on board. We're going to need solid evidence to get their attention."

"You could be right. I testified before a government committee about the damage being done to the seas. They nodded their heads and looked sympathetic, but in the end, nothing happened. I even picketed fish markets, trying to bring attention to the damage fishermen were doing. Again, crickets."

Deep in her soul, she firmly believed that if mankind didn't wake up, they wouldn't have any sea life that they desperately needed to survive. Picketing was one thing. Diving where there could be a possible mercury leak was another. She'd be putting her own life at risk. But if a leak continued to go unchecked, there would be grave consequences.

Then she thought of something. "Could you dive down there without me and get the evidence?"

"In my current state, I don't know." Jonathan's kind and caring gaze met hers, begging her to understand. "At the shack, I had more of a mortal form, but I never went in the water when I saved people from drowning. I have no idea if I can even swim, let alone dive." Jonathan sat in the armchair. "Can a spirit even go into the water?"

She eased down on the edge of the bed. There were so many uncertainties. They were both learning as they blindly stumbled along, unsure of what to do but also knowing how very important it was for them to solve this problem.

At that moment, a tap came on her grandfather's bedroom door.

Grandpa blinked his eyes open.

In walked her mother carrying a pill bottle. "I'm so glad you two have been able to visit, but it's getting rather late." She walked to the nightstand and poured Grandfather a glass of water. Then she stopped and seemed to notice an indentation in the armchair's cushions. She leaned close to Gloryanna. "Is Jonathan here too?"

"Yes." Grandpa cleared his throat. "He is."

Her mother nearly dropped the glass in her hand but caught it. "Dad, you can see him too?"

"It's only because I've met him before." He nodded his balding head and shrugged like it was no big deal. "When he was alive, near his shack."

Her mother stepped back and turned to Gloryanna. "What happened in here? What's going on?"

Gloryanna rose from the bed, moving so her mother could give Grandpa his medicine.

Her mom took the hint and handed him the pill and glass of water.

Grandpa took them, tossed the medication into his mouth, then chased them with a drink. Handing the glass back to Gloryanna's mother, he said, "I'm too tired to go through it again. Starbuck, explain it to her." His vibrant spurt of energy had quickly deflated.

"Explain what to me?" Gloryanna's mother looked between her father and her daughter.

"It's a long story, Mom." She gave her mother a hug.

"I don't care. I want to know what's going on." Her mother didn't notice that Grandpa yawned.

"Why don't I fill you in over a piece of blackberry pie? I saw one in the fridge." Blackberry pie was Gloryanna's favorite. She knew what she had to tell her mother would be earth shattering. The pie could help soften the blow, especially when she learned what Gloryanna and Jonathan had to do tomorrow after graduation ceremonies.

"I picked it up to celebrate your earning your degree." Though worry furrowed her brow, she smiled.

"Thank you." She gave her mother another hug. "That's so thoughtful. With everything that has been going on, I hadn't even thought about celebrating."

"Well, you should." Grandpa yawned. "I want to go to my granddaughter's graduation." He motioned for them to leave. "Let this old man sleep."

"Are you sure, Dad?" Her mother tucked him in.

He merely nodded and looked at her. "Honey, I'm sorry." His eyes closed.

Her mother turned to Gloryanna. "What does he mean? Sorry for what?"

Gloryanna went to the door. "Come on, Mom. I'll tell you downstairs."

"I'll be right there." Her mother leaned over to kiss the top of her father's head.

Jonathan and Max joined Gloryanna, and the three of them stepped into the hallway. Jonathan stopped. "Your grandfather said there was a crate of Hitler's gold on board the ship, right?"

"Yes. And don't forget the mercury." That was what had her concerned.

Jonathan shook his head and looked at her. "Frank was always looking for gold, remember?"

"That's what you told me." She was still trying to put two and two together.

"The captain of the German sub must have paid him with a bar of gold. They couldn't have gotten all the gold out before the ship went down, but they could take one bar. That's why Frank could afford that swanky rest home." Jonathan rubbed his chin. "And he probably killed me so I wouldn't report him to the authorities. That gold could be why someone has been trying to kill you after you saw the sub."

"Thomas saw it too." The stark reality hit her hard.

Jonathan nodded. "And someone shot him."

"You think Ralph knows about the gold?" Was that why he'd loaned her his camera, because he knew it was down there and he wanted proof?

"Someone does. And they want it all. We've got to prove the gold and liquid mercury are down there and take the information to the authorities fast."

"I've always wanted to do more to fight for a cleaner ocean. Now I can." The words sounded more courageous than she felt.

"Your mother will try to talk you out of diving," Jonathan cautioned.

"I know." She hated to be the one to tell her. But if her mother knew the truth, it might help her understand what Gloryanna and Jonathan wanted to do. Had to do. And the sooner, the better.

The light in Grandpa's room went out, and her mother quietly closed the door. She motioned for Gloryanna to follow her and headed downstairs. Stopping at the fridge, she grabbed the pie while Gloryanna collected two plates, a knife, and two forks.

So she could face her mom, Gloryanna had Jonathan get in the booth first, then she followed.

Her mother served the pie, and as they ate, Gloryanna recounted everything Grandpa had told her.

Her mother quit eating midway into her slice. "My father was on a U-boat and is German?" Shock and denial quavered in her voice.

"That's what he told me." Gloryanna felt for her. Then she told her that Grandpa had seen Jonathan and his dog murdered.

"Oh my stars. So, not only was my father a sailor in the German fleet, but he was also an accomplice in Jonathan's murder?" Her mouth hung agape.

"No, Mom. He couldn't have stopped Frank from shoving Jonathan over the cliff. And he tried to help Max but couldn't. Remember our countries were at war at the time." Not the best excuses, but they might calm down her mother.

"Dad must be hallucinating." Her mother folded her arms. "He watches too many war movies, that's all."

"No, Mom." This was harder than she'd thought it would be. "It's true. Jonathan remembered it."

"What should we do? Who do we call?" Her mother's face paled.

"Let me tell you the rest." Gloryanna took a deep breath.

"There's more?" Again, her mother's mouth hung open.

Gloryanna told her about seeing the conning tower of what could be the top of a U-boat on the ocean floor. However, she didn't tell her about the gold or the mercury. "I need to dive down there and check it out."

"I should say not!" Her mother stood and walked to the kitchen island, then turned to look at Gloryanna. "You promised you wouldn't dive in that area again." Her cheeks flushed red.

Gloryanna went to her mother, took her arm, and guided her back to the bench seat across from her. "I only agreed so you and Dad wouldn't worry. But, Mom, if we're going to prove what Grandpa told us, someone has to dive. And that someone is me."

"I'll go with you if I can," Jonathan added, drawing Gloryanna's attention.

"Jonathan said something, didn't he?" Her mother stared at his space.

"He said he is going with me." She didn't add, *If he can.* She needed to stay positive, not only for her mother's sake but for her own. Even though she'd planned to do this dive, it had been before knowing what was really down there. This was going to take more courage than even she could imagine.

"Are you going after the graduation ceremonies?" Her mother nervously tapped her index finger on the table.

Gloryanna gave a lone nod.

"What am I going to tell your father?" Mom leaned back against her seat. "Couldn't someone else go? Your professor?"

"No!" Gloryanna said it too forcefully, making her mother flinch. She tried to explain. "Remember, I told you that Grandpa's U-boat had two men who were Imperial Japanese. I think one of them has a connection to Professor Takahashi, because she knew Frank." Gloryanna felt in her bones that she was right. "Maybe you could research officers in the Japanese Army."

"I see what you're doing. You're trying to take my mind off you diving again and the fact that my father lied to me." She rubbed her chin.

Gloryanna said nothing, just looked at her mother.

Finally, reluctantly, her mother said, "Well, Takahashi wouldn't be foolish enough to go by the same name. I could look for Japanese officers who disappeared. A lot of them committed hara-kiri."

"It's true," Jonathan said. "Even before the war ended, I heard stories that instead of enduring the humiliation of being captured, many officers killed themselves."

Maybe it was the weight of all that had happened and the tremendous mental drain it had been, but Gloryanna was suddenly bone-wearyingly tired. She slumped in her seat.

"Sweetie, I think you should go to bed." Her mother cleared their plates, setting them in the sink.

Gloryanna glanced at the time. 1:00 a.m. Her mother was right. If she was diving tomorrow, actually today, she would need to be alert. "Okay."

She rose and started for the stairs.

Jonathan followed her. "It will be all right. Now that I know what happened to me and Max, I also know I'm here to help you. We have to do this."

"But how do you know?"

"Did you say something, honey?" Her mother had gone to the alcove to sit in front of her laptop.

"What are you doing?" Gloryanna crossed the distance to see what her mother felt was more important than going to bed herself.

"Just a little more research. There's no way I'll be able to sleep. My father lived a lie all my life." She pulled at her bottom lip, then took a deep breath. "I'm still struggling to accept it, so I might as well see what I can find about XB U-boats and those Japanese soldiers who could have been on my father's ship." She motioned Gloryanna away. "You go to bed. Don't worry, I won't be long."

Any other time, Gloryanna would have stayed and helped, but she was truly exhausted. Fighting back a yawn, she said, "Please, Mom, don't be much longer. Dad will be home in the morning." She paused. "What are we going to tell him?"

"The truth," Jonathan said.

"Yes, but maybe later." It would take time to convince him, time that she desperately needed for the dive.

"I agree." Her mother cleared her throat. "I could never keep something from your dad."

"Mom, did you hear what Jonathan said?" Gloryanna wouldn't doubt it after all they'd been through tonight.

"No, dear. But I heard your reply, and I just knew. Your Jonathan is a stickler for being honest." A hint of a smile graced her mother's lips.

"I've said it before, and I'll say it again. I like your mom." Jonathan nearly beamed.

"It's a pity she can't see or hear you. You'd get along swimmingly." Gloryanna headed for the stairs.

"What did he say?" Her mother stopped her.

"That he likes you."

Her mother nodded and smiled, then turned back to her laptop.

Gloryanna climbed the stairs. Though tomorrow was going to be a monumental day, at least her mother wasn't fighting her about the dive. She should have told her about the gold and the mercury but felt it better to spare her that worry.

Even though Jonathan planned to go with her, Gloryanna would have to face those worries alone.

CHAPTER TWENTY-FOUR

Jonathan stayed with Gloryanna until she fell asleep. Once certain she wouldn't need him, he and Max returned to the kitchen. He wanted to watch over her mother. She'd suffered quite a shock.

He found her still working on her laptop, sitting on the couch in the alcove. All seemed peaceful, except for the noise of her madly typing on the keys.

Max curled up at her feet, staking out his territory. Jonathan stood behind the couch and gazed at the screen as she read about holdouts of the Imperial Japanese force.

In the 1950s, some men had been found in the Philippines, and over eighteen had been found on Anatahan Island.

She scrolled from story to story of more holdouts that dated into the 1960s and '70s. Some had been captured in Guam, and one soldier wouldn't surrender until his former commanding officer was flown in to relieve him of duty.

Gloryanna's mother stretched her arms, moved her laptop to the coffee table, and got up. Max scrambled out of her way and hid behind Jonathan as she went to the microwave to reheat her tea. As Jonathan watched her, he realized Gloryanna had inherited the woman's beautiful eyes and high cheekbones, though Gloryanna's mother's eyes now had fine lines at the corners and her cheeks were less pronounced. Her brown hair was highlighted with streaks of blonde, much like her daughter's, but there were also threads of gray mixed in.

She settled on the couch, placed her cup back on a coaster, and picked up the laptop. She clicked on another page with stories of Japanese holdouts discovered in the 1980s on the Solomon Islands.

For some reason, Jonathan found that reading about those poor men who had believed in their cause for several decades after the war had ended made him feel better. He and Max, in a way, had been holdouts patrolling the beach even though they were dead. He stroked Max and rubbed his ears.

Another page appeared that had a picture of Japanese soldiers who had never been found. There was something strangely familiar about one of them who had been reported as missing in action. Jonathan drew closer.

Gloryanna's mother's finger was poised, ready to click and change the screen. He couldn't let her do that. He had to figure out what the deal was with this man. Spying her teacup, he summoned his gift and tipped it over, spilling newly warmed aromatic tea over the table and onto the floor.

"Oh, for heaven's sake." She jumped up and grabbed a towel, then quickly returned to sop up the mess. She took the dripping cloth to the sink and rinsed it out. Returning, she mopped up the last little bit, then once again rinsed the cloth. She hung it on the oven handle to dry. As she returned to her spot on the couch, she slowed down and stared at the cup, deep in thought. She stopped and glanced around the room. "Jonathan?"

"Yes, I'm here." She couldn't hear him. How could he let her know? Maybe . . . Once again, he tipped over the cup.

"You really are here." Her hand covered her mouth. "I wish I could see you." She glanced at her laptop. "Did I stumble onto something?"

How could he tell her yes? She hadn't righted the cup, so once again, using his gift, he set the cup upright.

She plopped down on the couch and froze.

Was she scared or relieved?

She slowly picked up her laptop and peered at the screen, reading about the man in the picture. "Do you recognize him?"

That was a good question. Jonathan stared at the photo. The name below read Sergeant Fumio Yokoi. The name meant nothing to Jonathan, but as he gazed at the man, he suddenly realized this soldier had been with the Germans Frank had helped. He had been with Gloryanna's grandfather.

The elderly woman at Frank's assisted living center had said that Professor Takahashi had visited once a month. What if Yokoi was the professor's father and Frank had helped him hide? That would give Takahashi a reason to visit his old partner. It wasn't a far leap. In fact, it made sense.

Gloryanna's grandfather had hidden among civilians, taking on a new identity and even marrying and having a family. Yokoi could very well have done the same thing, though he'd have had to find his way into a Japanese internment camp. What better way to disappear than to live among the enemy? If Yokoi was the professor's father, there was a chance she might know more about the submarine than anyone else.

That she'd visited Frank and moments later he'd coded made Jonathan even more suspicious of the woman. And then his mind raced to what had happened to Gloryanna. Though it would have taken a good disguise, Takahashi could have compromised the gas line to the stove. She could have cut Gloryanna's brakes, put poison in her drinking water, *and* she very well could have sabotaged Gloryanna's scuba tank.

But something still bothered him.

Gloryanna had mentioned that she'd told Takahashi about her grandfather's delusional ramblings regarding his serving on a submarine that sank. What if Takahashi knew about Hitler's gold being on board? She may have known the general vicinity where the sub had gone down but wasn't sure. She could have planned to have Thomas and Gloryanna help her find the sunken U-boat and then kill them afterward. She could have easily taken their remains and dumped them far away from the sub. But why? Why would she do such a thing? A crate of gold bars would be enticing, but the woman made good money as a professor. Something else must have motivated or threatened her.

Ralph was another suspect in this. He had tried to kill Thomas.

Was there a connection between Ralph and Takahashi?

Questions whirled around Jonathan, questions he wished he could talk to someone about. He was so close to finding answers. He felt they were right there, staring him in the face.

Gloryanna's mother moved the pointer on the screen and clicked on the words *Save As.* "I wonder if my father knows this man or, at least, what happened to him. If he's coherent in the morning, I'll ask him. But I must warn you"—she looked to the side of her and in back, having no idea where Jonathan could be but still acting like she knew he was near—"my father has good days and bad, as you're probably aware. And, Jonathan . . ." Tears welled up in her eyes. "I need to thank you for saving my little girl's life. Please, oh, please keep her safe tomorrow."

Jonathan's heart melted for this woman who had never believed in an afterlife but now embraced her new knowledge. He wanted her to know that he'd do everything in his power to protect not only Gloryanna, but all of them.

Could he try to type a reply? He should have done that before instead of dumping her tea on the table. Summoning his gift, he tapped the letter I. He hit the space bar and typed "will."

She stared at the screen as tears spilled down her cheeks. "Thank you."

CHAPTER TWENTY-FIVE

Gloryanna awakened early despite her late night. The morning sun streamed through her bedroom window, announcing that the rain from last evening had cleared out. Today, she would receive her undergraduate degree . . . and return to the ocean floor—by herself.

Danger would be twofold possible mercury poisoning and the vortex current. She'd be lying if she said she wasn't scared. She wished she could hand this burden to someone else. But Jonathan was right. No one in the Coast Guard or the EPA would take seriously her grandfather's claim of a sunken sub with possibly leaking mercury canisters without proof.

Even though she was putting her own life at risk, she couldn't stand by and do nothing. Everyone who went diving in that area would be exposed. And she didn't want anyone else in danger, so that meant she had to dive alone immediately, which increased the risks exponentially. But she'd take every precaution she could to stay safe. Preparation would be crucial. She'd better get a move on.

She crawled from under her covers to find Jonathan sitting in the armchair at the foot of her bed and Max waiting on his haunches beside him. "We thought you'd never wake up."

"What's going on?"

"First, let me tell you that your mother is amazing." Jonathan clasped his hands together.

"Thank you. I'll tell her you said that. So, what amazing thing did she do?"

"She found information about Japanese soldiers that is quite interesting." Anticipation showed in his eyes.

"Did she talk to you?" She hoped so.

"Yes." He explained how he'd communicated with her and that she'd learned about Yokoi and saved his picture. "So it's still a lot of conjecture that he might be Takahashi's father, but it's something."

"After last night, it doesn't seem far-fetched at all. I hate thinking the professor might have something to do with this. We still have other suspects, right?"

"Yes. But I'm wondering if there's an alliance between Ralph and Takahashi." He rubbed at his whiskery chin.

If that were the case, that would mean two people that she thought highly of had purposely deceived her. She wanted to scream and rant, but that would solve nothing, so instead, she reined in her emotions and put on her slippers. "Is Mom up?" She reached for her robe that lay at the foot of her bed.

"I think so. I heard noises coming from the kitchen, but I wanted to stay close to you to tell you everything I could as soon as you woke up."

"Takahashi will be at the graduation. I could ask her about Ralph there." She pulled on her robe.

"I doubt she'd outright tell you. If Yokoi was her father, she's changed her name and doesn't want people to know who he was. And she won't give up the truth easily. It would be best to ask her when you already know the answers."

Heading for the door, she stopped. "That doesn't make sense. Why ask if you already know the answer?" Sometimes Jonathan bewildered her. No, change that to most times he bewildered her. "How in the world am I going to find the answers without asking the questions?"

"By talking to Ralph first. We need to check into Skip and Minnie just in case they figure into this too." Jonathan's eyebrows rose.

She took several deep breaths. "I would need to go to the county jail to talk to Ralph. I highly doubt he'd be allowed visitors." She thought a moment. "But didn't Mom say Ralph might get out on bail?" She needed to fully wake up. "Let me go slap some water on my face and comb my hair. Be right back." She took off.

As she refreshed herself, she tried to think what to do. First, she'd go to the Fish Tail to see if, by chance, Ralph was there.

On her way back to her bedroom, she passed Grandpa's door. After everything he'd told them last night, she wondered if he knew about Professor Takahashi and who her father was. And if he knew, there was a slim chance he might know if there was a connection between Ralph and the professor. That would save Gloryanna from having to face Ralph yet again, and it would save precious time.

She listened at his door and heard her mother talking. Gloryanna gave a light tap and went in.

"Oh, sweetheart." Her mother smiled at her as she took the breakfast tray from Grandpa's bed. "You look much better this morning."

"Starbuck! We need to go whaling on the *Pequod* today. Might catch a glimpse of the great whale." Grandpa smiled at her. His mind had slipped into dementia and blended his life with Captain Ahab's. Obviously, his confession last night had overtaxed his mind. He would be no help in finding out more regarding Ralph or Takahashi.

"Sorry, Dad. But *Gloryanna*"—her mother emphasized her name—"has graduation today, remember?"

Grandpa thought a moment. His eyes stared blankly ahead as he fought with his memory.

"It's okay. We'll go another time." Gloryanna kissed his forehead, then followed her mother, who carried the tray out of the room.

"He's worse today." Her mother headed down the hallway. "I think he should stay home."

Gloryanna trailed her downstairs. "Jonathan told me that last night you found something." She should have stopped at her bedroom and told him she was going down with her mother, but maybe he was already there.

"Yes, I did. I couldn't find anything on the U-boat, but there was a ton about Japanese soldiers after the war. Did Jonathan tell you about the one guy we found?" Her mother placed the dirty dishes in the sink and wiped off the serving tray before returning it to the rack.

"A little." No sign of Jonathan in the kitchen. About to return and get him, Gloryanna noticed a package on the counter with her name on it. She glanced at the return address. Nikon. "Good, the camera I ordered for Ralph is here. I paid for express mail but never dreamed it would be that fast."

Her mother drummed her fingers on the countertop.

Gloryanna's stomach growled. "By the way, Jonathan thinks you're amazing. I should run up and get him, but first, I'll get some waffles cooking." Gloryanna grabbed a couple from the freezer and dropped them into the toaster.

Jonathan and Max came downstairs. "So, this is where you got off to?"

"Sorry. Mom and I were talking, and before I knew it, we were in the kitchen." Gloryanna pointed to the camera. "Look what came."

"Jonathan is here?" Her mother glanced around as she loaded dirty dishes into the dishwasher.

"He is." Gloryanna motioned for him to sit in the nook. Her waffles popped up. She retrieved them, slathered them with maple syrup, and slid into the booth. In between bites, she told her mother what Jonathan had told her and what he suspected about the professor.

Her mother sat on the bench across from them. "Oh my stars! Tell him I knew the picture of Yokoi was important."

Jonathan smiled and nodded.

"He knows, Mom. He can hear you just fine."

"And he thinks your Professor Takahashi could be that Sergeant Yokoi's daughter?"

Gloryanna bobbed her head. "Not only that but because Ralph shot Thomas, Jonathan also thinks that, somehow, Takahashi and Ralph have some kind of connection."

He gave a nod that she was right on target.

"Oh, I almost forgot." Her mother placed a hand to her chest. "On this morning's news, they said the judge set Ralph's bail. They released him."

"Good," Gloryanna said. "I guess I'd better talk to him before I see the professor." She glanced at the clock on the wall. 830. "I need to shower, get dressed, and get my gear ready for this afternoon's dive before heading to the university." She started for the stairs. "Can I take your car again, Mom?"

"Yes. But don't you think we should call the police to let them know what's going on?" She crossed the distance to her daughter, took her hand, and smoothed a wild curl behind Gloryanna's ear.

Jonathan stayed in the booth, watching the mother-daughter scene.

"Not yet. We need proof of what Grandpa told us." She took a resolute breath. "And if I find it, we should probably get a lawyer for him."

"Why?" Her mother stepped back.

"What do you think they'll do to Grandpa?" She hated to be blunt, but they needed to face reality. "I've heard of some German soldiers who were found years after the war being sent to prison. I don't think we want Grandpa's last days spent there."

"No, we don't. That U-boat has been down there all this time. Maybe we should leave well enough alone, at least until . . ." Her mother didn't finish. She didn't need to.

As much as she hated to say it, Gloryanna finished her mother's thought. "Until Grandpa dies? We can't." But she also couldn't tell her mother about the gold or the mercury. Instead, she said, "Grandpa told me last night that he wanted the truth to come out. I want to honor that and find proof." She looked at the package. "And luckily, I'll have a camera with me. We'll discuss getting the police involved if and when I find some evidence."

Her mother took a deep breath. "I'll keep you in my prayers."

"Mom?" She gaped at her mother, surprised by what she'd said.

"Well . . ." Her mother dipped her head. "After everything that's been going on, I can't ignore that there's something to all this religious stuff. Especially now that I know Jonathan."

He left the nook and came to stand beside her mother, like he was grateful that she believed in him.

Gloryanna put her arm around her mom.

Her mother kissed her cheek, then stepped away. "After your grandfather's ramblings this morning, I think I should give him another dose of Donepezil. If it clears his mind, he still might be able to attend your graduation."

"I hope it does the trick." Gloryanna nearly flew up the stairs as she thought about the many questions she wanted to ask Ralph.

***

Jonathan watched Gloryanna arrange the scuba things in the back of her mother's SUV, going over her list of primary gear. She checked off BCD, weights, releases, air, and camera. She also went over the redundancy equipment, extra air tank, regulator, and masks. Packing a folding wagon to haul the gear to the boat, she closed the hatch. "I think that's it. I even wrote up my dive plan. I'll give it to Mom before we leave, just in case."

She seemed to have thought of everything, but he wanted to make sure. "Did you remember the key to the boat?"

She checked inside her cross-body bag and pulled out the anchor key chain. "I think I'm ready to shove off." She dropped the key back inside her purse.

About to get in the driver's side, she stopped as her mother entered the garage. "Honey, your grandfather wanted me to tell you something." She paused and shook her head. "It doesn't make sense. And I don't know why, but I promised him I would tell you."

"What is it, Mom?"

Her mother took a deep breath. "He said to tell you not to save Pip, or the whale will get away. Whatever that means."

Jonathan had read Moby Dick many times. Pip was the cabin boy who had become tangled in fishing line and had to be cut out. Upon saving Pip, Moby Dick got away. Maybe the old man was more coherent than they thought. His confused mind had somehow sent Gloryanna a warning of what could happen, though Jonathan wondered if the old man thought Jonathan was Pip. He hoped not.

She turned to him. "Do you know what he could mean by that?"

"It's probably his way of telling you to be careful." Jonathan didn't want to frighten her by relaying the story.

Giving her mom a hug, she said, "Tell him I won't let the whale get away." Then Gloryanna got in the vehicle.

Her mother motioned for her to roll down the window. She peered past Gloryanna and looked at the passenger seat. "Jonathan, please take care of her."

"Tell her I plan to." He wished he could tell her himself.

"He said he will." Gloryanna pulled an envelope from her purse and handed it to her mother. "It's my dive plan. You need to know where I'll be."

Her mother's forehead furrowed, and worry framed her eyes.

"Mom, I'll be fine. I've been trained for solo dives."

"I know, sweetheart. A mother can't help but worry." She kissed her daughter on the cheek and then stepped back.

Gloryanna pressed the ignition button and pulled out.

The drive to the Fish Tail was quiet. Jonathan understood. Gloryanna had a lot on her mind. The most important thought right now had to be what to ask Ralph, Skip, and Minnie. But on top of that would be her grandfather's confused warning. Hopefully, she'd let that go.

She pulled up to the café/scuba-supply shop and shut off the engine. She turned in her seat to face Jonathan. "I don't see Ralph's van. Maybe I can talk with Skip and Minnie before he gets here."

"That would be good, especially without their boss around."

"Let's do this." She got out and brushed a stray hair from her skirt.

Jonathan and Max left the vehicle. There was no way he was letting her leave his sight for one minute.

In all the flurry of getting ready, Jonathan hadn't taken in how drop-dead gorgeous Gloryanna was. Dressed in a navy-blue dress that hung to her ankles, she looked stunning. The material had swirls of silver and light-blue flowers on it. Her curly hair draped over her shoulders and trellised down her back. "They'll be speechless when you walk in."

"I hope not." A smile lit her oval face. She hurried to the back door and went inside with Jonathan and Max.

Jonathan glanced around at the messy storage area. How did Ralph keep track of his merchandise? He trailed her as she passed the office to the scuba store. On one side was all the gear, and on the other side was the café.

A short and squat woman was in the process of taking chairs off the tables and preparing to open the café. She stopped. "Gloryanna! You're stunning! How are you?"

By the tone in her voice, Jonathan could tell that Minnie thought a lot of her coworker.

Skip, smoking a cigarette behind the counter, quickly snubbed it out in the ashtray and attempted to wave away the smoke.

"I'm better. Thanks for asking, Minnie." Gloryanna smiled.

"Ralph isn't here yet," Skip said as he moved the ashtray behind the counter where it couldn't be seen.

"That's okay. I wanted to talk to both of you."

Minnie guided Gloryanna over to a table she'd cleared. "What do you want to know?"

"If it's about your work schedule, we leave that up to Ralph." Skip came around the counter and plopped into a chair adjacent to them.

"No. It's not that." Gloryanna sat on a chair close to Minnie.

Jonathan stood across from Skip, watching his every move. Max sniffed at the merchandise and then came to join him.

Gloryanna focused on Skip. "Ralph said you filled my tank before the dive a few days ago."

He huffed and shook his head. "That again. Yes, I did. And like I told him, I filled it to 2440, just like you want us to. I checked the lines, and they were all working. If something happened to your tank, it happened after you left here."

Gloryanna glanced at Jonathan as though she were hoping that he could tell if the man was lying.

Jonathan wished he could. He didn't care for the guy. His cocky attitude bothered him, but some people were just like that.

"You know," Minnie piped up, "I stay away from all the scuba do-dahs. My only concern is the grill." Her face lit up. "Oh, it's cherry Danish day. I'll get one for you." Without waiting, she hurried away.

"Now that Minnie is gone, ask Skip some harder questions." Jonathan stared at the man, hopeful to see a crack in his tough-guy veneer.

She gazed at her lanky coworker. "So, Skip, I can't remember, but did you help load our gear into the professor's van before we left?"

"Yes. I think you were talking with Minnie." He crossed his ankle over his knee. "Thomas helped too. In fact, he was in the vehicle, and I handed them to him so he could place them in the back."

"Was the professor with you?"

"If I remember right, she and Ralph were arguing over something in his office." He coughed into his hand.

"Question him about that." Jonathan wished he could help her out more.

"They were arguing?" Gloryanna acted like that was news to her. Good.

"Yeah." He nodded. "Whenever she stops by, there's a row of some kind. I just thought since her students were with her, they wouldn't go at it."

"I can't believe I didn't know she came by that often." Confusion floated over Gloryanna's face.

"She usually comes on your days off. They had a major blowup the day you were found."

Minnie returned with a white pastry bag. "I thought you'd want to take it with you. You're graduating today, right?"

Gloryanna nodded and gratefully took the treat.

The back door slammed shut.

"Sounds like the boss has arrived." Skip got up. "You want me to tell him you're here?"

Gloryanna stood. "No, I can. It was good to talk to you both. Sorry I haven't worked more."

"No problem." Minnie glanced at Skip, then she said, "We understand."

He gave a reluctant nod.

Jonathan was tempted to stay behind to see what the two would talk about once Gloryanna left the room, but he also wanted to be with her when she spoke with Ralph. He really didn't think either one did anything to Gloryanna's tank. But that left the professor and Ralph as the main suspects. Possibly Thomas too.

He trailed her to the office in the supply room.

Gloryanna inhaled a deep breath, looking at Jonathan like she wanted to talk but couldn't.

He gave her a thumbs-up.

She knocked on the door.

"Come in," came a growl.

Gloryanna opened the door a crack and poked only her head in. "Can I talk to you?"

"Of course!" The man's deep voice sounded friendly enough.

She opened the door more, and Jonathan got his first in-person view of the man named Ralph. He was dressed in beach garb and looked heavier than he had on the TV.

She went into the office.

Ralph shot to his feet. "What are you all dolled up for?"

"Graduation."

"Oh, that's right." He sank back into a squeaky swivel chair behind his desk.

The man reminded Jonathan of Frank. All at once, he wondered if Ralph could be Frank's son. If Yokoi was indeed Takahashi's father, he could have introduced his daughter to Frank and Ralph.

A lot of "ifs." But stranger things had happened.

"I forgot. What's Ralph's last name?" Jonathan asked Gloryanna, despite knowing that she was in a tough spot to answer him.

"Why, Ralph Wagner, aren't you going to my graduation?" She'd done that perfectly.

But there went Jonathan's theory. Frank's last name was Becker. However, maybe Ralph used a different name.

"I don't think it's a good idea for me to attend after what happened between Thomas and me." He stroked the top of his head.

Gloryanna eased down on the folding chair in front of his desk. "Mind telling me why you shot him?"

"I think my lawyer would tell me not to." Ralph shrugged. "She told me to avoid you at all costs."

Gloryanna's face pinched. "Why?"

"Afraid I might say something that would make matters worse. But I want you to hear it from me. After your visit the other day, I asked Skip about your tank. He promised that he'd checked it over. I started blaming myself for not seeing to it personally. I'm ashamed to say it, but I got drunk. Haven't had booze for quite some time. And the more I thought about you nearly drowning and walking through the forest by yourself, the more I knew Thomas did something to your tank. Skip had helped Thomas load it in the professor's van. Knowing that with his rich father they could pay to cover up the truth, I snapped. I decided to confront Thomas and make him fess up." Ralph gave a curt nod.

"This is a good time to ask about the professor," Jonathan said. He didn't know if she'd heard him or not.

"Skip said that before the dive, you and Professor Takahashi were arguing." Gloryanna's eyes never left Ralph. Jonathan couldn't have been prouder, especially since he knew how much she revered this man.

Ralph jerked back in his seat. "Skip said that?"

"Yes." Gloryanna stared at him.

Ralph rolled his eyes. "Okay. I wanted her to pay her bill." He shuffled papers on his desk like he was looking for an invoice. "The woman has run up quite a tab. I swear, she dives more than a seal."

"Doesn't the university pay for it?" Gloryanna asked.

"Yeah, but not for her personal dives." He leaned back in his chair and scrubbed a hand over his face. "She's been searching for something for years. Even takes a Geiger counter with her."

Without thinking, Jonathan asked Gloryanna, "Did she take it on your dive?"

"She didn't take one the last time we went out." She was getting good at answering him by seamlessly slipping her answers into the conversation. "What do you think she was looking for?"

Ralph thought a moment, then shrugged. "I don't know, and I don't care. I just want her to pay her stupid bill. I'm not running a charity here."

Gloryanna glanced at the clock. "I better get going. By the way, I've ordered you a new camera. Again, I'm so sorry for losing yours. I know how much it meant to you."

"You shouldn't have done that," he scoffed.

"Yes, I should have." She held the sack Minnie had given her and started for the door.

"Let me walk you out." Ralph escorted her to her car.

Jonathan and Max brought up the rear and got in.

Once Gloryanna started the vehicle and pulled away, she said, "Do you believe that?"

"The woman had to have been searching for the U-boat. And that's why she visited Frank. She thought he knew. She sent you and Thomas on that dive to look for it." Jonathan could hardly stand it. They were so close to learning the truth.

"But if that is the case, why did she try to kill me?" Gloryanna glanced at him, then returned her eyes to the road.

"Because you told her that your grandfather told you about a sunken submarine. He was no threat, but you were. You're a diver. And what better way to cover up the murder than to have you die while diving? If Hitler's gold is on that ship, that's high motivation to get rid of someone who might want a cut of the money once it's found." Jonathan felt confident about that. But pieces were still missing. "And didn't you say she and Thomas were studying coral when you went off on your own?"

"Yes." Her teeth worried her bottom lip.

A new disturbing thought rippled through him. Jonathan drew a deep breath. "I hate to say this, but what if Thomas is in on it with her?"

CHAPTER TWENTY-SIX

GLORYANNA DIDN'T KNOW WHAT TO say about Jonathan's new theory that Takahashi and Thomas may have been working together. She thought they had crossed Thomas off the suspect list, but now he was solidly back on it. The possibility of the two working together against her made her angry and sick at the same time. She drove to the university stadium without saying anything, trying to digest the gravity of her situation.

The caps and gowns were in the locker room, so Jonathan and Max waited patiently at the door while she quickly found her gown size and slipped it on. The staff gave her the cap as she exited onto the playing field.

The Astroturf was filled with rows of folding chairs, where the graduating class would start their long walk up to the podium to receive their diplomas.

The previous evening's rainstorm had not made them change venues. Eager to have this over with and grateful to have Jonathan with her, Gloryanna scanned the sea of students.

"Wow. There's a lot of people here," Jonathan said.

Speaking softly so that no one close would hear, she said, "That's why they hold it in the football stadium, so families can come and celebrate with those graduating. In fact, do you see Mom and Dad?"

She skimmed over the people in the stands, trying to find her family, but all the faces blurred together.

"Ah. They're on the front row on the other side." Jonathan pointed them out.

Gloryanna's heart warmed. There they were Mom, Dad, and even Grandpa. He was in his wheelchair, his legs covered with a throw, but he was here. She waved to them.

They waved back.

"They're very proud of you." He had a loneliness in his voice mixed with a touch of envy as he followed her to her assigned seat.

"I'm proud of them too." Luckily, she was on the end with no chair on her right side.

Jonathan settled on the ground, and Max lay at her feet.

"Fancy meeting you here." Thomas eased into the seat on her left, his arm in a sling.

Startled, a frisson flashed over Gloryanna's skin as she spat out, "What in the world are you doing? You should be in the hospital. Did you sneak out?" He was the last person she wanted to be sitting beside her. Not only did she not trust him, but she also couldn't imagine that his doctor approved. She wasn't ready to have him near her. Last night, she'd thought he was on her side, but now . . . What if Jonathan was right and Takahashi and Thomas were working together?

"You didn't call to let me know what happened. And I might add that you are as bad as my mother." He leaned a little to one side and winced.

Trying her best to ratchet down her fear, she said, "So, your parents know you're here?" She scanned the stands, trying to see them.

"Don't you remember?" Jonathan drew her attention. "His parents stopped by his apartment to grab his suit."

That's right. She gave a slight nod.

"My parents are the ones who brought me. I'm too drugged up to drive. I wasn't about to let a little bullet keep me away from graduation. I've worked four long years for this." Thomas grimaced a bit. "Besides, I needed to speak with you."

"I'll just bet he does," Jonathan said.

She didn't look at him, wanting him to be quiet so she could take care of Thomas as soon as she could and get him on his way. "I own a cell phone. You could have called."

"And miss seeing the shock on your face?" He chuckled a little and then held his shoulder. "Nah, it was worth the pain. Besides, I promised the doctor I'd check back with her after the ceremony."

"What's so important that you're willing to sit on these torturous folding chairs for a couple of hours?" She tried to hurry him along.

"After you left last night, I started wondering about the grant that Professor Takahashi told us about. Remember, she said it was so new that they hadn't posted it yet? She seemed awfully anxious for us to go on that dive."

The subject of the grant caught Gloryanna off guard. "What do you mean?"

"Well, from the very beginning I was a bit skeptical about either one of us being able to write a paper that would be accepted in a scientific magazine.

I mean, even professionals have a hard time publishing. It takes years. But when she said she'd help us, I thought maybe she had connections."

A group of graduates scooted by to sit in the empty seats on the other side of them. All except one, a skinny guy with black-rimmed glasses and greasy hair. He stood in front of Thomas, staring at him.

"Can I help you?" Thomas glared.

"You're in my seat." He pressed his glasses up on the bridge of his nose. "They sat us alphabetically."

"They only do that so we're in order to receive our diplomas on the podium. They'll call the entire section to line up when it's our turn. You can get in order then. Dude, I'm not budging."

The guy frowned like he was going to grab someone and make Thomas move.

Ordinarily, Gloryanna would have let him, but she needed to hear what Thomas had to say. "Look, he was shot yesterday and really shouldn't even be here. Could you cut him some slack?" She smiled at the guy who only wanted to do things the right way. She added, "I promise I'll make him go where he's supposed to when they call our section."

"Where are you supposed to sit?" he asked Thomas.

"With the C group. My last name is Clifford."

Again, the greasy-haired guy pressed his finger to his glasses. "As in Clifford Hall, Clifford?"

"Yep." Thomas nodded.

The guy's eyes grew as wide as his glasses frames. "Sure. No problem." He hurried away.

"Nothing like having a wealthy father." Gloryanna leaned closer to Thomas. "What did you find out about the grant?"

"There is no Pacific Biological Oceanography grant." He bit his lips together and shook his head.

"Why would she make something like that up?" Gloryanna rubbed the side of her head, feeling a headache coming on. "She had to know that we'd eventually find out."

"Not if you were dead and Thomas was in on it." Jonathan injected himself into the conversation.

"But why would he tell me about the grant if he were?" Though grateful for Jonathan's input, she hoped he was wrong.

"Keep pressing him," Jonathan said.

"Who are you talking to?" Thomas stared at her.

"You. " She tried to think how she could get Thomas to slip up. "Takahashi must have been the one who did something to my tank. But why?"

"Good. You're on the right track." Jonathan sounded as anxious as she felt. "Bring up the gold and see how he reacts."

She turned and looked at Jonathan. "I don't know which is more important, the gold or the mercury."

"Gold? Mercury? What are you talking about?" Thomas gave her a wide-eyed stare.

Had she said that out loud?

"Wait a minute." Thomas glanced to the other side of Gloryanna. "Are you talking to that Jonathan ghost guy again?"

She really didn't want to get into it. She'd already said too much. Several teachers, the dean, and even Professor Takahashi had walked onto the dais. They were getting ready to start. She stared at Takahashi. How could that woman go on like everything was normal? How could she put on such a show? And how could Thomas conspire with her against Gloryanna?

She stole a calming breath and leaned close to Thomas. "I can't explain right now."

"But you will later?"

In that moment, Gloryanna saw true concern in his brown eyes. He really did care about her, maybe even loved her in his own way. But love made people do strange things, like kill the person they're supposed to love. She forced a smile to her lips. "I will."

Jonathan scooted closer to her. "This shores up my theory that Frank was paid with a gold bar."

Jonathan was right. Had his other theories been right as well?

The dean got up and went to the mic. "Welcome to the graduation of the Class of 2023."

Everyone applauded.

Gloryanna tuned out what the dean was saying. Her mind stuck on Jonathan's theory. Anger pulsed through her. She thought about how Takahashi had acted like Gloryanna was her favorite, and all along, she was using her, trying to find out what her grandfather remembered.

She glanced at Thomas. And Takahashi may have used him too. Gloryanna hoped so. She didn't want to think Thomas was so evil as to feign feelings for her while at the same time plotting to kill her.

Thomas caught her gaze. "Are you okay?"

"No." She stared down at her lap, not wanting to see him, not wanting to look at Jonathan, and trying her best to sit there like nothing was wrong. But she couldn't keep it all in. Leaning close to Jonathan, she softly said, "But why, after I turned up missing, why didn't she kill Thomas when he told her that he'd seen the conning tower?"

Jonathan folded his arms and gave her a thoughtful look. "Because he already knew. You're going in circles. But I'm also wondering if she did a double-cross on Thomas and sent Ralph to kill him."

"That makes sense," she said out loud.

"People are staring at us." Thomas nudged her with his elbow. He must think she'd lost her mind.

She smiled at those around them and tried to listen to the dean as he introduced their commencement speaker. She whispered to Thomas, "I really need to know, Were you in on this with Takahashi?"

"No." Thomas's eyebrows rose, and he looked offended. "Why?"

"Because if you were, she may have sent Ralph to kill you."

He reared back. "What?" He glared at her like she was insane.

People shushed them.

Gloryanna leaned into Thomas. "She was doing what all villains do kill-ing those who might know too much."

Thomas sat there. Was he dumbfounded to have been found out or shocked by Gloryanna's accusations?

If what she and Jonathan suspected about Takahashi was true, the woman was truly diabolical. What would stop her from not only killing Gloryanna but also her entire family to ensure that no one learned about the U-boat or the gold or the mercury? That was why she'd done something to the gas stove at Gloryanna's parents' house, to kill them all.

Gloryanna had to do everything she could to stop her.

CHAPTER TWENTY-SEVEN

GRADUATION WAS A BLUR AS Gloryanna wrestled with what she believed were Takahashi's motives and the fact that Thomas may have been her accomplice and was sitting right next to her. She needed proof, and that was exactly what she planned to get.

She barely remembered walking onto the stage and accepting the cylinder that symbolized her degree—the real thing would be mailed to her—but she felt Takahashi's eyes on her the entire time.

Did the woman know her master plan was about to be uncovered? Had she seen Thomas and Gloryanna talking during the speeches and put two and two together to realize they were finally on to her? She certainly had no clue that Gloryanna was going to the dive site to expose the truth this very day, unless Thomas had told her.

Walking down the steps from the dais, Gloryanna found Thomas waiting for her, along with Jonathan and Max. She walked past all three.

Thomas caught up. "Are you still planning to dive?"

"You'd better believe it. And don't you dare tell Takahashi." Gloryanna prayed he was on her side.

"I won't. I'm coming with you." Thomas stood in front of her, his arm in a sling and pain creasing his face. His pills must have worn off.

"You can't dive!" she said.

"No, but I can drive the boat." He looked past her. "I see my parents coming. I'll get rid of them. Just wait here." He took off.

"Wow, I didn't think he had it in him." Jonathan sounded surprised.

She let his remark go and watched as Thomas's parents gave him a hug. "I'm not waiting. He can't come. He's still recovering. And besides, I'm not sure I can trust him."

Knowing Jonathan and Max were with her, she raced to her mother's SUV, where she checked the time on the dash. "It's two thirty. The drive to the harbor will take a good hour. Then I need to load the gear into the boat."

Jonathan saluted her. "Max and I will help. We're your crew."

"I think you should reserve your strength for the dive. I might need you, and if you're too weak to help me—"

"Don't worry. I'll be ready." He sounded sure of himself, which gave her great comfort.

"Getting to the site on the boat will take some time, but I'm fairly certain I know the longitude and latitude of where it is. As soon as I get in the water and gain my bearings, I know I'll be able to find the shipwreck."

"Just stay aware of the vortex current," Jonathan added.

"Don't worry. I learned my lesson. And this time, I've brought two ties for the new camera. This one isn't getting away from me." Her words sounded more confident than she felt.

***

Jonathan clutched the armrest on the door as Gloryanna weaved in and out of traffic. Just when he thought she would run into the bumper of the car ahead of them, she'd switch lanes and step on the gas. He'd never ridden in a car that traveled so fast. Several times, he'd put his foot down as if to apply the brakes, but it did no good. "You should have been a race car driver."

"Sorry." She shrugged as she passed yet another car. "We don't have a lot of time. Besides, I'm not bad. You should ride with my father."

Jonathan glanced in the back seat, where Max lay. The German shepherd had his head down, not watching out the window like he usually did.

Just as Jonathan was getting used to Gloryanna's driving, they reached the harbor. "I'd kiss the ground, but I was never in danger, was I?"

"Seeing as you're already dead, no, I don't think so." She parked and grabbed her purse. "The scary part is ahead of us." She took a deep breath, then got out, rushing to the rear of the vehicle.

By the time Jonathan and Max joined her, she had unloaded the collapsible wagon and opened it.

A few people walked down the dock. "I could levitate your gear, but they might see," Jonathan said, tilting his head toward them.

"I'm fine." She kept working. "Really. I've done this a lot. And like I said, you need to save your strength for the dive."

It didn't take as much time as he thought it would. Soon, Jonathan and Max followed Gloryanna as she wheeled the wagon full of equipment onto the bobbing dock and came to the chain-link gate that kept the public away from the boats. Using Thomas's keys, she opened the lock and pulled the wagon through.

The gate closed behind them with a bang, and they continued down the dock until they reached the slip where Thomas's father's Bertram 35 Flybridge was moored.

"This is it." Gloryanna loaded the tanks and scuba gear into the stern. Once done, she collapsed the wagon and stored it. Then she grabbed her long fleece underwear and Thomas's dry suit from a bag and said, "I'm going to change while we're in dock. Once we arrive at the location, I don't want to struggle putting the suit on. Fortunately, Thomas's suit is a little too big. I'll have more flexibility and can get my hands and feet to pass through more easily." She disappeared down into the sleeping berth and closed the door.

Jonathan settled on a blue-and-white-striped cushioned seat in the stern. This vessel was mighty impressive three levels and gleaming like a shiny jewel. He'd often admired these kinds of boats from the shore and wondered what they were like up close.

Max let out a loud bark as he stared at the marina.

"What is it, old boy?" Jonathan tried to see what had his dog concerned. His gaze stopped on Professor Takahashi's black Jaguar pulling into the parking lot.

He moved closer to the door Gloryanna had disappeared behind. "We're going to have company. I think you'd better come up here."

She burst out of the berth. She had on long black underwear, but only half the dry suit; the top half hung from her waist. "Who?"

Jonathan pointed to the professor, who was now out of her car.

"I wonder if Thomas told her. That's the only way she would have known."

"Or she followed you when you left the dais. But she couldn't have kept up with you." Flashes of their ride to the bay raced through his mind.

"All she had to do was follow us to the freeway and she'd know exactly where I was going. I hope that's what happened and that Thomas didn't betray us." Gloryanna disappeared back into the interior of the boat, then came racing out, the key in her hand. "Can you untie the boat and pull in the buoys?"

She didn't wait for him to answer but scurried up the ladder to the upper deck.

Without questioning her, Jonathan focused on both the front and rear cleats, untying the ropes at the same time with his mind. The riggings floated in the air, looping together and drifting to the storage bin.

The engines roared to life as he levitated the plastic foam floats that kept the boat from bumping into the berth. Water rippled from them as he brought them onboard, and he used his mind to keep the boat from bumping against the dock. He quickly glanced back to see where Takahashi was.

The woman had wheeled her gear onto the wharf and was heading for them. How had she gotten through the gate?

It didn't matter, because she was heading their way.

"Hurry!" he yelled at Gloryanna, dividing his attention between keeping the boat away from the dock and watching the professor.

The boat slowly motored from the marina and floated into the channel that led to the open seas.

"Come back!" Takahashi yelled. She'd reached the slip where they'd been docked.

Jonathan glanced up at Gloryanna steering the vessel from the second level. Gloryanna paid the professor no mind. Once they were safely out of the harbor, she opened the throttle, and the ship sped over the water.

Jonathan and Max went to the upper deck. "That was close," he yelled to be heard over the engines.

"Too close." She held on to the steering wheel as the boat bumped and cut through the waves. "I'm just worried she might hire someone to bring her out to the site." Gloryanna stole a look at him. "You've faded a bit."

"I know. That's why I'm here with you." He sat in the seat next to hers. "How long until we reach our destination?"

"Twenty minutes to a half hour." She checked the gauges near the wheel, then looked to the stern and back again.

"Max alerted me that she'd arrived."

"Thanks, Max." She gave the dog an appreciative smile. "I wish I could pet him."

"I'll do it for you." Jonathan patted the animal and gave him a good rub.

Wind pulled at Gloryanna's wild hair, and a mist of sea water covered her face. She tightly gripped the wheel. "As we walked down the dock, I noticed there were several boats for hire. I don't think we'll have much time until she's on us again." She kept her focus ahead on the open water.

"It's late though. She might not be that lucky." Jonathan hated to give Gloryanna false hope, but he didn't want to tell her that he agreed. Such words would not be helpful and would only add to her stress. She needed to remain focused on what lay ahead of them and not worry about that woman.

"I hope you're right. But she's very determined. Remember what she did to Frank." Gloryanna said it like she knew Takahashi had killed Jonathan's old partner . . . and had also tried to kill her. "I've been thinking about the vortex current the shipwreck is under."

"Yes?" He waited, anxious to hear what she had to say.

"It's been there for years. That's probably why the U-boat was never discovered until now. It's like the whirlpool has been protecting it."

Jonathan inclined his head. That made sense.

She looked at him. "Do you think the vortex current has anything to do with you?"

Taken by surprise, Jonathan didn't know what to say.

"You saved me from the current, like you've saved other people, but what if . . ." She bit at her lip.

"What?" he asked.

"What if, like the vortex current, you and Max have been the guardians of the shipwreck?"

He thought a moment. "I've saved a lot of people from that current over the years."

"Yes, but none of them saw you until I came along." The wind whipped her hair behind her. She squinted at him. "Jonathan, as I fought for air on that dive in the vortex, I saw flashes of you. It happened fast, and then I passed out. But when I came to on the beach and you were standing there, it was weird, and I didn't understand. I've thought about it, though, and at first, I believed that maybe the glimpses of you were to comfort me. Now, however, I think the vortex was sending me to you."

The vision he'd had of her as he'd lain dying on the rocks came to him. Could she be right? Could it be that all this time he and Max had been stuck here in limbo, they had been connected to the U-boat and the current and were waiting for Gloryanna to find them? "You might be onto something."

"Jonathan, we were meant to meet so we could save the ocean." She fought back emotion as the truth she'd just spoken obviously touched her.

He gazed into her beautiful brown eyes with flecks of copper. Warmth and love filled his being even though he was scared to his core. Yes, just as he'd thought, their paths had been meant to cross. Perhaps because her grandfather had been present when Jonathan and Max had died, it had somehow sealed their fates. What was supposed to happen now? He would save her, she would save him, and the truth would be told. All of that needed to be done to expose the danger that lurked at the bottom of the sea. He knew that the treasure meant nothing to Gloryanna compared to saving her beautiful Pacific.

A love deep and powerful swelled within him. In many ways, he'd spent decades fighting the war, continually trying to keep the beach safe, but now, all he wanted was to fight with all his might to save the woman he loved. He prayed he'd be successful. That whatever power had set up this circumstance would see them through.

CHAPTER TWENTY-EIGHT

GLORYANNA CHECKED HER PRIMARY AND redundancy gear, making sure her bases were covered. She'd mounted her backup air supply tank to her main tank and pulled the yellow tubing in front, attaching it to the diving necklace. After her last dive, she wanted to make sure she'd have enough air to reach the surface should anything happen. Her objectives were to find the shipwreck, discover its identity, and, if possible, locate the mercury tanks and gold. That shouldn't take too long. She quickly calculated her surface air consumption rate because it was tank specific, then she divided it into thirds. One third to get where she was going, one third to get back to the boat, and one third that she always left in the tank.

She tied the new camera to her wrist twice, like she'd planned. She also secured a light to her wrist and made sure she had many submersible lights in her diving pouch. She sat on the boat's edge and pulled fins over her booties.

Jonathan stood in front of her. She knew he was anxious. She couldn't blame him. He'd never tried diving before.

"Are you ready?" she asked.

"Don't we need some kind of hand signals?" His dark eyes peered into hers. "I'm a ghost, not a mind reader."

She should have thought of that. "You're right. Okay, I'll give you the basics." She made a circle with her thumb and index finger and had the other three fingers sticking straight up. "This means 'okay.'" She made a fist with one hand. "If I move my fist up and down, it means I need help."

The boat rocked back and forth, making her very aware that every second was precious. She thought of another important signal. "A fist straight out means danger."

Max barked and growled.

Gloryanna looked in the direction the dog faced. A boat headed toward them. "Looks like Takahashi found a ride. We don't have time for anything else." She quickly secured the dry suit around her neck, arms, and legs. She'd already twisted her hair into a knot, so she pulled the hood over her head, then spit into her mask and spread the saliva around. She tugged the mask on, shoved her hands into diving gloves, put the regulator in her mouth, and fell backward into the ocean.

The whoosh of water wrapping around her had always been comforting before, but not this time. For one frenzied moment, she wanted to swim back to the surface. She hadn't been in the ocean's embrace since she'd almost drowned. Pushing past the panic and slowing her breathing, she turned on the light attached to her wrist and adjusted her regulator, trying to calm her nerves. Bubbles burst out at first, then fell into a familiar rhythm. She went over her mantra Plan your dive and dive your plan. She waited for Jonathan. Would he merely appear? Or dive in? She didn't quite know what to expect.

She adjusted her weights and checked her BCD. Then she turned, and there was Jonathan, in the water. He looked just like he did on land. The water hardly affected his outward appearance. But his hair waved in the water. He smiled and gave the okay signal.

Grateful that he'd be with her, she gave him the thumbs-down and started her descent, kicking her fins. She swam over unfamiliar, barren rock formations. Had she gone to the right place? She glanced at the compass on her wrist. She was off course. She motioned for Jonathan to follow her and turned a bit to the left.

Finally, she came to the swaying green sea kelp she'd found on the other dive. The pull of the current grew more intense. She adjusted her weights and continued. Soon, she came to the glove sponges among sea cucumbers. This was very close to the same spot.

She spied the dark-purple and vermilion sea anemones. Their colors had dulled even more than what they had been last time. Something was very wrong.

The vortex current dragged her. She adjusted her weights yet again. The wild whirlpool had grown larger, its tentacles reaching for her. Trying her best to remain calm, she stared through the turbulent waters and saw the conning tower on the ocean floor. She needed to somehow dive under the furious whirlpool.

She gave Jonathan the thumbs-down signal.

He looked at the revolving vortex, then back to her, and frantically shook his head.

But she knew what she needed to do. There was no way she could go around the current. And she could only go a hundred feet down before she'd run into trouble. She glanced at her gauge. She was at fifty.

If she didn't try, she'd always regret it. Without waiting for Jonathan, she descended deeper.

The current tugged at her. She kicked harder and harder, glancing between her depth gauge and the wreckage. Finally, she had descended far enough that the vortex's pull eased and she was able to swim toward the conning tower. A massive darkness lurked beneath. As she neared, she shined her diving light at the shadow, and there rested the shipwreck.

Silt and barnacles covered the U-boat. She turned on the light to the camera and took a few pictures, then turned it off and swam deeper, nearer the vessel. She came upon a hole the ship must have sustained as it crashed to the ocean's floor. The opening was large enough for her to make her way inside.

Jonathan swam in front of her and put his fist out. Danger. Yeah, she knew that. This entire venture was dangerous. But she'd ignored him once before and didn't want to now. She'd follow his direction on this because there was only so much time and so much air.

She motioned him to trail her along the outside of the U-boat until they came to the conning tower. On the deck lay a long barrel-like tube. It had to be a cannon of some kind. She swam to the front of the tower and swiped her gloved hand along crustacean and rust patches, stirring up silt. She could see no identifying logo or name to prove it was a U-boat.

What did she think? That she'd dive down and, bingo, the name would be right there? This could very well be the *SS Lamut*. She had to make sure it wasn't. She took several more pictures, then swam over the top rail and found the hatch open. A ladder went down into the ship.

Every nerve in her body tingled.

She pointed to the open hatch, showing Jonathan she was going in.

He held his palm up to her.

She stopped.

Jonathan pointed with two fingers at his eyes and then to her. Without her showing him, he'd given her a signal to watch him and follow.

He entered first. She placed a small submersible light on the railing just in case they needed it to find their way out, then went after him.

A long vertical tube, which must have been a periscope, was to her right. Jonathan kept descending into the ship and turned down a long corridor. Gloryanna attached another submersible light on the wall. They were moving into the forward torpedo room. Long, huge cylinders lined the walls. Bunks stood underneath. She knew from her nautical history class that war ships stored supplies in the forward.

Jonathan stopped over a large crate. Sea salt had corroded the wood in places, but here were markings of some sort. Gloryanna brushed away the silt. There, barely legible, was a Nazi swastika. She took a picture of it.

Jonathan squinted and focused on the deteriorated top, like he was trying to levitate it. The lid bobbled. Then bobbled some more. He was able to move it enough for her to stick her hand inside. Letting the camera float beside her, she pulled with all the strength she could muster without being able to gain leverage with her feet. She yanked and yanked again. The lid fell apart in her hands.

Brown silt swirled in the water. Finally, it settled, and she saw inside the crate. Gold bars, all imprinted with the familiar swastika. The treasure Hitler had attempted to send to Japan. One bar would be worth a fortune. It could help take care of Grandpa and make it so her mother wouldn't have to work. For that matter, her father wouldn't have to either.

No! This was not hers to keep. It was evidence needed to prove that the gold was down here and Hitler had sent it. She grabbed the camera and took more pictures. Then she grasped one of the heavy bars and placed it in her dive pouch, which made her too heavy. She dropped the weights on her belt until she balanced. She wished she could put the lid back, but its pieces were floating all around her. Gloryanna didn't have time to hide the treasure. If Takahashi made it down here, she'd find it.

Gloryanna motioned to Jonathan that it was time to leave. But he shook his head and pointed to canisters scattered all over the floor.

They looked like scuba tanks. She brushed silt from one and saw a huge red Hg.

Jonathan pulled her away, then made a fist.

Danger.

She looked back at the tanks. Could these be the tanks of liquid mercury Grandfather had told her about? She stared at the large red Hg, the universal sign for mercury. The hazard she'd feared was real. But there had to be more than just a few canisters. She looked around and saw what appeared to be the door to the keel.

Jonathan got between her and the door, motioning for her to leave.

But she couldn't. Not until she checked. She opened the door and shone the light inside. Canisters stacked as far as she could see filled the space. It looked like possibly seventy tons' worth. Seawater had been eating away at their seals. If liquid mercury had leaked out, it could be poisoning all the sea life. And now she was exposed. Afraid, she swam away, but stopped. No way could she just leave. Not after what she'd just seen. Besides, she didn't want to expose someone else to this danger. She had to do something. Her first impulse was to shut the door, but she had to get proof. She pulled the new camera into position and took several shots of the tanks. As soon as she finished, she closed the door.

Jonathan motioned for her to follow him again, so she swam into the passage and stopped. Near the submersible light at the end of the hall was another diver.

Takahashi.

CHAPTER TWENTY-NINE

JONATHAN NARROWED HIS EYES AT the professor blocking the way. He was in no danger; the woman couldn't even see him. But she could hurt Gloryanna. She had chased Gloryanna down, knowing full well that she would lead her to the treasure.

Weak from diving and loosening the crate lid, Jonathan tried to think of a way to get Gloryanna safely out of the sub. With only one passageway, there wasn't a way out. She couldn't move through walls like he could.

The professor crushed the light on the wall. It blinked off. Jonathan could see only shadows now.

Gloryanna must have realized the light on her wrist was a beacon. She switched it off.

Calling upon his power within, Jonathan used his ghostly vision to see through the murky water. The only movement was bubbles from their regulators, and a trail headed toward them. The professor was an expert diver and would be on them in no time.

And then she drew a gun.

Jonathan had seen underwater weapons used during the war, but this one was more compact and probably performed no matter the depth. Its bullets would be metal darts of some kind. Even if a dart didn't mortally wound Gloryanna, it could do damage to her scuba gear, which would be deadly in itself.

What could he do?

A burst of bubbles sprang from Takahashi's weapon, and a dart raced directly for Gloryanna.

Summoning energy he didn't know he had, Jonathan moved his hand, forcing the water to the side and deflecting the dart into the U-boat's metal wall. It impacted, then sank to the floor of the ship.

Takahashi pulled a knife and pushed off toward Gloryanna.

Jonathan tried to lift a pipe on the floor but could only make it wobble.

Gloryanna pulled a knife from her sheath. He should have known she'd have one too. It made sense that a diver would always carry a trusty knife.

Takahashi swam through him in her pursuit for Gloryanna.

Gloryanna parried the woman's attacks and shoved Takahashi against a torpedo launcher. Takahashi jerked free, her knife wildly stabbing at Gloryanna.

But Gloryanna deflected each jab. How long could she keep this up?

Jonathan had to do something, fast.

Again, he focused on the pipe. This time, he was able to propel it straight at Takahashi, striking her from behind. He then tangled it in her regulator octopus that fed her oxygen. The professor backed off her attack as she desperately tried to untangle the lines.

Gloryanna swam past her, but without the submergible light by the hatch, she missed the exit. Jonathan didn't have the strength to stop her. He had only enough to follow her deeper into the sub, past the galley.

She stopped, and to his surprise, she turned on her flashlight. The beam would give away her location, but then he saw why she'd done it. She'd come to the hole they'd seen when they'd first approached the sub. He could tell she was debating if she could fit through with her gear, but then she looked behind her, and without further hesitation, she swam for the opening. Her tank hit the lip of the U-boat, jerking her backward for a moment, but she adjusted and swam out of the vessel with Jonathan right behind her.

Takahashi would be on them any second. Gloryanna swam toward the bottom of the vortex, the same way she'd come. A flood of bubbles escaped from her. And then he saw the problem. Takahashi must have nicked Gloryanna's oxygen tube as they'd fought in the sub.

Gloryanna flipped on the valve of her redundancy air.

Out of nowhere, Takahashi collided with Gloryanna. Somehow, the woman had freed herself from the pipe. Takahashi jabbed her knife at Gloryanna.

Gloryanna swirled around, deflecting the blows.

Bubbles roiled the waters.

Takahashi grabbed the yellow tubing attached to Gloryanna's backup air and yanked.

More bubbles burst into the water.

Jonathan looked at the vortex current. Gloryanna had told him that she thought the vortex was connected to him. The current that had caught her before and brought her to him might actually save her life. But it could also kill her and erase him from his ghostly existence. He didn't care what happened to him. All that mattered was saving Gloryanna. Wielding a blade, Takahashi raised her arm. Before she could deliver the killing blow, Jonathan grabbed Gloryanna and wrapped her in a protective embrace. She'd grown limp from lack of air. Panicked, he summoned all the energy he had and plunged them both into the current.

***

Gloryanna felt something on her cheek.

A lick? And was that a dog panting?

Where was she? Her head pounded, and her body felt weighed down and cold—freezing cold. Forcing her eyes to open, she stared through her scuba mask at the dark of night.

What had she been doing?

Diving—but she obviously wasn't in the water now. Her mouthpiece wasn't even in her mouth. In fact, she lay on her side on solid ground.

Working sore muscles, she managed to pull her arms from the BCD and sat up to find Max standing a few feet away.

She tore off her mask and took several deep drafts of air through her nose and mouth. "Max, we left you in the boat. How did you get here? And where's Jonathan?"

She scanned her surroundings, looking for him. Where had her diving light gone to? It wasn't attached to her wrist and wasn't anywhere on the ground. Moonlight shone on the turbulent ocean as waves crashed to shore not far away. She took off her gloves and the diving pouch. She undid the ties to the camera and yanked her feet free from her diving fins. She jerked her head from the hood of her suit before forcing herself to stand. The wind blew through her damp hair that escaped her bun.

Her mind raced through what had happened on the dive she had found the gold and the leaking mercury tanks, and she'd fought with Takahashi. The mad woman had come at her with a knife to kill her. She'd nicked Gloryanna's oxygen tubing. And she'd even yanked off the line to her backup air. The panic that had surged through Gloryanna made her catch her breath even now. But in the midst of thinking she would surely die, Jonathan had pulled her into his arms.

He had used so much of his strength helping her during the dive. What if his gallant act of saving her had been too much? What if . . . She didn't want to think of the horrible possibilities. What would happen to a ghost if said ghost depleted all his gifts to save a mortal?

She had to find him. And then she saw a body lying down the beach a ways. Her feet pounded the sand as she ran to it, and she collapsed to her knees when she discovered it was Jonathan. She studied him. Moonlight lit his chiseled cheekbones and short beard. He no longer appeared ghostly. No, he seemed alive, like he had when she'd first met him. She dared not touch him, not knowing what would happen.

"Jonathan," she said.

His eyes blinked open, and he stared at her. "Gloryanna?"

"Yes!" She so wanted to throw her arms around him but restrained herself, though she couldn't tear her eyes away from him. "We made it."

He seemed to drink her in as well.

Her breathing slowed; every nerve in her body tingled.

He leaned close to her. "I never told you, but I saw you as I lay dying on the rocks below Purgatory Point all those years ago." He reached to touch her but stopped short like he, too, worried about what might happen to them. "Your curly, curly hair with a mind of its own encircled your porcelain face like a halo. You came to me in my last moments of life, you found me when Takahashi was messing with my past, and now you're here, sitting beside me." A smile upturned his lips. "You did it."

"No. *We* did it." She looked down the beach where she'd left the scuba gear, the camera, and the pouch that held the gold bar. "We found the evidence. Now all we have to do is take it to the authorities."

They both rose to their feet and hurried to the gear, Max joyfully keeping pace with them.

She picked up the pouch and the camera. "These are heavier than they look."

"Here, let me."

"Are you sure?" She did a double take. "You used your gift to bring us here. Don't you need to get closer to your shack to restore your energy?"

"It's the strangest thing. I'm tired, but I don't feel weak like I usually do." Jonathan slung the strap of her pouch over his head and took the camera from her.

She could hardly believe it. He held her gear like a normal person. "You didn't levitate it."

He looked at what he'd done. "This is amazing, but I'm not going to question it." Then, with his free hand, he grabbed the diving tank. "Why don't we leave this by your things that you stashed in the twinberry bushes?"

Gloryanna quickly scooped up the rest of the gear she'd borrowed from Thomas, and they walked toward the cliffs. They reached the bushes and her gear and set Thomas's beside it. Jonathan kept the pouch and camera.

"We should be able to use the diving light on your camera to get through the forest to the mountain meadow, and then you can take it from there to the other forest." He clicked it on, lighting the trail carpeted with spongy mosses beneath the towering spruces.

As she followed him, Gloryanna said, "What do you suppose happened to Takahashi?" Even though the woman had tried to kill her, Gloryanna had a hard time sorting out how she felt about her mentor and supposed friend, and why the woman seemed to value wealth over morals and even people's lives.

"Don't know." Jonathan sounded thoughtful. "But I rather doubt she made it."

They came to the shack. Gloryanna headed toward it, but Jonathan hung back.

"What's wrong? I thought you'd want to go in and get recharged," she said.

"I don't think I need it. Besides, you don't have time. Your parents will be worried about you, and your grandfather will be beside himself." Jonathan turned away.

Max started down a different path that led to the cliffs.

"Max, come back here," Jonathan called to him. The dog reluctantly turned around and hurried to him.

"Is that Purgatory Point, where you two . . . well, where you were both pushed over the edge?" She didn't know if Jonathan wanted to talk about it or not. But she wanted him to know she cared and would be here for him, if he needed her.

"Yes. But I'll deal with what happened in my past later. Let's get you home." He led the way to the path through the forest.

Gloryanna had only the diving booties on her feet and could feel most every rock and rut, but she didn't complain. They hiked for quite a while with Jonathan scanning the forest, checking the area, and scouring the path. The usual night noises of animals scurrying through the bushes and owls hooting overhead followed them.

They finally came to the spot on the trail where Jonathan had first touched her. With everything they'd been through, that moment five days back seemed so long ago. He stopped. "Remember what happened here?"

"Oh yes. I remember it very well. I was so afraid of you and wondered if you were some crazy person, and then you touched me and . . ." She couldn't finish.

"And everything changed," he finished for her.

"For you too?" She was amazed.

"Yes, for me too." He stared at her. "I hadn't touched a woman in decades. The feel of your soft skin was almost more than I could bear. Not far down this path, Max and I will be sent back to the shack." He set the camera on the ground. "Last time, I wanted to kiss you, and I'll be honest, I want to kiss you now. I don't know if I'll be able to, but I'd love to try. It will be one more thing I can hang on to to remember you by. Do you mind?"

"But—" She could hardly stand the thought of going on without him. "Jonathan. I'll come back. I promise. We can have a life together."

"I once thought the same thing, but I no longer do. I don't want you stuck here like I have been. You're meant for better things." His low, husky voice tore at her heart.

She gazed at his face cast in lunar shadows and wished she could see his eyes more clearly. He stepped closer to her and cupped her cheeks in his hands. Immediately, an electric sizzle flashed over her body. He could touch her! Perhaps they'd been given this one last gift. She stood mesmerized, waiting, yearning, wanting. She could hardly draw a breath.

He lowered his lips to hers and kissed her softly, tenderly. He tasted of life, of dreams, and of hope.

She wrapped her arms around his neck, pulling him closer as she melted into his embrace, never wanting this magical moment to end.

Max whined, and Jonathan finally stepped away, breaking the spell. "It's time." He picked up the pouch and strapped it on her shoulder. He handed her the camera. "Be careful. And know that I love you and always will."

She didn't want to leave. Her bottom lip trembled as she said, "Please walk with me until it takes you. Please."

"Of course."

This time, as they approached the meadow, Jonathan walked on one side of her and Max on the other. Jonathan inhaled deeply.

They slowed and took one cautious step at a time until they were in the meadow.

All three of them!

Jonathan stopped abruptly. "Wait. What just happened?"

"Nothing! You're still here!" Gloryanna looked down at the dog. "And so is Max!"

Max barked.

"I can't believe it." Jonathan scooped her up in his arms and swung her around before he set her on her feet. He patted his chest. "I'm here!"

Max jumped up on him. "And so are you, old boy!" He hugged his dog.

Happiness bubbled through Gloryanna, making her laugh and cry at the same time. "What do you think happened?"

"You!" Jonathan stared at her. "You're what happened. I knew you would free us from the limbo. I just didn't know how or that I'd have another chance at life. A life with you. Somehow, saving you and helping you gather evidence about the submarine has bought me another chance to live."

She set the camera and pouch on the ground, reached up, and pulled his head down, planting another kiss on his warm, inviting lips. As the kiss deepened, he moaned and drew her to him.

At that moment, a loud whoop, whoop, whoop sounded above them. She glanced up. A helicopter hovered overhead. Its searchlight scanned the mountain meadow and settled on them. As the chopper descended, she saw the words Pacific Gas written on the underbelly.

"That has to be Thomas's father," Gloryanna said.

The helicopter landed, and two people got out. One had his arm in a sling. Thomas? And the other man must be his father. "Do you think Thomas is here for Takahashi or because he wanted to help me?"

"We're about to find out." Jonathan fisted his hand.

"Do you think they'll see you?" Gloryanna looked at Jonathan.

"I hope so." His optimistic words filled her with encouragement.

As Thomas drew nearer, she saw relief capture his whole face. "Are you all right?"

"Yes." Even though he sounded friendly, Gloryanna was cautious. "Are you sure you should be here? I mean, you're still recovering."

Seymore Clifford approached her. "When my son gets an idea in his head, no one can talk him out of it. He wanted to help you and was really upset that you thought he'd conspired with Professor Takahashi."

"She tried to kill me," Gloryanna blurted.

Jonathan stood by her side. "She would have, too, but Gloryanna beat her at her own game."

Thomas stared at him. "And you are?"

"This is Jonathan." Gloryanna smiled and took hold of his hand.

Thomas stepped back. "But he's . . . Isn't he a—?"

"We'll talk about it later," Jonathan said.

Gloryanna hadn't a clue how to explain what had happened to Jonathan. She was still processing it.

Max yipped. "And this is my dog," Jonathan said.

Thomas's father cut in. "It's great to meet you, but could we perhaps save this conversation for later? I'd like to get Thomas back. He's been sick with worry, and he needs to rest."

Gloryanna reached to pick up the camera and pouch, but Jonathan beat her to it. Everyone made their way to the chopper. Setting the camera and pouch inside, Jonathan gave Gloryanna a boost up while Thomas and his father helped Max scramble on board. Jonathan was the last to get in, and he settled in a seat next to Gloryanna.

She looked at Thomas and yelled over the sound of the chopper's blades slapping the air above, "We've got a lot to tell you."

"Best to wait until we land," he yelled back.

The helicopter rose above the trees and flew over the forest. Soon, they came to the cliffs, and the spotlight shone down on Jonathan's shack. He took hold of Gloryanna's hand and squeezed it.

She squeezed back. They'd been through so much in just a few days and had so much left to do, but she could face anything with Jonathan by her side.

CHAPTER THIRTY

JONATHAN STUDIED SEYMORE AND THOMAS as the helicopter flew them toward town. He admired their father-and-son relationship.

Thomas looked up and caught Jonathan's gaze.

What must he be thinking? Jonathan hadn't a clue. If he were in Thomas's shoes, and his ex-girlfriend had told him a ghost had saved her, and had then said the ghost had turned out to be alive—well, there weren't words for that.

A small part of Jonathan still wondered about Thomas and how involved he was with Takahashi. But his showing up and giving them a ride out of the primitives gave him a few extra points. Jonathan would be willing to listen to the guy tell his side of the story and straighten things out.

Thomas reached down and petted Max. The dog let him. If Max trusted him, that was a good sign. And at least Thomas hadn't questioned them in front of his father about Jonathan's transforming from ghost to living.

The chopper landed at Mercy Hospital, and they disembarked. Jonathan took the underwater camera and the diving pouch from Gloryanna.

A group of doctors and nurses hurried toward them.

"I called ahead so they'd be ready for us," Seymore said. "I hope you don't mind, Gloryanna, but I called your parents, too, and let them know you're okay. They asked me to drop you off at their place instead of your condo when we're done here. I guess your grandfather has taken a turn for the worse."

Gloryanna grabbed Jonathan's arm. "I've got to get to him."

Thomas's father noticed the exchange and gave Jonathan another measuring look but said to Gloryanna, "In due time. You've got to get checked out first. You've been through quite an ordeal."

As the doctors and nurses whisked her, Jonathan, and Thomas into the building and toward the triage area, Max tried to follow.

A nurse stopped. "He can't come with you."

Thomas's father took hold of his collar. "Max can stay with me while we wait."

Max barked and tried to get away.

"It's okay, old boy," Jonathan told him. "I'll be right back."

The dog calmed down but didn't look at the man who had stopped him, staring instead at Jonathan until he was out of sight.

A nurse guided Jonathan behind a curtain, where she had him sit on a gurney. She took his temperature and recorded it. Next, she wrapped a rubber tubing around his arm. "Make a fist, please."

"What are you doing?"

"The doctor will want to do a full panel on you. You're going to feel a pinch."

He hadn't had his blood drawn since he'd signed up to join the Coast Guard and had become a sand pounder. This might be interesting. He watched as she stuck a needle in his arm. She was right. He did feel a pinch. Blood filled the vial. His actual blood. He marveled again that he was truly alive. Next, the nurse checked his blood pressure and made more notes on his chart.

A doctor with a stethoscope looped around his neck pulled the curtain aside and took the clipboard from the nurse. He read the notes, then glanced at the top of his chart where Jonathan's name was written. "Mr. Dawson, you seem to be in great shape. What happened out there?"

"It's hard to put into words. I'll let Gloryanna fill you in." He knew she'd know how to dodge their questions. He might say something wrong.

"And you live at the peninsula?" The doctor's long face peered at him skeptically.

"I did. I do. But I'm thinking of moving soon," Jonathan said just as Gloryanna came around his curtain.

"Doctor, I'm sorry to interrupt, but I just learned my grandfather may be dying, and I'd really like to see him before he passes. Is it okay if we go now?" Her pretty face glowed in the overhead light.

"Aren't you Celia Griffin's daughter?" The doctor studied her more closely.

"Yes. She works here."

He inclined his head as he studied her. "You have your mother's eyes. She's one of my best nurses. I'm sorry to hear about your grandfather." He motioned for the nurse to hand some papers to them to sign.

The nurse pointed to the line. "Put your John Hancocks here. If either of you start feeling sick, please come back."

They both signed.

Before they left, the doctor said, "Tell your mom our thoughts are with her."

"Thanks, Doctor." Jonathan retrieved the camera and diving pouch, then followed her.

They found Thomas and his father waiting down the hall. Max pulled away from Seymore as soon as he saw Jonathan.

"The police want to talk to all of you." Thomas's father stood as they approached. "But I told them what's going on with your grandfather, Gloryanna, so they backed off. You can give them your statements in the morning. I want my best lawyers with you when you go."

"Have you heard anything about Professor Takahashi?" Gloryanna asked.

Thomas rose a little slower to his feet. "She's in custody, which is the reason the police want to speak to you. Well, to all of us."

Jonathan could hardly believe the woman had survived. But she was not going to hurt Gloryanna again. He wouldn't let her.

Through the glass doors of the main entrance, a media mob awaited.

"Let's use the back door." Thomas's father guided them away.

"How did they know?" Jonathan hadn't a clue how word had spread so fast.

"When Thomas told me Takahashi sabotaged your tank, Gloryanna, and how she faked the grant, I made a few calls," Seymore said. "They must have gotten wind of something happening." This man, who oozed with power and wealth, from his brightly white-capped teeth to his pinkie ring, said it like it was no big deal. "They picked her up at the Neah Bay marina and will hold her for twenty-four hours before actually charging her with a crime. By then, my people will have learned everything there is to know about Nakano Takahashi."

They came to the area in the hospital where Gloryanna and Jonathan had come in when they'd visited Thomas in the ICU. She stopped. "Wait a minute. Thomas. You were in the ICU just yesterday."

"Yes, that was *yesterday*. I'm much better today." But his face looked a little pale, and he favored the side where he'd been shot.

His father opened the hospital's back door. "I tried to get him to ease up, but he was determined to make sure you were all right. I donated the money for this entire hospital wing, so they take extra care when it comes to my family. He probably didn't need to stay in the ICU, but he is my son. Besides, he wouldn't let any injury keep him from setting things right with you."

Gloryanna paused, looking at Thomas. "You and your folks must have had some talk."

"According to them, my life is an open book." Thomas grimaced.

"What you need to understand is parents will always look out for their kids no matter how old they are." His father gave them a curt nod.

Those words pierced Jonathan's heart. He wondered, Had his parents been watching over him from the other side? Had they been helping him through the years he and Max had spent at the shack? He'd like to think so.

They left the building, and this time, no employees sat on the bench, smoking. At the curb, a limo waited. The driver got out and opened the back door. Thomas's father waited while Gloryanna, Jonathan, Max, and his son got in, then he followed.

Mr. Clifford talked with the driver, then closed the privacy window between the back seat and the front, and they were on their way.

Gloryanna fidgeted. Jonathan took her hand. Her grandfather's outing to her graduation had possibly been too much for him. Jonathan hoped they could see him one last time and tell him what they'd found. It might give him peace.

"Guess I should fill in the blanks for you now." Thomas sat across from them, next to his father.

Good, Jonathan thought. *This might take her mind off the possibility that her grandfather might die before she reaches him.*

"See, when you left after graduation, I told Dad what was going on. Everything."

"Everything?" Gloryanna looked at Jonathan, then back to Thomas.

"Yes," his father answered for him.

But Thomas gave them a sideways glance that said no. At least that was what Jonathan hoped that look meant.

Seymore continued. "I have connections in the Coast Guard, and I have them looking into reports of missing U-boats and if one could have sunk off our coast during World War II."

Jonathan felt the weight of the gold bar in the diving pouch. "Sir, I have solid evidence that there was one." He glanced at Gloryanna. She nodded. He pulled out the gold bar with the swastika stamped on it. "We found the submarine, and in it was a crate of these." He proceeded to tell them exactly what had happened how they'd found the gold and Gloryanna had found the keel full of tanks of liquid mercury, and how Takahashi had tried to kill Gloryanna. By the time he finished, both Thomas and his father seemed shocked.

Jonathan handed the bar and the camera to Thomas's father. "Would you mind having your people check these out? I'm pretty sure that's real gold, and Gloryanna took a lot of pictures."

"You bet." He took them from him. "I'll give them back once they're done. I'll also alert my friends at the Coast Guard about those tanks. They'll know what to do."

Jonathan trusted him because, after all, the man had believed his son enough to take a helicopter out to find them. "I'd appreciate it. Thank you."

Jonathan glanced at Gloryanna. Though her forehead was lined with worry for her grandfather, she managed to give him a heartfelt smile.

He studied Thomas.

Thomas looked at them both, but he leaned close to Jonathan and said, "I don't know quite what to think of you, but I trust Gloryanna. And don't worry. My father will get to the bottom of what Takahashi was doing."

Jonathan believed him. And though he'd mistrusted Thomas during all the chaos of figuring out what had happened, he was beginning to think he wasn't such a bad guy after all.

***

Gloryanna, Jonathan, and Max got out of the limo at her parents' home. She thanked Thomas and his father, and the vehicle pulled away.

She glanced at Jonathan as they walked toward the kitchen door. "I can't wait to tell Grandpa what happened and for him to see that you and Max are here, that you're no longer ghosts to be frightened of, and that everything worked out." She looped her arm through his.

"And we'll be right by your side." Jonathan patted her arm.

They reached the door, and Jonathan opened it, letting Gloryanna and Max go in before he did. The kitchen stood empty; the house was eerily quiet.

"My folks are probably upstairs with Grandpa." She couldn't imagine what her parents would think seeing Jonathan and Max in the flesh. They would want to know everything that had happened. She didn't know if she had the energy to tell it again. But the story could wait until after she had seen Grandpa. They hurried to the stairs and took them two at a time.

They stopped at Grandpa's door. Gloryanna took a deep breath and went in. Dad rose from his seat and hugged her. With one arm still around her, he used his other to shake Jonathan's hand. "I understand you saved my daughter."

Her mother sat on the other side of the bed and beamed as she stared at Jonathan. She must have a thousand questions, but she was also grieving inside.

Jonathan gave both of Gloryanna's parents a humble nod.

Her father kissed Gloryanna's cheek. "I'm so proud of you."

"Thanks, Dad." Her attention went to Grandpa, who lay so still in his bed.

His wrinkly lidded eyes were closed. He looked peaceful. Her mother got up and motioned for Gloryanna to take her place. "I think he's been waiting for you." A lone tear escaped down her mother's cheek. She swiped it away.

Gloryanna sat where her mother had been, and Jonathan came to stand beside her. She took Grandpa's arthritic, blue-veined hand in hers.

A faint smile pulled at his aging lips. "Is that Starbuck?" His eyes opened slightly. Then he saw Jonathan, and his eyes widened. He caught a deep breath and held it, then let it out slowly. "I see Pip saved you instead of the whale."

Jonathan chuckled and nodded.

"We didn't let the whale get away. We captured him," Gloryanna said. "This is Jonathan. Remember?" She wanted her grandpa to understand that he shouldn't blame himself for Jonathan's death.

"I do. Yes, I do." He sucked in another deep breath. "Give me a full report."

"I found your old U-boat." She told him everything, and as she spoke, tears puddled in her grandpa's red-rimmed eyes. Jonathan handed her a tissue. She dabbed at the tears as they slid toward his ear.

"It's going to be all right, Grandpa." She rubbed his arm. "Thomas Clifford's father has connections, and soon, everyone will know what happened on that night so long ago."

Grandpa glanced at Jonathan and closed his eyes. "The harbinger is at peace, I see."

Instead of going into a long explanation, she said, "Yes, Grandpa. He is." "Good." He drifted off.

She stroked the top of his balding head. A peaceful look came to his face.

Her mother leaned near Gloryanna. "He's resting now, sweetie. Why don't you change your clothes and put on something more comfortable while I make you and Jonathan something to eat. A repairman fixed the stove, so I can heat up anything you want."

Gloryanna would have loved to get out of the scuba suit, but instead, she said, "Thanks, but I'm okay, Mom. I just want to sit here with Grandpa for a while."

She couldn't put into words the tangle of emotions inside her worry, loss, love, fear, but mostly deep appreciation. The last few days, she'd had the privilege of being with Jonathan and of righting a wrong her grandfather had been a part of so many years ago. In helping Jonathan, she'd also helped her grandfather.

Jonathan rubbed her shoulder. She took his hand.

She didn't want to leave Grandpa just yet. She and Jonathan would be with him, reassure him that all was well, and comfort him as he progressed from this life. Grandpa no longer needed to fear. Because he'd told her the truth, they could save the ocean, and Jonathan and Max would be right by her side.

EPILOGUE

Three months later

Gloryanna and Jonathan gathered the scuba gear they had hidden behind the bushes and set them in Gloryanna's collapsible wagon. "I'm so glad to finally collect these."

He took hold of the pull handle and started up the trail to the shack. Max trotted ahead of them. "I know you've been worried about this stuff, but we had to be available in case the police wanted to question us more regarding Takahashi. I must say, I'm glad Ralph had nothing to do with her."

"So am I. I can't believe worry over me made him drink again. Mixed with his anger and Thomas grabbing for the gun and . . . well, I'm just glad neither one of them was killed." Gloryanna walked behind the wagon.

"I think Ralph looks to you as his little sister or something." Jonathan stopped and got a better grip on the wagon's handle.

"You could be right. Thomas isn't going to press charges against him, but Ralph still has to do community service. I told him I'd help out at the Fish Tail more." She hoped she had the time. "I showed Ralph a picture of the camera I'm giving him. He was impressed, even more so when he learned about the pictures I'd already taken with it. Once the authorities finish getting everything they need off the camera, they'll give it to Ralph."

Jonathan stopped while she caught up to him. They were near the top of the path.

"I spoke with Ralph about his drinking. He promised to go to AA." Gloryanna wanted to do as much as she could to support her friend.

"Good. I'm glad he's getting the help he needs." He sounded like he meant it. She hoped that Ralph and Jonathan would grow to like each other.

She'd been so caught up in this trip to collect her gear that she'd forgotten to tell him her other news. She couldn't on the ride up here. Her parents had come with them, and they all planned to stay the night and head out in the morning. But now was the time. "Did I tell you the dean over the marine biology department called me?"

"What did he want?" Jonathan pulled the wagon up to more level ground. The shack was only a few feet away.

"He told me that he'd been watching the case with Professor Takahashi, and he's been impressed by how I handled her and how I found the sub. I guess she'd been living a lavish lifestyle and was heavily in debt at the university credit union. She was on the verge of losing everything. She wanted to find the gold to not only pay her debts but to help her save face too. For exposing her, the dean wants to help me."

"By doing what?" Jonathan stopped in front of her.

"He offered me a spot in the master's degree program. He wants me to apply, and they would give me a full-ride scholarship." She still couldn't believe it.

Jonathan scooped her up in his arms and hugged her tight. "That's what you've always wanted."

"I know." She stared into his eyes. "But that means that things are going to be crazy, and I won't have much time to spend with you." Which was the main reason she'd hesitated to tell him. Even though they'd been super busy testifying and settling issues in regard to the submarine, Jonathan had been right by her side the entire time. She didn't want to leave him, even to attend classes.

He set her down. "I wanted to talk to you about that."

"You did?"

"Yeah. I think we need to make some changes." He started pulling the wagon toward the shack again.

"Changes?" Gloryanna had been dreading this. She knew he'd been growing restless living in the apartment over her parents' garage.

"I think we need a place of our own." He paused, looking at her, waiting.

"We? But, Jonathan, my parents are very old-fashioned. They'd never understand us just living together."

"Wait a minute. Let me finish." He got down on one knee and pulled out a small velvet ring box. He flipped open the top. A beautiful diamond shone up at her. "Gloryanna, you are the only woman for me, and I'd love to make it official. Will you marry this beat-up, old sand pounder?"

Joy rushed through her like a vortex current. She jumped into his arms. "Yes!" She kissed him soundly, like it was the very first time. He returned her passion. Pure bliss rushed through her body.

The door to the shack opened. She pulled back in time to see her mother running toward them.

"Finally! We've been waiting for days for him to pop the question," her mother said.

Gloryanna hugged her mother. "You knew?"

"We did." Her father stood behind her mom, holding the blue-banded burial urn containing Grandpa's ashes. "Jonathan came to us and asked our permission. How could we say no? He's going to work with me. I will finally have someone to pass my business down to. Though we need to have a talk about that table and chair set you made in there." Her father winked and shook Jonathan's hand.

"What? You didn't like it?" Jonathan's brows bunched together.

"Actually, my good man, I think we'll need several sets just like them. I want to expand my business and offer my clients hand-made furniture. I expect your table and chairs will be hot sellers." Her father gave him a nod.

Gloryanna's eyes went to the urn her dad held. They'd come here for two reasons to pick up the scuba gear and to spread Grandpa's ashes over Purgatory Point. She took the urn. "Mom, do you mind if I do the honors?"

"I think that's exactly what your grandfather would want." She handed the urn to her.

Together they walked to Purgatory Point. Jonathan stood on one side of her, and Max and her parents stood on the other.

Gloryanna took a deep breath. "Before I do this, I want to say a couple of things I often heard Grandpa quote from his favorite book. 'There is, one knows not what sweet mystery about this sea, whose gently awful stirrings seem to speak of some hidden soul beneath. Let faith oust fact; let fancy oust memory; I look deep down and do believe.'"

Gloryanna opened the urn and handed the top to her mother. Then she turned it over and set free her grandfather's ashes. They fluttered in the ocean breeze, trickling down to the craggy rocks below. She could almost hear him say, "Well done, Starbuck."

Her mother sniffed and took the urn. Then together her parents headed back to the shack.

Jonathan's arm came around her waist. "He would have been proud."

With Max at their side, they turned away from the cliffs and looked forward to their new life together.

FACT OR FICTION

WAS THERE A DIVISION IN the Coast Guard called sand pounders? Yes. They patrolled the coastlines of both the Atlantic and Pacific Oceans. Their mission was to detect and observe enemy vessels operating in coastal waters and transmit information to the navy or army commands, to report attempts of landing by the enemy and assist in preventing landings, to prevent communications between persons on shore and the enemy at sea, and to rescue those in need and police the areas.

 https//www.hsdl.org/?view&did=19425
 https//sweetheartsofthewest.blogspot.com/2017/04/sand-pounders-of-wwii.html

Did the sand pounders help in an actual rescue? Yes. The *SS Lamut* was purchased by the Russian Merchant Marine and operated between the US West Coast and the Soviet East Coast. Caught in a horrible storm, the crew lost its bearings and grounded the ship on Teahwhit Head, south of Cape Flattery.

 http//www.researcheratlarge.com/Pacific/USSRShipwrecks/Lamut.html

Did the Germans send U-boats to Japan? Yes. I based my story around U-boat U-864, destined for the Japanese military industry. Their mission had the code name Operation Caesar. The cargo included steel canisters of metallic mercury that had been stored in her keel, which would have been used to manufacture explosives. The ship's cargo list also had parts and engineering drawings for German jet fighter aircraft and other military supplies for Japan. Among her passengers were Messerschmitt engineers Ralf von Chilingensperg and Riclef Schomerus, Japanese torpedo expert Tadao Yamoto, and Japanese fuel expert Toshio Nakai. U-864 sank with all of its crew during an altercation with the British submarine *HMS Venturer* on February 9, 1945.

https//en.wikipedia.org/wiki/German_submarine_U-864

Did they have gold on board U-864? It was not listed on the ship's cargo list.

https//en.wikipedia.org/wiki/German_submarine_U-864

Did U-864's canisters of mercury start leaking? Yes. In August 2005, using a remotely operated underwater vehicle (ROV), researchers found that the steel canisters were leaking and posed a severe environmental threat of mercury poisoning. They found that cod, torsk, and edible crab around the wreck were contaminated. The rusting mercury bottles and live torpedoes on board made any attempt to raise the ship very dangerous. Debates over how best to handle the situation went on for years. Finally, in 2018, the Norwegian Coastal Administration (NCA) decided to cap the U-boat to stop the spread of contaminating sediment. It was thought it would be completed by the summer of 2020. However, the Green Warriors of Norway have sued the NCA, stopping them as of this writing.

https//en.wikipedia.org/wiki/German_submarine_U-864

Is the fishing industry putting the oceans in danger? Yes. According to the Netflix documentary *Seaspiracy*, they are. The film is loaded with facts and video taken at great risk of the filmmaker. Other noteworthy information in the film

- Sharks are harvested for their fins, then thrown back—shark fins are a billion-dollar industry.
- 300,000 dolphins, whales, and sharks are killed each year.
- Fishing boats discard ropes and lines in the ocean.

I only listed a small number of interesting facts. Please watch the documentary to learn more.

Was there really mercury contamination in Minamata Bay, Japan, in the 1950s? Yes. The bay became contaminated with mercury from a nearby factory. The mercury bioaccumulated and biomagnified in the muscle of fish. Over two thousand people died, and thousands more experienced crippling injuries to their central nervous systems. It became known as Minamata disease.

https//www.healthandenvironment.org/environmental-health/social-dontext/history/mercury-the-tragedy-of-minamata-disease

Were there really Japanese holdout soldiers? Yes. Some were spotted in the '50s, '60s, '70s, and even the late '80s.

https//en.wikipedia.org/wiki/Japanese_holdout

ACKNOWLEDGMENTS

I MUST THANK MY HUSBAND, Bruce, for supporting me as I worked on this book. His health has declined, and still, he champions my writing, never complaining about the hours, days, weeks, and months that I sequester myself in my office to write a book. He is always ready to listen to me as I go through "what if" scenarios, always ready to read anything I've written, and always ready to do anything I ask him to do. I've been truly blessed to have him in my life. I love you, sweetheart!

I must thank my writers group. They have listened to several chapters, giving me wonderful feedback. I especially need to thank Kathleen Dougherty, Kerri Leroy, Maureen Mills, and Charlene Raddon. Thank you so very much for your help!

I want to thank my publisher, Covenant Communications, Inc. Their entire team works very hard to make each book the best it can be. I especially need to thank my editor, Samantha Millburn, for her patience and guidance. I thank my lucky stars that she is my editor. The covers of my books have been outstanding, and I'd like to thank Kevin Jorgensen for doing the cover for this novel. He has an amazing talent. Also, a huge thank you to Jessica Bybee for her awesome marketing skills.

As always, I thank my family and friends, whose support I don't deserve but very much appreciate.

And thank you, dear readers, for buying my books. I'd be lost without you.

ABOUT THE AUTHOR

KATHI ORAM PETERSON LEARNED TO write the hard way, by spending years practicing her craft. Her path to publication took a detour as she raised her three children. During those years, she read all the how-to books on novel writing that she could find. When her last child graduated from high school, Kathi returned to college and earned her BA in English. She was fortunate to do an internship for the University of Utah's *Continuum* magazine, where she learned to edit and write articles in the "real" world. Shortly after graduation, she was hired by a curriculum publisher to write and edit concept and biography books for children. She worked shoulder to shoulder with artists and computer programmers as she watched her children's stories come to life. But the desire to write full-length novels called to her. Upon leaving the workforce, she focused her attention on writing romantic suspense and YA time travel novels. The thread she sews in both genres is faith in a higher power.

She currently resides in Salt Lake City. You can contact her through her website, www.authorkathiorampeterson.com.

And please feel free to sign up for her newsletter http//eepurl.com/cE52Y1.